DELTROIT
AND THE VALLEY OF
HILLAS CREEK

A Social and Environmental History

With best wishes

Nicola

24. Jan 2014

DELTROIT
AND THE VALLEY OF
HILLAS CREEK

A Social and Environmental History

Nicola Crichton-Brown

M

MELBOURNE BOOKS

Published by Melbourne Books
Level 9, 100 Collins Street,
Melbourne, VIC 3000
Australia
www.melbournebooks.com.au
info@melbournebooks.com.au

National Library of Australia Cataloguing-in-Publication entry:

AUTHOR: Crichton-Brown, Nicola

TITLE: Deltroit and the Valley of Hillas Creek:
   A Social and Environmental History

ISBN: 9781877096235 (hbk.)

SUBJECTS: Crichton-Brown, Nicola.
   Deltroit Station (N.S.W.)–History.
   Farms–New South Wales–Wagga Wagga Region–History.
   Country life–New South Wales–Wagga Wagga Region.
   British–Australia–Biography.
   Wagga Wagga Region (N.S.W.)–Social life and customs.
   Wagga Wagga Region (N.S.W.)–History.

DEWEY NUMBER: 994.48

FRONT COVER: On the Murrumbidgee at Yabtree, c. 1900.
Daisy McCarthy (back facing), Isabel Richardson, Mary Agnes Horsley
and Lo You (Chinese gardener at Yabtree, slightly obscured, rowing).
The flat-bottomed boats at Yabtree were made by Dennis McCaig,
Mary's brother and usually called 'Lurline'.

BACK COVER: The author moving cattle along the Deltroit Road.

For my parents, who taught me the solace

to be found in hard work and scholarship and

who died before this book was completed.

Contents

Author's Note

From London to Gundagai is a giant leap — so vast, in fact, that few people these days would contemplate it. While Skype, email and other internet facilities have diminished the isolation of rural Australia from the rest of the continent and the world, there is little else that has helped to bridge the gap in attitude and outlook. Aside from a handful of competitive and modern agribusinesses, the Gundagai district remains left behind and largely forgotten while the major urban centres of New South Wales, especially Sydney, move ahead with comparative optimism, energy and speed.

I first came to live at Deltroit part-time in early 2001 with my husband, Anthony, and our twelve-week-old daughter, Antonia, before moving here full-time in April 2006. When Anthony and I married in 2000, he was Chief Executive of Lumley Insurance, whose headquarters were in Bishopsgate in the City of London. Every day, he went to work in a Saville Row suit and Hermès tie, professing to enjoy the many cultural pursuits that we regularly indulged in together. Although I knew, when we met, that Anthony owned a property in New South Wales that he hungered for and where he hoped one day to settle down, I thought of this as merely a romantic dream. I was happy to share the notion of living there at some stage, but I believed this would either never materialise or, if it did, would only be in the very distant future.

I could not have been more wrong. Within three years of our marriage, Lumleys was sold and Anthony retired from the city, deciding almost overnight to become a New South Wales farmer. Nothing in my background had prepared me for a life in rural Australia, though I did have some strong Australian connections. My grandfather was Samuel Wynn, the founder of the iconic Australian wine label Wynns Coonawarra, and my father, Victor, had been born and raised in Melbourne. My mother was a German immigrant during the Second World War who also spent her schooldays in Melbourne, before meeting my father at university there. Although for career reasons my parents went to live in London almost immediately after their marriage, they retained firm ties with Australia. I was regularly brought on holiday to this distant land, both as a child and throughout my teens, so that by the time I was a young adult I had travelled more widely in Australia than many Australians.

On the other hand, my experience of country life anywhere was almost nonexistent and was chiefly limited to weddings and shooting parties in England, Scotland and northern France. Moreover, my professional skills were irrelevant where I was now going. Having been at school in London and subsequently studying law at London University, I went on to become a solicitor in the city for nine years, specialising in commercial litigation, before becoming a student again, this time of history of art at the Courtauld Institute. Two years as a fundraiser in the arts followed, before I set up a distribution business importing Australian skincare and fashion brands into the UK.

Once Anthony and I began to spend an increased amount of time at Deltroit, meeting regularly with neighbours, I noticed that it was hard to raise the conversation above the drought and the flies. I am ashamed to admit that, in my ignorance, I scorned it then, but gradually came to understand why the lack of rain, especially, was such a predicament and how its scarcity ate steadily away at the psyche of all those people dependent on the land. Our decision to live full-time at Deltroit coincided with the worst drought in New South Wales for over a hundred years, yet it took the actual experience of several poor seasons before I fully comprehended the potentially disastrous consequences. Climate change was the foremost topic in the Australian news, though it barely received a mention in the UK at that time. The burning question on everyone's lips was: were we living through just another drought, or was this evidence of insidious and drastic global warming?

Even though I had begun to feel acute sympathy for my husband's battle with Deltroit and those of our neighbours on their properties, I thought that, nonetheless, I would die of loneliness, boredom and lack of stimulation. On returning each day from the monotonous school run to Gundagai, I was overcome by the immutable silence that cloaked the homestead and garden, broken only by the occasional screeching of cockatoos or the demonic laughing of kookaburras.

Frequently riding my horse alone through the dusty paddocks, I began to lose the ability to communicate, becoming taciturn and as mute as my surroundings. Haunted daily by thoughts and images of London, my friends and family there, I dreaded contact with neighbours who would enquire anxiously how I was enjoying my new life. Before I had any time to answer, they would tell me straight and with absolute authority that 'You can take a girl out of the city, but you can never take the city out of the girl'. With every day that dawned, I began to feel that they were right.

In the garage at Deltroit, I had a large bag packed permanently in case I needed to run away. It contained some of my favourite clothing from London, which I thought would give me confidence in my new role as farmer's wife, and included a vintage red lace Valentino ball gown that I quickly discovered had no possible use at Deltroit. Other items in this suitcase were an array of designer shoes and handbags as well as various Ralph Lauren outfits that were equally redundant in the harsh environment to which I had come. Not only were these items unsuitable because of their luxurious materials and delicate forms, but I also quickly realised that outward appearance, and feminine dress in particular, had little value in this Australian setting. Similarly, and to my consternation, intellectual abilities went more or less unrecognised. What mattered was a woman's capacity for physical work and, ideally, this ability should be the same as a man's.

In a short time, I learned that 'a great bird' was a woman who rose early; fed the horses, chickens and poddy calves or lambs; cooked a hot breakfast; got her children to school; cleaned the house; brought 'smoko' to the yards or shearing shed midmorning; prepared lunch; laboured on the farm or in the garden until the school bus returned; supervised homework and attended to farm accounts; prepared dinner; and then, with this myriad of tasks finally completed, cheerfully bedded her husband. She was supposed to do all this, day in, day out, without complaining and with a smile on her face. It mattered not that she looked as if she had slept in the paddock, only that she got everything done. Such is the very male orientation of the Australian rural scene that has prevailed since white settlement and which appears to have changed little over two centuries.

From the beginning, I knew that I would not and could not meet these expectations of female performance. Farming itself did not interest me, and I had no desire to devote myself entirely to the domestic sphere. Casting around for something to do to alleviate my unhappiness and sense of isolation, I remember vividly returning from Gundagai one day in June 2007. As usual, I had dropped Antonia at school and driven back towards Deltroit with a heavy heart, wondering how on earth I was going to fill the emptiness of the day. Suddenly, I thought of the women who had lived at Deltroit before me and wondered how they managed to make a life for themselves here. I realised that I had no idea who these women were, so, instead of turning into the Deltroit Road from the Hume Highway, I continued on to Wagga Wagga.

Arriving at the public library, I asked the librarian if she had any information on Deltroit. I was shown to the Local Studies section and handed a thin manila folder that contained just two items: a condition report from the 1980s on the Junction Hotel (now part of Deltroit), prepared by the Gundagai Shire; and a funeral notice relating to the death of a member of the Ryder family, who lived on a neighbouring property with a very similar name. After checking with the librarian that this was indeed all the information available on Deltroit, I was shocked that such a well-known and obviously historic property should have so few records properly documenting its past. I reflected momentarily that this was typical of the utilitarianism of the Australian approach to life, which I had felt so keenly on my arrival at Deltroit: preserving heritage has, of necessity, always been a low priority for most hard-pressed rural communities. In a flash, I realised that I had found a vocation — to discover the history of Deltroit and the valley of Hillas Creek where it lay.

With this newfound purpose, I began a fascinating journey in which the parallels between my own situation and that of the Richardson and Fraser family who lived at Deltroit for three generations were gradually revealed. More importantly, my research took me into the very heart of the community where I now live and gave me something worthwhile to share and to contribute. After four years of systematic and at times intensive investigation, this book is the result of my efforts.

Nicola Crichton-Brown
March 2012

Deltroit homestead, 2009

CHAPTER 1

Deltroit

*A*nyone who has ever been to Deltroit speaks of it in revered and hallowed terms. Frequently described as one of the finest properties in the Riverina,[1] it has captured the imagination of locals, agents and outsiders for more than a century, and appealed to both their romantic and practical ideals. Situated at the junction of the South Western Slopes and the far eastern Riverina, a legendary grazing area of New South Wales, Deltroit lies halfway between Sydney and Melbourne, 30 kilometres south of Gundagai. Here, the property extends on both sides of the Hillas Creek along a narrow but fertile valley. Beautiful, lightly timbered creek flats almost two kilometres wide and largely sown with lucerne give way to gradual, undulating pastures that stretch towards the Mundarlo hills to the north and the Tarcutta hills to the south. Comprising just under 6500 acres, the expansive view from the entrance on Deltroit Road is of a timeless landscape, divided by a sandy creek that winds its way along the valley floor between the slopes and ridges. Crowned on either side with eucalypts, kurrajongs and outcrops of granite boulders, these hills spread out along the valley as far as the eye can see.

Heritage

The fairytale effect of the landscape is completed by the large, majestic and single-storey homestead dating from 1903. This magnificent house, encircled entirely by a deep verandah, stands on a gentle rise overlooking the creek in a 15-acre garden redolent of an English park. Mowed lawns and huge elm trees, planted over a hundred years ago amid eucalypts and white cedars, create an oasis in the increasingly dry surrounding landscape. At dusk, the slopes to the north are bathed in a soft, rosy light as the sky liquefies into pinks, oranges, reds and mauves, and the multitudinous birds break into cacophonous song accompanied by the frogs and the crickets. As darkness falls on summer evenings, a cool breeze referred to affectionately by locals as 'the Hillas Creek Doctor' comes up from the creek, reducing the ambient temperature that regularly hovers around 40 degrees Celsius in the hotter months.

Aside from its beauty, Deltroit has long had a reputation as one of the greatest wool- and stock-producing properties south of Sydney,[2] and grew famous in particular for its herd of Shorthorn beef cattle. In spite of this, almost nothing has ever been written about Deltroit before. It seems to have escaped the interest of local historians and even the notice of the National Trust. Local knowledge of Deltroit's history is thin, and few people know that the property was established by a pioneer from northern England, William Richardson, initially in partnership with his brother, John. If the two brothers, their families or descendants kept any diaries, journals, ledgers or registers, these have all mostly disappeared, together with any correspondence, maps and plans. The only family papers that remain are a small postcard collection belonging to William's niece; a pocketbook kept intermittently by his eldest brother, Thomas; and a variety of photographs. Fortunately, there are some other valuable sources, too. These include a handful of contemporaneous accounts in newspapers and journals, occasional references in the diaries kept by squatters and selectors on neighbouring properties, a limited number of government and official records, and the oral testimony — irreplaceable over time — of those families with connections to Deltroit or the valley of Hillas Creek.

On the other hand, there exists a great deal of material about the early Riverina and the discoveries by Hamilton Hume and William Hovell in 1824 and by Charles Sturt in 1829 of the rich, well-watered pastures along the nearby Murrumbidgee River. These discoveries initiated the greatest wave of land settlement in Australian history,[3] as settlers raced to harness the agricultural potential of this new land with scant regard for title or security of tenure. Being outside the boundaries of the Nineteen Counties of New South Wales drawn up in 1825, this unauthorised settlement became known as the 'squatting movement'. It went through Yass and Gundagai and across the Murrumbidgee toward Port Phillip, taking in the country along the Hillas Creek which flowed into the river from the south-east at the famous squatting run of Yabtree. The eventual transformation into pastoral paradise of what was described by early colonists as 'wilderness' was recorded in the *Town & Country Journal* of 22 May 1880. It lauded the Riverina as 'doubtless the great pastoral area and wool growing district of New South Wales' and asserted that 'its vast natural resources, reproductive wealth and ever accumulating industry, render it always an object of vital interest to the colonist and a special attraction to the squatter, the free selector and the merchant'.

The Wiradjuri

The Aboriginal history of the Riverina and the Wiradjuri tribe that roamed the area is also reasonably well documented. Although the precise number of Aboriginals in the Murrumbidgee district before white settlement is not known, Henry Bingham, the Commissioner of Crown Lands in the area, estimated that in 1841 there were between 1600 and 2000.[4] These Indigenous people lived in the district, hunting and gathering animals both large and small, including birds, reptiles, fish, and insects such as the popular Bogong moth. The forests of eucalypt were habitats for possums, a main culinary standby, while the more open, grassy hills and plains were ideal for kangaroo and emu. In the Murrumbidgee River and its tributaries, such as Hillas Creek, swam platypuses, turtles and perch. Wild ducks and water fowl

OVERLEAF
View above
Deltroit, looking
north, 2011

nested in the reeds. In addition, after times of flood, there were freshwater mussels and yabbies, and edible aquatic plants in the creeks, lagoons and the river. While meat was valued by the Wiradjuri, vegetable food also formed part of their diet, which included roots of yam daisies and kurrajong, kangaroo grass seeds, orchids, lilies, herbs and berries.[5]

However, as in so many other parts of Australia, this 'pristine' landscape — so-called by white settlers because of the absence of any civilisation comparable with their own — became the site of several massacres and smaller incidents. Settlers took ownership of what they perceived to be 'empty' land, introducing sheep and cattle that trampled and tore up the fragile native grasses with their sharp, cloven hooves and destroyed the vegetable food on which the Aboriginals and their game relied. Deprived of their traditional food sources and hunting grounds, the Wiradjuri were obliged to help themselves to stores belonging to these presumptuous colonisers and speared their livestock as though these were kangaroo or emu. Even without malice, violent confrontation was almost inevitable as the European concept of exclusive land and property ownership clashed with the Aboriginal idea of communality. Moreover, most settlers believed they had a God-given right to take possession of land, of which, they argued, the Aboriginals were only 'inhabitants' and not 'proprietors'.[6]

In this way, the numbers of the Wiradjuri declined dramatically through murder and starvation, but also through diseases, especially smallpox, influenza and syphilis, caught from contact with the settlers. The situation became distressing even to the most hardened colonists as evidence mounted that the Aboriginals were 'fast being swept away from the face of their native soil'.[7] By 1849, Bingham reported that there were only about 1250 Wiradjuri left in his district, either camping in small groups by the river or working on the stations as stockmen, shepherds or domestic servants. Bingham thought them 'a shrewd, cunning, and intelligent people' with great powers of observation and imitation, but, although he regarded them as ideally suited to stock work, he recognised the difficulties of assimilating them into the employment structures of most white settlers.[8] Instead, he called for a large reserve to be created for the area's Indigenous people so that they could continue to hunt and fish, and for a school to be built adjacent to the reserve for the education of their children.[9]

For another three decades, however, the Wiradjuri tried to continue their traditional lifestyle, moving about the countryside and camping by the river. A few found work on the stations and smaller properties owned by settlers, and were paid in rations. The Wiradjuri were invaluable in times of flood, cutting canoes from the bark of trees and rescuing men, women and children from their huts, ultimately saving them from a watery grave.[10] The most notable instance of this was during the great flood of 1852 in Gundagai, when Yarri rescued a total of 49 people. Of these, one was R. F. Horsley, whose property, Yabtree, was also on the Hillas Creek and encompassed the land that is now Deltroit. Notwithstanding these times of extreme humanity on the part of the Indigenous people, conflict and tension between Aboriginal and settler remained, and in the 1880s the Brungle Reserve near Tumut was created. Aboriginal dispossession in the district was then effectively completed.

It would have been instructive for the early settlers to take note of how the Aboriginals lived *with* their land rather than merely *on* it. Had they done so, they might have avoided some of the impoverishment their pastures faced subsequent to white settlement, which is as much a part of the history of Deltroit as of other Riverina properties. The Aboriginals had recognised that in an arid climate with inconsistent rainfall patterns it was imperative to allow their hunting grounds the opportunity to regenerate. They did this in part by being in a constant state of migration, but also through using fire extensively, albeit in a controlled manner that was the responsibility of an experienced member of the tribe.[11] While fire may have had some negative effects, it nonetheless enabled the native pasture to renew itself by stimulating fresh growth after summer and autumn rain, eradicating pests and clearing dead ground cover that precluded germination. In contrast, the white settlers on Hillas Creek, as elsewhere, applied European farming practices to a much more fragile landscape than they were used to, and quickly 'made one blade of grass grow where two had grown before'.[12]

Origin of the name 'Deltroit'

Having lost their land and traditional way of life, the Wiradjuri nonetheless retained their language, and numerous settlers even chose Aboriginal words for the names of their runs. Deltroit (pronounced '*del*-troy', with a silent 't') is a prime example. The name is neither American nor French nor Old English, as many have supposed, but probably derives from the Wiradjuri word *dhaldhuray*, meaning 'having food' or, if stretched a little further across the language, 'eating place' or 'feasting ground'. Wiradjuri language experts believe that the name can be split into two parts: 'del' being an attempt to spell 'dhal', the stem of the verb 'to eat' and pronounced '*dull*'; and 'troit' being a transliteration of 'dhuray', meaning 'having' and pronounced '*dra*'.[13] The sense of the word as 'eating place' or 'feasting ground' is consistent with the abundance of wildlife on the Hillas Creek. Turtles, which are still plentiful there, were known to be a favourite food of the Wiradjuri, and a property called Gundillawah on Deltroit's western boundary, owned by the Horsley family and originally part of Yabtree, is thought by them to be named after the Wiradjuri word for this small, amphibious creature.

Further evidence that the name 'Deltroit' was originally from Wiradjuri can be found in the existence of other, almost identical place names nearby. Not only is there the similar-sounding Dellateroy Creek ten kilometres away towards Tarcutta, but just south-east of Deltroit, also in the Tarcutta direction, used to be another property that, from at least 1873 up until the early 1900s, was known as Delatroy (or Deletroy) Station, Tarcutta.[14] This property, which has since been renamed, was owned by the Ryder family and was never part of the property known as Deltroit, Hillas Creek. In 1900, Delatroy Station, Tarcutta, was said to be a holding of 4600 acres, partly grazed by sheep and partly under cultivation with wheat and oats. There was also an extensive and beautiful orchard planted with choice trees.[15] Another, even larger property south-west of Deltroit, at Lower Tarcutta, was called Delatroy Estate. This latter holding comprised about 7000 acres, and until 1907 was owned by James Dennis, the brother of George Dennis of Parkley, located just east of Deltroit.[16] With so many places nearby bearing almost the same name, it seems likely that the whole area must at one time have been known to the Wiradjuri by a word that sounded like 'Deltroit'.

When the current spelling of Deltroit was arrived at is uncertain, as is the date when the name began to be used by the Richardsons. Ascertaining the spelling of any Aboriginal word or name was difficult for settlers, not only because Aboriginal languages were never written, but also because many of the sounds produced differed from those in European languages. Moreover, the poor literacy of many early settlers, including those in charge of keeping records, meant that mistakes and inconsistencies were bound to occur. Finding the exact Aboriginal word from which a property name derives is therefore never easy. Early land title documents and other official records suggest that Deltroit may in fact have been called 'Hillas Creek' to begin with. The first references to the Richardsons' property as 'Deltroit' appear in the diary entries of R. F. Horsley dated 30 May 1876 and 29 July 1878. To complicate the matter further, Horsley recorded the name as 'Deltroy', and the property's current spelling is not found until as late as 1895 in the Australasian Federal Pastoral Directory.

Origin of the name 'Hillas Creek'

The naming of Hillas Creek itself has a far simpler explanation, deriving from the surname of two of the first squatters in the area, John and James Hillas. Originally spelled 'Hillas's Creek' and then 'Hillas' Creek', the apostrophe was finally dropped and its current spelling adopted about 1888. John and James Hillas were the sons of free, assisted migrants from Yorkshire in England who arrived in Australia in 1801 and settled in Parramatta. John had been born in England in 1797 and James was born in Australia in 1808. Initially, John had a property named Hillas Mount near Taralga, 30 miles north of Goulburn in New South Wales, before 'squatting' in 1830 or 1831 with his younger brother on the Murrumbidgee near the junction of what is now Hillas Creek. They called their run 'Yabtree' (another name deriving from the Wiradjuri language), and herded sheep and cattle over an area of about 50,000 acres.[17]

Although John owned the stock,[18] he apparently went back to Hillas Mount and left James in charge of Yabtree. Subsequently, James became embroiled in an adulterous relationship with the wife of a local stockman, Samuel Collins, who, in a jealous rage, murdered James in his hut at Yabtree on 3 March 1835. The case became a sensation when Collins, described as 'a quiet harmless good sort of man', was sentenced to death yet, according to the Judge, 'had received the greatest provocation which one man could receive at the hands of another'.[19] In particular, there was much evidence that James had made Collins a laughing stock by going about the country singing a song that included the following verse:

> When Sam went home and found his wife gone,
> He mounted his horse, and off he did ride,
> It was funny to see how he scampered along
> With Jobbins's butterknife slung by his side,
> Across the plains he did caper and quiver,
> And swore he'd surprise all the lads by the river.

The case was referred to Buckingham Palace for the consideration of King William IV, and Collins's death sentence was ultimately commuted to fourteen years' transportation to Van Diemen's Land.

The Robertson Land Acts and the emergence of Deltroit

While the history of Yabtree is largely beyond the scope of this book, it is relevant to the extent that it was out of the original Yabtree run, established by the Hillas family, that Deltroit first emerged. This was a result of the new land legislation introduced into New South Wales in 1861, which was designed to end the squatters' monopoly and enable more settlers to acquire land for agricultural purposes.

After the scramble for land beyond the legal limits of the Nineteen Counties following the explorations of Hovell, Hume and Sturt, squatters had been given some rights of occupation, initially in 1836, by the granting of a £10 annual licence. This reform was marginally improved in 1847 by the introduction of a fourteen-year lease at £10 per annum for 4000 sheep (or the equivalent in cattle), and a further £2 10s per annum for every 1000 sheep (or the equivalent in cattle) thereafter. Neither system restricted the amount of land that could be occupied, though, under the new lease arrangements, the squatter was obliged to describe his boundary. These laws led to vast tracts of land, commonly between 20,000 and 25,000 acres and sometimes as much as 50,000 acres,[20] as in the case of Yabtree, being occupied by squatters, to the exclusion of other settlers arriving in the colony.

It was this iniquity that led to the introduction of the new land legislation into New South Wales in 1861. The *Crown Lands Alienation Act* and the *Crown Lands Occupation Act* (also known as the Free Selection Acts or the Robertson Land Acts, after Sir John Robertson, Minister for Lands and champion of this legislation) implemented the principle of free selection of land before survey and, with few exceptions, applied to all Crown lands, including those already leased. The provisions were complex but, broadly, enabled any man to select a block of unimproved Crown land between 40 and 320 acres (later raised to 640 acres) for £1 per acre, provided that the land was part of neither a mining nor a water reserve. The selector was to pay one quarter of the purchase price immediately, and at the end of three years he could either pay the balance and obtain freehold title, or pay interest on the outstanding balance at the rate of five percent per annum indefinitely. These selections were conditional upon residence and the carrying out of improvements, and were known as 'conditional purchases'. After one year, the selector was allowed to transfer his land to anyone who could fulfil the residency and improvement requirements. Additionally, the selector could apply for a 'pre-emptive lease' to secure the right of grazing on adjoining land three times the size of his selection, but this was often impossible if that land had already been selected by another person.

When this new legislation came into effect, Yabtree had already passed out of the hands of the Hillas family and was held under a lease by R. F. Horsley and his then business partner, Richard Whittaker. The lease was transferred into the sole name of R. F. Horsley in 1866 but expired at the end of that year. It was then a battle for Horsley to retain his holding, buying back, under the new conditional purchase scheme, land that he had previously leased and resorting to the common practice of using 'dummies', reliable employees and friends who took up land on his behalf when he himself had used up his land quota under the legislation.[21] However, many acres were permanently alienated, including the area that is now Deltroit. By virtue of the Robertson Land Acts, the Richardsons were able to 'pick the eye' out of Yabtree, selecting in 1866 and 1867 two prime 320-acre blocks

Sunset at Deltroit, 2009

with frontage onto the Hillas Creek, already reputed at that time to be a continuous and reliable source of water. Over the next twenty years, the Richardsons made many other conditional purchases of valley country along the creek as first title holders, as well as buying numerous portions from other selectors who had taken up land in the same way.[22] Thus, by the mid-1880s Deltroit extended to about 7500 acres, all of which had been part of the original Yabtree squatting run.

Several other neighbouring properties also emerged out of Yabtree and still exist today, including Parkley to the east of Deltroit, and Happy Valley, owned by the Derrick family on Deltroit's northern boundary. The Derricks are the only family other than the Horsleys to have selected land on the Yabtree run and who have remained on their selections ever since. While the Horsley family still own Yabtree, it is significantly reduced in size and has been divided into two further properties, Gundillawah and Yaven, both of which are held by family members. Many other selectors on Yabtree were eventually forced by drought, depression or poor pasture and farm management to leave the district. In most cases, they either sold their conditional purchases back to the Horsleys or on to the Richardsons.

The Robertson Land Acts were very controversial, creating a great deal of animosity between squatters and selectors. It is not hard to imagine, then, that relations between the Richardsons and R. F. Horsley might initially have been cool. Nevertheless, at some stage this was to change, and R. F. Horsley was sending weaners to Deltroit by 1876[23] and was even buying rams from the Richardsons by 1882.[24] In the course of many years of occupation on the Hillas Creek, a close relationship developed between the Horsley family at Yabtree and the different owners of Deltroit, including the Fraser family who were direct descendants of the Richardsons. Whatever the sense of injustice that R. F. Horsley might have felt when the selectors first appeared, the isolation of the surroundings at Hillas Creek and the struggle to make a living from the land that all settlers faced ensured that, ultimately, the Horsleys and the Richardsons became loyal friends — or 'mates', in the best Australian bush tradition.

Earliest known
photograph of
William Richardson,
The Pastoral Review,
April 1920

CHAPTER 2

William Richardson

William Richardson, who established Deltroit in the mid-nineteenth century, was born on Christmas Day 1839 in Bleatarn, a tiny hamlet of six houses in the Parish of Warcop, County of Westmorland (now part of Cumbria), in the far north-west of England. His parents were Michael Richardson and Dorothy Dent, the offspring of yeoman farmers from nearby Sleagill and Soulby respectively. The couple had married five miles from Bleatarn on 6 February 1836 in Kirkby Stephen at the parish church known locally as the 'Cathedral of the Dales'. By then Dorothy was already pregnant, as her first child was born only five months later.

Birthplace

At the time of William's birth, the family was living at Walkers House and Barton Fields, the house and farm owned by Michael's mother, Margaret Richardson, and which Michael later inherited upon her death on 27 June 1847. There were already two older children: Thomas, born on 2 June 1836; and John, born on 13 August 1837. According to baptism records, two younger children, Henry and Mary Isabella, were born subsequently in 1851 and 1854 respectively, but there are no birth certificates to confirm the exact dates. There may have been further children between the

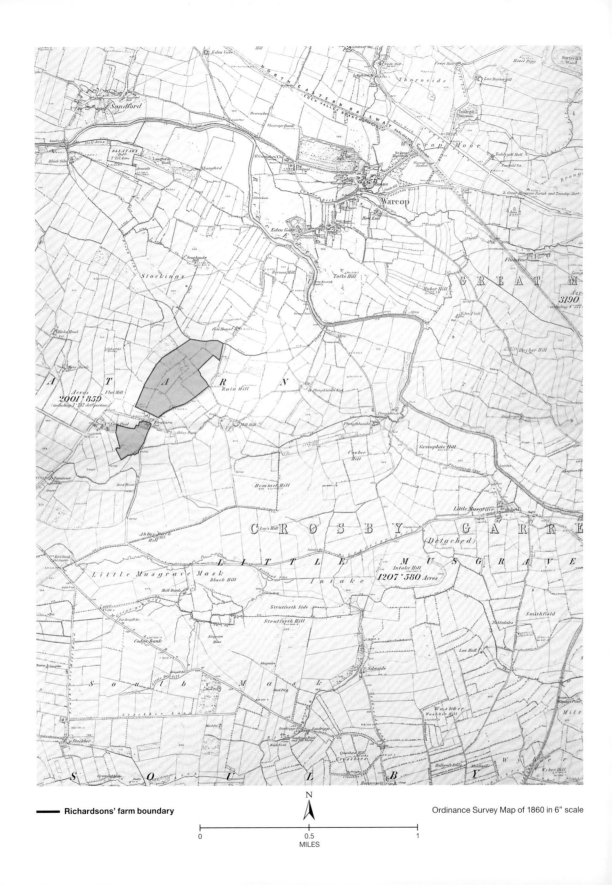

Richardsons' farm boundary

N

0   0.5   1
MILES

Ordinance Survey Map of 1860 in 6" scale

births of William and Henry, as there is a twelve-year gap between them, but the names of any such offspring have not survived.

Walkers House, which still stands today, is a simple two-storey dwelling built from the local red sandstone. Surrounded by a low dry-stone wall of the same material, the house is adjacent to a small stable block and byre or barn for keeping cattle. This 'bank barn' is typical of the area, being on two levels, with an upper storey for threshing or storage reached by a bank and the lower level used for livestock. There appears to have been an orchard behind the house within the confines of the garden wall, and there were also one or two fields beyond, though most of the 75 acres of farmland lay over the road from the house towards the north-east in the direction of Warcop.[1] Bleatarn itself (pronounced '*blay*-a-tarn' and meaning 'blue' or 'dark pond') was so called because of the tarn or marshy ground in the area due to the claylike quality of the soil.[2] The marsh has since dried up, possibly drained, but the small stream or beck that ran alongside the southern end of the hamlet remains.

From Bleatarn, it is possible, even today, to walk along a quiet country lane for just over one mile to Warcop, the village that gave the parish its name and where William was baptised on 22 January 1840. Crossing the Eden River over a three-arched medieval bridge, the countryside here is both hilly and open, with extensive views of the nearby low-rising mountain

OPPOSITE
The Richardsons' farm, Walkers House and Barton Fields in Bleatarn, Westmorland, 1846

RIGHT
Walkers House, Bleatarn, where William Richardson was born

The garden and orchard at the back of Walkers House, Bleatarn

range, the Pennines. There are woods and coppices, hedgerows and streams, and a patchwork of bright green fields delineated by traditional dry-stone walls. Rounded hills give way to broad lowlands stretching towards the more rugged, flat-topped Pennines, a treeless landscape of high moorland known locally as 'fells' and blanketed with snow in winter.

The countryside is largely unchanged since William's birth, and it is not hard to imagine the young Richardson family walking (or possibly riding in a cart) on the day of his baptism to the twelfth-century church at Warcop dedicated to the Irish Celtic saint, Columba. In the cemetery there are several Richardson tombs that testify to the family's long association with the region. Intriguingly, hanging inside the church is a massive portrait in a carved oak frame of one of William's distant relations by marriage on his father's side, Eleanor ('Nelly') Breeks. Her family were also local yeoman farmers but, in addition, had trading interests in the Far East. She was a year younger than William and, in her youth, fell in love with John Lewis, the proprietor of a new shop in London's Oxford Street. Nelly's proud family would not allow her to marry this suitor and, after her death in 1903, John Lewis, who by this time had married another and built up an emporium that is still a household name in England, endowed the Warcop Church on condition that Nelly's portrait hang permanently in its vestry.[3]

TOP
Medieval bridge
over Eden River
between Bleatarn
and Warcop

BOTTOM
Warcop Church

The farming community in Westmorland

Such romantic stories were probably few and far between in this largely rural community of exceptionally hard-working people. In spite of industrial development in or near certain towns and the growth of the textile and mining (notably coal, lead and graphite) industries, agriculture remained the foundation of the economy in both Westmorland and neighbouring Cumberland throughout the nineteenth century.[4] Farmers in Westmorland, especially, received national praise for their 'unceasing work' and 'intensity of industry', and consequently no other part of England was so little affected by the later agricultural depression of the 1870s and 1880s.[5] One commentator noted:

> This industry is a thing to be witnessed with admiration, and even sometimes astonishment. In fact, it is almost impossible to exaggerate the laborious activity of each member of a Westmorland famer's household.[6]

By concentrating on the traditional enterprises of breeding and rearing cattle, sheep and horses and growing only limited crops on the lowlands mainly for the use of feeding livestock, this farming community enjoyed modest prosperity throughout the nineteenth century.

The Richardsons themselves were a good example of this economic reality. They were part of the yeomanry, a social group that had been well respected in Britain since the Middle Ages and which was made up of farmers who held land under either freehold, leasehold or copyhold (including customary) title. While below the rank of gentry, yeomen were generally prosperous small farmers with political rights, often employing servants or labourers, and were distinct from gentleman farmers, who did not labour with their hands. The amount of land they owned and their wealth varied, but the Richardsons were probably better off than many in their class. Evidence of this is in the relative extent of their assets.

William's paternal grandfather, Thomas Richardson, had freehold land of just over 100 acres called Whitestone in Sleagill, which had been in the Richardson family since 1757. Thomas bequeathed Whitestone to William's uncle Henry, the eldest son, leaving legacies of £400 each to two more of his children, including William's father, Michael.[7] There was a further legacy of £1000 to the youngest son, Septimus, who was still a minor. For the times, this estate was not insignificant. Moreover, William's paternal grandmother held Walkers House and Barton Fields in Bleatarn in her own name before she left them to Michael on her death. When Michael himself died in 1888, long after his four eldest boys had emigrated to Australia, he left a considerable estate that included legacies totalling over £1000 and a farm at Scargill in Yorkshire known as Rutherford House, having previously

The traditional byre barn at Walkers House, Bleatarn

transferred a separate 220-acre landholding elsewhere to James Richardson, a son by his second marriage and thus William's half-brother.[8]

Although only 75 acres, the farm at Bleatarn where William grew up was of a size common in that period. More than 70 percent of farms in this area of Westmorland around the time of William's birth occupied 100 acres or less.[9] The Richardsons' land was held under customary tenure, an ancient form of landholding dating from the twelfth century, which meant that although the Lord of the Manor owned the freehold, the customary tenant had the right to sell or pass on the land to his or her heirs. This right of alienation was in return for various services such as mowing hay or cutting peat, as well as 'fines' or rents payable upon certain events, including leaving a property or the death of the Lord of the Manor during the tenancy.

While the number of small landholdings and customary tenures might suggest an inward-looking, feudal society based on subsistence farming, this could not be further from the truth. Farmers in Westmorland had long

Views over Barton Fields towards the Pennines

traded their livestock at the important fairs in Rosley, Appleby and Brough Hill that attracted stock from all over northern England, Scotland and even Ireland. By the mid-nineteenth century, with the arrival of the railways, many locally-bred animals and other farm produce were being transported south.[10] Although Westmorland was far from any densely populated region of England, it was on the main route between London and Scotland by road. Moreover, as early as 1846, a railway between Carlisle in Cumberland to the north and Lancaster to the south was opened, which ran through Westmorland before joining the main railway line to London, thereby linking Westmorland to the capital.

A number of regional railways followed, including the Eden Valley branch line completed in 1862 from Kirkby Stephen to Penrith via Warcop. This line joined the Carlisle-to-London service, creating even greater opportunities for local farmers. Apart from extending their markets by using the railways, many entrepreneurial farmers began to increase the scale of their operations by enlarging their landholdings.[11] William's father is a good example. By 1861 he had moved his family to nearby Great Ormside and was farming 200 acres. Then, by 1871 he had moved his family again, this time to a farm called Northside, comprising 200 acres (later increased to 220 acres), in Bowes, North Yorkshire.[12]

Westmorland farmers were also known for their skills in animal husbandry and, in particular, for raising well-bred Shorthorn cattle. It was said that the Shorthorn were 'the greatest boast of Cumberland and Westmorland agriculture', and that they had become 'the grandest race of cattle which, apart from show and fancy herds, can be found in any quarter of the Kingdom'.[13] Shorthorn cattle owned by William Fawcett of Sandford, just two miles from Bleatarn, were even being sent from Westmorland to Australia and winning prizes in Melbourne in the 1870s.[14] It is hard not to speculate whether Fawcett was known to William Richardson, as both men were from the Parish of Warcop and emigrated to Australia about the same time. It is also highly likely that the Richardsons farmed Shorthorn cattle since William subsequently ran this particular breed at Deltroit, becoming a noted Shorthorn judge in Australia.[15] About 50 percent of the Richardsons' farmland at Bleatarn was classed in the Tithe records as 'pasture' or the more valuable 'meadow',[16] and was therefore ideally suited for running cattle.

Aside from producing beef, the Richardsons may have had dairy cows or sheep at Bleatarn. In addition, they appear to have grown crops, as a number of their fields were designated arable land. No doubt the brothers and probably also their sister helped out on the farm to keep costs to a minimum, although the family also employed a labourer.[17] 'Work, and that of a hard and unceasing kind,'[18] was the daily occupation of each member of a typical Westmorland farming family. Whether Michael Richardson had a second occupation (as many small farmers did), such as a carrying business (which was William's first business venture in Australia) or inn-keeping, is unknown, but it is likely that the family lived simply, investing any surplus funds in their livestock or on farm improvements.

Lack of water was never a problem in Westmorland, which encompassed the Upper Eden Valley. The Eden itself is a river of exceptional clarity and quality, consisting of 90 miles of rushing water that tumbles northwards over rocks and boulders into the Solway Firth. Along the way, the river is fed by many streams, running off the Pennines to the east and from several lakes to the west, where there is an abundance of birds and fish, mainly salmon and trout. The annual rainfall in this area is about 38 inches and increases to almost 78 inches in other parts of the valley. In contrast to Westmorland's soft, wet landscape, the dry and brittle environment of Australia was far less forgiving. What is more, the grasslands in the new colony that the early settlers spied with such delight had never before been grazed by sheep or cattle.

Details from the Bleatarn Tithe records of 1846 showing Michael Richardson as landowner and describing the state of cultivation of his fields

Published by W. H. Beynon & Co. Cheltenham

The Old School Sedbergh.

Education in Westmorland

Front view of
original main
schoolhouse of
Sedbergh School,
c. 1870, now the
school library

William's education is likely to have included a period in a local village
school, probably followed by a grammar-school education at either Kirkby
Stephen, where his parents were married, or Appleby, where his second
cousins Thomas and Arthur Richardson were sent in the 1870s. There
was neither a primary nor a secondary school in Bleatarn or Warcop
when William was a boy, though there were schools of both descriptions
within a five-mile radius at Great Musgrove and Soulby and in the much
larger market towns of Kirkby Stephen and Appleby. This was an area of
England where a substantial part of the population was fully literate and
education was highly valued.[19] There were at least six newspapers published

Recent view (back) of Evans House, Sedbergh School, fomerly the headmaster's house

in the region during the 1830s and an astonishing sixteen by the 1860s. Moreover, Kirkby Stephen claimed to have the largest circulating library in the north of England during the same period. Even a Reading Room was founded in Warcop in 1859, albeit too late for the young William to enjoy.

Unfortunately, until 1880, when schooling became compulsory up to the age of ten, few schools kept attendance records and, even if they did so, many of these records have been lost. Among the registers remaining, there is no evidence of William's education at all; however, it is clear from the handful of his letters that still exist and from his handwriting that he was an educated man. Moreover, according to one of his obituaries, once he had settled in Australia he read the *Sydney Morning Herald* daily for fifty years,[20] indicating not only his literacy, but also the interest he took in affairs beyond the immediate district in which he lived. Similarly, there is no record of the education of any of William's siblings other than his eldest brother, Thomas; and a much younger half-sister, Sarah, who attended a ladies' boarding school in Barnard Castle.

Traditionally, the sons of yeoman farmers would be sent to either a grammar or boarding school (if the latter could be afforded), and this was invariably the case with the eldest son.[21] While family tradition maintains that Thomas was educated at Eton, there is no record of his attendance there at any time. Instead, it seems clear that he was sent 20 miles away from his home at Bleatarn to the prestigious Sedbergh Grammar School. Founded in 1525 by the Provost of Eton, Roger Lupton, it is probably this Eton connection that later caused confusion among Thomas's descendants as to where he was educated. Thomas commenced his schooling at Sedbergh in August 1850 at the age of fourteen and interestingly, during his time there, boarded with the Lupton family (presumably descendants of the original founder) on their nearby farm.[22] The fact that the school chosen for Thomas was beyond the immediate district where his family were living, even though there were good grammar schools in nearby Appleby and Kirkby Stephen,

Back view of
original main
schoolhouse
of Sedbergh
School, c. 1870

OLD SCHOOL-HOUSE, SEDBERGH

suggests that the right education was very important to the Richardsons
or that there was a family connection with the Luptons, making Sedbergh
School the natural choice.

No record exists as to how long Thomas stayed at Sedbergh, but
according to many family sources he aspired to enter the Church, which was
one of a number of professions that the sons of yeoman farmers commonly
pursued after schooling. Unfortunately, in spite of this strongly held belief
in the family, no firm evidence has been found of Thomas receiving a
theological education. There is an entry for a Thomas Richardson in the
Michaelmas Term of 1852 at St Bees Theological College in Cumberland,
about 40 miles west of the Eden Valley and situated on the coast. However,
because further information is unavailable, it cannot be ascertained whether
this Thomas Richardson is the same as the one from Bleatarn. He would
have been only sixteen at the date of entry for this two-year course and
one of a hundred students 'expected to be well versed in the classics'.[23]
At the time, there were no other theological colleges in the region that
Thomas could have attended, but it is of course conceivable that he went

further afield. Alas, nothing concrete has been established to confirm this. A check in the archives of St John's College, Cambridge, which had close ties with Sedburgh School in the nineteenth century, has elicited no material to suggest that Thomas was a student there. Similarly, there is no evidence in the relevant records of his having attended a theological college in any of the major cathedral cities in England. It therefore remains a mystery as to whether he ever answered his calling.

Death of Dorothy Richardson

Wherever the Richardson children were educated and whatever they were engaged in immediately after leaving school, their lives were to change suddenly after the death of their mother, Dorothy, on 26 November 1855. Dorothy was only forty-two when she passed away from cancer of the uterus. While Thomas, John and William were nineteen, eighteen and almost sixteen respectively, Henry was just four and Mary Isabella was eighteen months old. Clearly needing help with the younger children, Michael Richardson employed as housekeeper his late wife's niece Mary Dent, who was working as a cook in Newcastle.[24] She seems to have also provided a warm bed for him, as about a year later the first of their five children, Joseph, was born on 27 November 1856 — just one day after the anniversary of Dorothy's death.

No marriage certificate can be found for Michael and Mary, and it is possible that their union was never formalised. Nevertheless, they proceeded to have four more children together: Michael Septimus, born on 10 January 1860; James, born on 10 April 1862; Margaret Ann, born in 1864; and Sarah, born on 16 April 1866. Prior to the birth of these last four children, the three eldest boys, Thomas, John and William, had left separately for Australia, only to be followed by the fourth boy, Henry, a few years later.

If William thought, upon his departure, that he could transfer successfully the totality of his early farming experience in Westmorland to the South Western Slopes of New South Wales, he would have a rude awakening.

CHAPTER 3

Emigration

*T*he 'remarriage' of Michael Richardson may partly explain why his three eldest sons, Thomas, John and William, emigrated to Australia one after the other, followed about ten years later by his fourth son, Henry. Doubtless, the boys saw that it was likely their father would have several more children with his new, much younger wife, and that their share of the family assets would be reduced. They may even have objected to the relationship developing so soon after the death of their own mother, Dorothy, and gone to the other side of the world in protest. While such explanations are possible, the reason for the mass emigration of the Richardson boys was probably far more complex. Clearly, John Richardson, who was the first to leave (probably departing only about two weeks after his mother's death), must have been contemplating a new life in Australia for some considerable time.

Emigration in nineteenth-century Westmorland

Although the popular perception is often that farming families have been rooted on their farms for generations, this did not invariably apply to small family farms in Westmorland.[1] Many of these families moved, as did Michael at least twice during his second 'marriage'. Moreover, movement was not limited to migration within the region. As in the case of other rural communities in Britain, the Upper Eden Valley was 'an exporter of people',

not only to other parts of the UK, but also overseas to North America, New Zealand and Australia.[2] From the 1840s, both the expanding railway system and the development of steamships encouraged travel and migration far beyond a man's birthplace.

Regular advertisements for sailings to Australia began to appear on the front page of regional newspapers from at least the mid-1850s. In the case of The Black Ball Line, readers were offered passage to Australia within sixty-five days by sailing boat from Liverpool for fourteen shillings and upwards.[3] These vessels were touted as being 'the largest, the finest and the fastest Merchant Ships in the World', even faster than the rival steamships that were, at this time, still carrying a full set of sails because of their inefficient engines and the lack of coaling ports en route. The sailing ships carried on board 'full Bands of Music, as well as Chess, Backgammon, and Draft Boards' for the amusement of passengers, and provided a milking cow and baths for their comfort.

Chief among the inducements for emigration to Australia was the news that gold had been discovered in significant quantities. From 1851, there was extensive coverage in the British press, including dozens of articles in the *Westmorland Gazette and Kendal Advertiser*, about these discoveries in New South Wales and the new colony of Victoria. According to several firsthand accounts received from Australia, the finds were so large and numerous that people were 'intoxicated' by the news and 'every person you meet speaks of gold and nothing but gold'.[4] It was reported too that 'all former occupations are at a standstill' and that 'all the shepherds are bolting'[5] to the gold diggings. In Bathurst, near Sydney, it was said that the average earnings of those who went to the diggings was not less than thirty shillings a day and that it was even possible in certain places to earn between £100 and £200 per month on the goldfields.[6]

Aside from the chance to join the gold rush, people were encouraged to emigrate by the glowing letters and stories from migrants overseas, often reproduced in newspaper articles, about the growth and opportunities in farming and agriculture in the colonies. One such compelling letter, which might have been read by William and his brothers a year before their mother died, appeared in the *Westmorland Gazette* on 4 November 1854.[7] This

OPPOSITE
Thomas Richardson, c. 1890. His watch-chain was reputedly made of gold from his own mine.

letter began with these words: 'The market for all sorts of dairy and agricultural produce is unlimited in Australia, and you may go the world over and not find a finer country and climate for stock, and one that presents fewer obstacles to the pursuit of agriculture than this.' The correspondent continues by saying:

There are very few of the labourers that came out two years ago that are not now landowners and fast attaining independence; whilst those who had a little money to start with are already prosperous farmers. [...] There are many Westmorland men — working men and small farmers — who, if they could but be persuaded to come out here would never wish themselves back again in England.

Louisa Richardson, one of Thomas Richardson's daughters

In addition to favourable reports such as these about farming, there were also many newspaper articles about the extraordinary growth of the Australian wool industry. In the *Westmorland Gazette* of 22 November 1851, a lengthy article appeared stating that Australian wool production had increased 300 percent in the last ten years and that the amount being exported to England alone was 40,000,000 pounds per annum. In addition to being huge, the wool clip's quality was such that it had apparently encouraged new branches of trade in the product. No wonder so many Westmorland farmers were eager to seek out the extensive and highly productive pastures to be found in the Colonies.

Exodus by the Richardsons

With news about gold discoveries in payable quantities and the thriving rural scene, many people, whether out of choice or necessity, began to seek what they believed to be a better life in Australia. They sought to create wealth for themselves and their families, to gain prestige and to rise above their station. The society of the Upper Eden Valley, where the Richardsons came from, was traditionally outward-looking and enterprising,[8] with trade links well beyond the region. It is therefore not surprising that William and his brothers felt able to contemplate a life in Australia, whatever their thoughts on their father's new arrangements at home. All four brothers appear to have had an enterprising spirit, combined with varying degrees of entrepreneurial flair. In William's case, there can be little doubt that he achieved far greater prosperity and position in New South Wales than he could have done had he stayed farming in Westmorland.

Another impetus for the Richardsons is likely to have been the earlier emigration to Australia of various cousins who were themselves seized by gold fever. Henry and Robert Richardson, the sons of William's uncle, Henry Richardson of Whitestone in Sleagill, emigrated in 1852 and 1854 respectively and sought their fortunes on the Victorian goldfields. Henry was very successful and ultimately settled with his family on a block of land in Wodonga, on the border of Victoria and New South Wales. The property, known as Barnawartha, became famous for grazing sheep and cattle and grew to about 10,000 acres in size.[9] Robert was not so lucky and struggled to support his wife and three children until his premature death in 1865.[10]

Other cousins also emigrated, including John and Thomas Dent. Their father, Joseph, was Dorothy Richardson's brother, and their sister, Mary, was Michael Richardson's new 'wife'. John and Thomas Dent went initially to Victoria in 1853, but later settled in New South Wales.[11] John Richardson was for a time in business with one of the Dents, probably Thomas, on a block of land in the Adelong district about 20 miles from Deltroit. Additionally, John Dent appears to have 'dummied' for William and John Richardson in 1869 on a parcel of land at Deltroit that was subsequently transferred into the Richardson name.[12] Clearly, the Richardsons were comfortable associating

Thomas Richardson's gold mine in the Adelong hills

with the Dents in Australia, suggesting that any family rift potentially caused by their father's 'remarriage' was neither too serious nor prolonged.

Perhaps inspired by their cousins, the Richardson brothers emigrated to Australia one by one, paying their own passage. According to recollections of various family members, John was the first to leave, though the date of his departure is uncertain. Relevant sailing records for the 1850s include over twenty passengers with the name of John Richardson. However, the most likely entry, taking into account the age and occupation of each migrant on the passenger lists, is that of a John Richardson described as a 'farmer' who left on the *Marco Polo* on 7 December 1855 from Liverpool, arriving in Melbourne on 26 February 1856.

William very likely followed eighteen months later on the same vessel, departing Liverpool on 7 June 1857 and arriving in Melbourne on 3 September 1857. Thomas then emigrated on 21 June 1858, departing Liverpool on the *Albion* and arriving in Melbourne on 12 September the same year. Henry left for Australia sometime in the late 1860s or very early 1870s, but it has not been possible to identify the date any more closely. In 1861, at the age of nine years, he was still living with his father, stepmother, sister and half-siblings in Westmorland, but by 1871 he was no longer at home.[13]

Among William's descendants there is a belief, which cannot be substantiated, that he arrived in Melbourne on 20 August 1857, the day that the *Dunbar*, a clipper from England, sank outside Sydney Harbour with the loss of 121 passengers and crew. This maritime disaster, one of the worst ever in Australia's history, captured the attention of the public and was written about in the Sydney and Melbourne press for several weeks afterwards. William would have heard or read about the catastrophe on his arrival in Melbourne and, over time, the two events may have become closely linked in the minds of William's family. However, between the day the *Dunbar* sank and the arrival of the *Marco Polo* on 3 September, there were no ships from England with any passenger by the name of William Richardson listed on board. It is therefore almost certain that William's true arrival was fractionally later than his descendants believe.

Crossing the oceans

While none of William's personal recollections of his voyage survive,
there nevertheless remains a detailed account of the journey[14] by a fellow
passenger, James Cooper Stewart, who became a prominent Melbourne
lawyer and alderman in 1872. The *Marco Polo* itself was a sailing ship
of 1613 tonnes under the command of Captain James Clarke and was a
favourite in the fleet of the Black Ball Line. There were 436 passengers on
board this particular voyage, which, according to Stewart, began on a foggy
morning with a two-gun salute, after a routine health inspection and solemn
address by a clergyman the night before. He describes his own intense
feelings of sorrow and those of the other passengers at 'leaving home and
its hallowed associations' and the separation 'from the friends of childhood
perhaps never to meet them again'.

As the voyage progressed, a more cheerful note is struck and, in spite
of some rough weather and terrible seasickness, the passengers began at
night to 'trip the light fantastic', even enjoying a ball arranged by the captain
in celebration of America's Independence Day. The weather improved,
becoming at first 'oppressively hot', before cooling down as the vessel
crossed the equator on 12 July. In accordance with tradition, a Ceremony of
Crossing the Line took place, during which a young sailor was dressed up as
Neptune. Those sailors who had not crossed the equator before were ritually
tarred from ear to ear and then shaved, before being brought before Neptune
in homage. There were other high points during the voyage, including the
sightings of a huge shark, a school of 700 or more porpoises in the Bay of
Biscay, and a vessel bound for London from Melbourne. Near the Cape of
Good Hope, the ship met with a fearful storm such that 'the sea was running
mountains high', with the waves rising to about 80 feet. The passengers were
clearly terrified and many sails were blown away and yards broken, but there
was no serious damage, though all aboard felt 'a lesson administered on the
precariousness of life'.

The vessel finally arrived in Melbourne on 3 September and, although
Stewart claimed to have landed 'almost a skeleton' since 'our food was not
eatable', the papers stated that the passengers were in excellent health and

The Marco Polo by
Thomas Robertson,
1859

delighted with the voyage.[15] The *Marco Polo*'s passengers presented their
captain with a testimonial written by Stewart as a mark of their appreciation,
but this can no longer be traced.

How William felt when he disembarked is a matter of conjecture, but
he no doubt experienced a mixture of relief and apprehension. His brother
John may have been there to meet him, or he may have had to find his own
way around in the first few days and weeks of his arrival. According to
family tradition,[16] he had fourteen shillings in his pocket, though this could
have been a reference to the cost of the passage from England which was
advertised for this sum.

As for Thomas, who travelled out to Melbourne one year later, he left a
record of his thoughts during the voyage in the form of a poem written in a
pocket book. The work is clearly that of an educated man:

On board Albion June 1858

Vesper fast is closing o'er the ocean's dusky waves
Day has sped away into oblivion's fretful shades
Night her sable mantle o'er the universe has cast
Which like its predecessor will fade away as fast.

The sun in ruddy vesture is setting in the west
With smiles of satisfaction being invited home to rest
Mankind has left his task of toil and now is homeward bound
But I upon the ocean wide do roam at large around.

The surging billow forms my pillow, my cradle and my bed
Can mortal say, but it may be – my sarcophagus when dead.
The porpoises, or whales, sharks, flying fish among
Or others of the finny tribe to gorge their maws upon.

The firmament above is decked in silvery sheen
The stars their influence lending to guide the paths of men
The moon in state majestic rides triumphant through the skies
Proclaiming God's Omnipotence to man's all-searching eye.

When the enemy comes, the brave best [*sic*] prepared
Survey your defence, and stand on your guard.

Thoughts of the Old Country

Leaving behind, possibly forever, his family, friends and all that was familiar,
Thomas was clearly plagued by bouts of melancholia on the voyage. Whether
this state of mind continued after his arrival in Australia is unknown. If he
was sometimes overwhelmed by a sense of profound desolation and even
despair, there would have been many other migrants, including his brothers,
lately arrived in the colony who shared the same feelings. It is inconceivable

On Board Albion June 1858.

Vesper fast is closing o'er the ocean's dusky
waves.
Day has sped away into oblivion's fretful shades
Night her sable mantle o'er the universe has cast
Which like its predecessor will fade away as fast.
The sun in ruday vesture is setting in the West.
With smiles of satisfaction being invited home
to rest
Mankind has left his task of toil & now is
homeward bound

But I upon the ocean wide do roam at large
around
The surging billow forms my pillow, my cradle
& my bed
Can mortal say but it may be — my
sarcophagus when dead.
The Porpoises, or Whales, Sharks flying fish
among
Or others of the finny tribe to gorge their
maws upon.
The firmament above is decked in silvery sheen

The stars their influence lending to guide
the paths of men
The moon in state majestic rides triumphant
thro' the skies
Proclaiming Gods Omnipotence to man's
all - searching eye
When the enemy comes, be brave & best
prepared
Survey your defence, & stand on your
guard.

OPPOSITE
Poem written
by Thomas
Richardson
during his voyage
to Australia, 1858

that the Richardson brothers did not have regular pangs of terrible homesickness — they were almost entirely cut off from England and had to face, without any prior experience of anything similar, the hardships of pioneering life in Australia. It would not be surprising if their thoughts often turned to those they cherished but had left behind: the green and rolling landscape of their birth, the fells and the dales, and the long-established and comfortable way of life in rural Westmorland.

Both William and his brother John returned to visit England in later years, but it is not known whether Thomas or Henry ever did. John was the first to visit England, returning in the late 1860s and taking with him the three orphaned children of his cousin, Robert Richardson.[17] These children were Thomas Wilkinson, Arthur Camplin and Elizabeth Ann, and were all under seven years of age when their parents died within a few weeks of each other. John, who was unmarried at the time, seems to have taken charge of the orphans and delivered them safely to their grandparents in England, where the two boys were sent to Appleby Grammar School. One of them, Thomas Wilkinson, later returned to Australia at the age of nineteen[18] and went to live with his unofficial guardian. Arthur Camplin emigrated to Canada for a time before returning to England, while Elizabeth Ann lived with an aunt and uncle, Barbara and William Thwaytes, at Crackenthorpe Hall near Appleby, before returning to Australia in 1884.

William returned to England on at least two occasions. The first time appears to have been with his youngest daughter, Mary Isabella ('Isabel'), in March 1902 for an extended trip of Europe and to install her in Rome, where she studied music. On the second occasion, William came to England in November 1905 at the time of Isabel's engagement to an Englishman. These trips were a luxury both in terms of cost and time, and, in the case of all four brothers, were probably undertaken only in exceptional circumstances. It is likely that the struggle to build new lives in Australia demanded their full attention and resources, and that, in spite of strong ties in England, they did their best to lead the lives they had chosen rather than seek out the one they had left behind.

Pattern of Land Acquisition at Deltroit
by the Richardsons from 1866

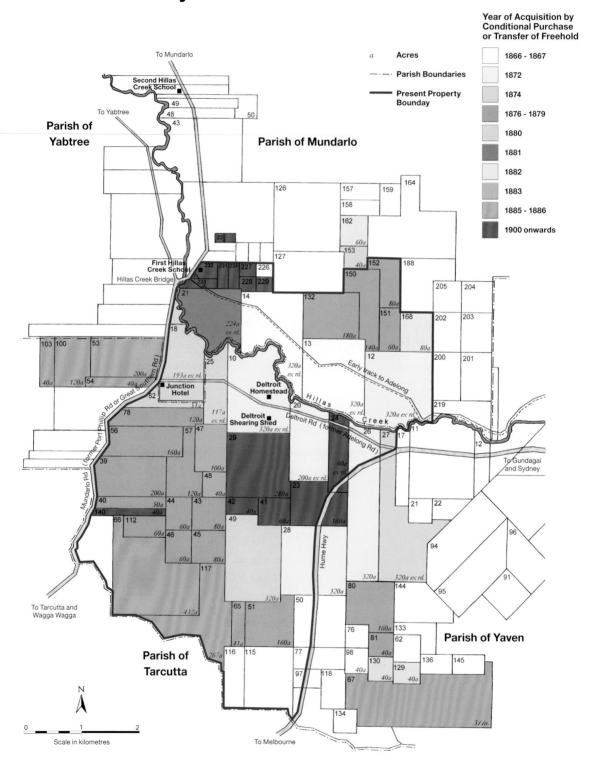

Year of Acquisition by Conditional Purchase or Transfer of Freehold

a Acres

–·– Parish Boundaries

— Present Property Bounday

- 1866 - 1867
- 1872
- 1874
- 1876 - 1879
- 1880
- 1881
- 1882
- 1883
- 1885 - 1886
- 1900 onwards

NOTE: This map is based on land title documents that are incomplete. Whilst every effort has been made to ensure accuracy, it should not be relied on for legal purposes.

CHAPTER 4

Birth of a Property

$\mathscr{A}$ ccording to family tradition, the seventeen-year-old William
Richardson made straight for the Victorian goldfields upon his arrival in
Melbourne and joined his older brother John, who was then a gold miner
in the colony.[1] In spite of extensive enquiries and research, there is no other
evidence of William's early life in Victoria apart from a brief reference in his
obituaries[2] which state that he 'became engaged in carrying pursuits between
Melbourne and Ballarat'.

Working the goldfields

'Carrying' — or 'carting', as it was also known — was often a more reliable
and lucrative source of income than gold mining. Transport was in much
demand as mining increased and new businesses and pastoral enterprises in
the vicinity of the goldfields flourished. Carriers used drays and wagons for
their work, pulled either by a team of horses or the more resilient bullocks.
The drivers were known as 'draymen', 'bullockies' or 'teamsters', celebrated in
verse and prose for their colourful language, resourcefulness, intractability
and sometimes trustworthiness. William, however, seems to have been
different. Known as 'Honest Bill'[3] and for being 'the soul of probity and
honour',[4] he was clearly a man of his word and had the utmost integrity.
Little else is known of his character or attributes, but he allegedly spoke with

a northern accent[5] or in what is now commonly referred to as Cumbrian, a brogue and dialect distinctive for its loose vowels and frequent use of Old Norse in place of standard English.

As for William's skills, apart from the likelihood of his having attended school and the certainty of a rural upbringing, almost nothing is known of his talents or training. According to his descendants, William was an excellent horseman, and he would no doubt have been familiar with the tradition of carting since there were numerous carriers in Westmorland still operating in the mid-1850s, in spite of the railways.[6] Additionally, William may have had a small amount of capital to start his own business when he arrived in Melbourne. His descendants believe that he came with only fourteen shillings in his pocket,[7] but when William's father died in 1888 he left William £50 less than his two surviving brothers.[8] Possibly this indicates that William had received an advance of £50 about the time of his emigration so that he could establish himself on his arrival in Victoria.

Whatever his circumstances when he first came to the colony, William made 'a great success' of his carrying business.[9] Subsequently, he left Victoria for New South Wales, settling in the Adelong district at the foothills of the Snowy Mountains in 1864 and continuing to operate there as a teamster.[10] His brother John had moved to Adelong a few years previously and, while the precise date is not known, John must have arrived in the area before 1862. His name appears in the Conditional Purchase Registers for the Adelong district in that year, and prior to this date he is known to have worked with his eldest brother, Thomas,[11] who was mining on the Adelong goldfields. Thomas had gone to Adelong immediately after his arrival in Australia in 1858. Either he intended to try and make his own way alone in New South Wales, or he went to join John, who may have already moved there from Victoria by this time. Family connections were likely to have influenced all three Richardson boys in deciding where to settle at first, and it is therefore unsurprising that they followed one another to Adelong at various stages. Moreover, the Dent cousins had also settled in the area, but the precise date of the Dents' arrival in Adelong remains unclear. It is known, though, that Thomas Dent married Mary Ann Crain, the daughter of a local selector, on 6 November 1862, while his brother married Mary's sister, Rachel, on 4 November 1873.

Adelong itself was, at this time, a growing community due to the discovery of rich deposits of alluvial gold in Golden Gully and Adelong Creek in the early 1850s. People of all nationalities flocked to this picturesque landscape of eucalyptus and kurrajong trees where hills strewn with granite boulders were coursed by creeks and waterfalls. Immigrants not just from Britain and Ireland, but also from China, Germany, France and even India settled along the banks of the creeks in slab huts and calico tents. When more gold was discovered in 1857, this time in veins running through the rocky banks of the Adelong Creek, an air of permanence descended on the area, and the huts and tents were replaced by more substantial buildings. By 1872, *The Town and Country Journal* noted that Adelong

> is one of the neatest and best conducted gold digging townships in the colony ... There are three churches, two schools, a bank, four public houses and about the same number of stores.[12]

Adelong was eventually to become so cosmopolitan, in comparison to other more provincial towns, that it was known as the 'Shanghai of Australia',[13] perhaps referring in part to a decadent side.

Notwithstanding, the life of a miner was exceptionally arduous, entailing hard, physical work from sun-up to sundown six days a week. Strength and endurance were vital in a pursuit involving much personal hardship and frequent disappointment, but those who persevered and were well equipped could be very successful. When alluvial gold yields in Adelong began to fall towards the end of 1859 and the expenses associated with reef mining in the area became prohibitive for the individual miner,[14] Thomas Richardson, who was as yet unmarried, went to the goldfields in Orange for approximately fifteen years and did not return to Adelong until about 1875.[15] It is not known to what extent Thomas made a success of his mining activities, but he ultimately managed to support a family of fourteen children on his gold findings, supplemented by income from farming and grazing.[16]

As for John Richardson, he determined that mining was not his vocation. About two years after Thomas's departure for Orange, John purchased 320 acres on the Adelong Creek on 6 May 1862.[17] This is the first record that can be traced of any of the Richardson brothers owning land in the area or anywhere in New South Wales. The land, which was situated on the west bank of the creek, was directly opposite the Conditional Purchase belonging to Irwin Crain, whose daughter, Mary Ann, married Thomas Dent later the same year. John appears to have gone into partnership on this block with one of the Dent brothers, probably Thomas, given that it was he who in effect married 'the girl next door'. Unfortunately, the only evidence of this partnership is the sale notice of the subsequent break-up of the business in 1866. This notice does not give the name of the Dent brother involved, referring simply to the partnership of 'Messrs Dent and Richardson', but it does indicate clearly the dairying nature of their business.[18]

Early selections on Hillas Creek

Two months before the dissolution of the Dent and Richardson partnership and despite prevailing drought conditions, John and William Richardson purchased the first two blocks of land on Hillas Creek, at what was to become Deltroit. A partnership began, this time between the two brothers, that continued for twenty years, until John's premature death in 1886. Together, they created a property of a size and quality far beyond the dreams of most Westmorland farmers. Extricating himself from his existing dairying business, John terminated his arrangements with Thomas Dent, and they placed an advertisement in the *Tumut & Adelong Times* on 1 March 1866 for the sale, without reserve, of their joint stock, including forty-five milking cows and an 'english [*sic*] patent barrel churn with the newest and latest improvements'. They also sold nine working bullocks, fourteen 'staunch draught and well bred horses' and two bullock drays, all of which were conceivably owned either wholly or in part by William and used by him in his carrying trade. Presumably, they would be surplus to requirements in the new grazing operation on Hillas Creek.

Unafraid of hard physical work and industry in the hostile environment of the driest continent on earth, the two Richardson brothers realised that in Australia a great deal of land was required to create an efficient pastoral

Deltroit wool bale

enterprise. They appear to have put aside any qualms to do with owning and managing hundreds and then thousands of acres, compared to the mere 75 acres that they were used to back home at Bleatarn, Westmorland. As for the acquisition of such large areas of grazing land, the Robertson Land Acts had made this a reality for thousands of settlers in New South Wales. In common with many other selectors, William and John stepped onto the ladder of opportunity afforded by the new land legislation and began the long climb to financial and social success that they so earnestly desired. As the eminent Australian historian Manning Clark wrote:

Land, after all, was the great source of wealth as well as the means to respectability and prestige, and of all the sources of wealth from the land, the most romantic, the most popular and possibly the most lucrative, was the grazing of sheep …[19]

It is clear that William and John were conscious of these imperatives. There was double security in sheep that could be grazed both for their wool and their meat. Although sheep might be more labour-intensive than cattle, requiring daily shepherding (in the absence of fences) and annual shearing, wool could be easily baled and transported, as well as shipped to Europe where it was in high demand. Notwithstanding these advantages, the grazing of cattle was still a major industry, and sheep and cattle were often run together as they were at Deltroit from the beginning. In fact, until the early 1860s, it was the grazing of cattle rather than sheep that predominated in the Riverina[20] even though the meat market was purely a domestic one, with refrigeration just beginning to be developed. However, as the price of wool rose, the emphasis shifted from cattle to sheep. Similarly, although the drought of the mid-1860s saw a temporary return to cattle, sheep numbers continued to rise afterwards, whereas cattle numbers remained stable. It has been estimated that between 1861 and 1891, sheep numbers in the Riverina climbed from one to thirteen million.[21]

Wool bales leaving
Deltroit, c. 1910

Although the Riverina was widely regarded as a most favourable grazing district, it seems that establishing a selection on Hillas Creek was not William's first choice. Before moving to New South Wales, he had tried to acquire land in Ballarat and Glenormiston, Victoria, but he had been unsuccessful because of 'too much grabbing going on'.[22] Subsequently, working as a teamster in the Adelong district, William must have noticed the beautiful Hillas Creek valley and seen its grazing potential. No doubt he and John ruminated on its possibilities. It is not known whether it was William who finally persuaded John to give up dairying in favour of a more ambitious, mixed-grazing enterprise in the vicinity, or whether John himself was behind the idea. Whoever was the true protagonist, the decision paid off handsomely.

The land on Hillas Creek that the brothers coveted straddled the Parish of Mundarlo to the north and the Parish of Yaven to the south. William and John began by purchasing two blocks, Portions 13 and 14 (Parish of Mundarlo), which they acquired as first conditional purchase holders on 4 January and 22 February 1866 respectively.[23] These blocks were 320 acres each of prime grazing country, situated directly on the northern bank of the Hillas Creek. They were also part of the unimproved section of the Yabtree run and, hence, were available for selection. Frontage country such as this was widely sought by pastoralists at the time to enable them to easily water stock. Land that was beyond a short walking distance from reliable water became known as 'the back blocks' and required improvements, such as a dam or tank filled by a windmill, in order to become viable and permanently usable. Selecting these creek flats, the Richardsons probably also had in mind the existing drought conditions[24] that prevailed for the rest of the decade and that reappeared again in the mid-1870s.[25]

However, as sometimes happened with free selection before survey (following the principle laid down by the Robertson Land Acts), the first two blocks at Deltroit taken up by the Richardsons were made part of a water reserve. These conditional purchases were therefore subsequently cancelled, only to be reinstated: in the case of Portion 14, on 27 December 1866 in the name of John Richardson; and in the case of Portion 13, on 28 November 1867 in the name of William Richardson.[26] In addition to these portions, and in accordance with the land legislation that also permitted a selector to graze three times the area purchased, both William and John had pre-emptive leases[27] of an additional 960 acres each, adjoining their blocks to the north. Some of these leases were eventually converted to conditional purchases between the late 1870s and the mid-1880s.

On the same day that William had originally purchased Portion 13, a local resident, Robert Tresilian, applied as first conditional purchaser of Portion 12 (Parish of Mundarlo),[28] another 320 acres on the northern bank of the Hillas Creek alongside William's land. This adjoining block was strategically important to the Richardsons, but, because of the inconvenient rule that only a maximum of 320 acres could be held by a conditional purchaser at any one time until the selection was paid off, Portion 12 was for the time being beyond their reach, even if they could have afforded it. On 3 January 1869, however, John Dent acquired Portion 12 as the second conditional purchaser. While it is possible that the Richardsons intended to bring him into their business, it is more likely that Dent took up this land on behalf of his Richardson cousins, acting as a 'dummy', with the Richardsons providing him the funds to cover the purchase. Such a practice was probably not contemplated by the framers of the legislation, but vicarious selection of this nature was within the law until it was made illegal in 1875.[29] There is no trace of any other blocks at Deltroit being purchased by John Dent, though he also simultaneously claimed another 960 adjoining acres as a pre-emptive lease. A year later, on 3 January 1870, Portion 12 was transferred into the names of William and John Richardson. Another of the earliest blocks at Deltroit acquired by the Richardsons was Portion 10 (Parish of Yaven), which was on the south side of Hillas Creek directly opposite John's first landholding. These 320 acres were originally taken up by a local selector, Frederick Bartholomew, on 27 December 1866,[30] but were transferred to William sometime before December 1872. Today, this land includes the homestead block and main cattle yards.

First mortgage

While these early selections brought the number of blocks owned by the brothers to at least four, William and John appear to have needed additional finance to purchase further adjoining land and to fund improvements. This was in line with the significant change brought about by the Robertson Land Acts, whereby an individual needed more capital to become a selector and to fulfil the conditions of purchase than if he had been a squatter who, in the early days of settlement, only had to buy a £10 licence that entitled him to occupy as much land as he could obtain.[31] Under the new legislation, land cost £1 per acre, not to mention the cost of required improvements equal to the value of the land, and selectors turned to sources of capital almost as diverse as their own backgrounds. In William and John's case, Portion 10 (Parish of Yaven), together with Portions 12, 13 and 14 (Parish of Mundarlo), were mortgaged[32] on 31 December 1872 to Edward Charles Williams, described as a 'gold miner of Adelong', who lent William and John the princely sum of £5000.

Also included in the mortgage were 2000 head of cattle at Hillas Creek and 7000 sheep 'running at Hillas Creek and at Sawyer's Creek Billybong

Inland Towns of New South Wales.——Adelong.

1. View of the Town.   2. The Falls, Adelong Creek.   3. Bridge of the Adelong Creek.   4. Quartz Crushing Works, Adelong Creek.
5. Travelling Shearers at Wayside Inn.   Business Houses.

[*sic*]'. Sawyer's Creek was a settlement near the present town of Holbrook, about 55 miles from Deltroit. According to baptism records in Tumut and Adelong, by 1872 Thomas Dent and his family were living at Sawyer's Creek, where Thomas was a sheep farmer at Billabong Station. Based on the security given in the mortgage, it seems likely that William and John Richardson had some sheep on agistment with Thomas (a common arrangement whereby livestock belonging to one party are grazed on land owned by another in return for a fee), or that there existed some other business arrangement between them. Possibly, the Richardsons themselves had land in the area, though this has not been proven.

When the Robertson Land Acts were amended in 1875 to increase the maximum amount of land that could be purchased at any one time from 320 to 640 acres,[33] the pressure on settlers eager to buy as much land as possible to make their businesses economically viable was multiplied. Borrowing became a theme in the rural community, especially as there was frequently a gap in cash flow between the receipt of profits on the sale of wool, meat and other produce and the need to make capital improvements. The Richardsons themselves were clearly not immune from this problem. However, the mortgage in favour of Williams was discharged on 18 January 1876 and, over a period of twenty years, the Richardsons managed to purchase more than forty blocks of various sizes on the Hillas Creek. Effectively, they put together, in a gradual and piecemeal way, a patchwork of land portions that were to become known as Deltroit. In some cases, the brothers were the first conditional purchasers or selectors, and in others they bought land from selectors who had purchased it previously and where the conditions of residency and improvements had yet to be fully satisfied. In a small number of cases, they bought blocks where freehold had already been acquired by an earlier selector. Without exception, all the land they purchased had once been part of the sprawling squatting run of Yabtree, then owned by R. F. Horsley.

The Hillas Creek locality

To what extent the Aboriginals in the area were a hindrance to the Richardsons while they were establishing Deltroit is not known. However, as the Aboriginals were by then so few in number in the Murrumbidgee district, being described at the time as a 'fast decreasing race', it seems likely that any interference by them was minimal. Nonetheless, they were still present in the area and continued to hold an annual corroboree at Tumut,[34] about 30 miles away. One or two may even have worked as shepherd or stockman for the Richardsons, having been forced by white settlement to give up their traditional lifestyle. They made good trackers and horsemen, like most Indigenous people, and could find water where there appeared to be none. By now, however, their traditional skills were coming under threat as they themselves stood helpless against the settlers on whom they became increasingly dependent for survival.

The timing of the Richardsons' arrival in New South Wales was fortuitous, as was their choice of Hillas Creek as a location. John's move from Victoria was shortly before the new land legislation was promulgated, giving him time to assess the potential of the Hillas Creek valley, especially the area that was to become Deltroit. Shortly after, when William arrived in the area, the brothers took advantage of the Robertson Land Acts, which enabled them to buy enough land on Hillas Creek to start a grazing enterprise and, moreover, to obtain security of tenure. Although there was as yet no proper settlement in the vicinity, the first blocks that the Richardsons purchased on Hillas Creek were just a mile to the east of the Great Southern Road, the main arterial route between Sydney and Melbourne. These major centres were respectively 270 and 300 miles away in opposite directions, but the location of the Richardsons' selections could not have been more convenient in terms of access to markets in both New South Wales and Victoria.

Furthermore, within two years of buying land on Hillas Creek, a neighbouring selector built a hotel or coaching inn one mile away from the Richardsons' selections. The Junction Hotel, as it was known, was the beginning of the main settlement of Hillas Creek, which over the next ten years developed to include a post office and a school. The Richardsons could have hardly asked for more on their doorstep. Deltroit and Hillas Creek were also roughly equidistant to three growing rural centres, with all the facilities and society that they too afforded. Adelong was approximately 20 miles east; Gundagai, about 26 miles north; and Wagga Wagga, around 29 miles west. Gundagai, in particular, had rebuilt itself after the devastating flood in 1852 and a bridge had been constructed over the Murrumbidgee River in 1867, making access to Sydney much easier. Until the bridge was built, the Murrumbidgee could only be safely crossed on horseback, by bullock wagon when the water was low, or by a small punt that was operated by some enterprising settlers.[35]

When the railway from Sydney reached Cootamundra in 1877, Wagga Wagga in 1881 and, finally, Albury in 1883, transport and access to markets and produce for local people was improved beyond measure. New South Wales was now linked directly to Victoria, and when a branch line to Gundagai was completed in 1886 it was possible for anyone living at Hillas Creek to reach Sydney within a matter of hours, compared to an uncomfortable coach journey of at least three days, which had been the only option previously. It is impossible to overstate the importance of these transport developments to the local populace and the change it brought about in terms of their social and business behaviour. Most significantly, the railway made places like Deltroit far more competitive than they would otherwise have been.

Aside from these amenities, the Hillas Creek valley had some very attractive geographical features. There was good annual rainfall compared to the plains of New South Wales further west, reliable water and fertile soil. The country was also gently undulating and may have reminded the Richardsons of their birthplace in the far north of England. There are discernible similarities in the contours of the landscape around Hillas Creek and Bleatarn, especially the rounded hills and gentle slopes that border the valley. The Hillas Creek itself, which at that time was described as an 'unfailing' water supply,[36] and the various smaller creeks that came down through Deltroit from the hills were perhaps reminiscent of the many becks that flowed into the Eden River. Certainly, the very cold and relatively wet

Misty morning
at Deltroit, 2010

winters with their heavy frosts and foggy mornings would have brought back
memories of a childhood in Westmorland and wintry scenes of Bleatarn with
clouds of mist rolling off the fells.

Realities of life

In spite of all these advantages, the realities of life as a selector were
sometimes at odds with the popular notion of gracious living in a pastoral
setting akin to that enjoyed by the British aristocracy. Most selectors in New
South Wales in the 1860s lived in primitive conditions, frequently in bark
huts with earthen floors, and slaved from sunrise to sunset on the land to try
and make a living. Challenged continuously by the harshness and volatility
of their environment, they fought heroically against the soil, the vagaries of
the markets and the extremes of weather, especially drought. Whether the

Richardsons lived a life of misery in the early days at Deltroit is unknown, but they probably had a simple and extremely hard-working existence, confronting the deprivations of rural life with stoicism and with the hope that one day they would be rewarded for all their efforts.

Living on the selection for three years until it was fully paid and carrying out improvements was a requirement of all selectors under the conditional purchase regulations. The site of the Richardsons' original hut or homestead is not clear. According to the Crown Plans of some of the earliest conditional purchases that the Richardsons made, huts worth £6, £20 and £30 were erected on Portions 26, 20 and 28 (Parish of Yaven) respectively, and there would have also been huts on the first two portions that they acquired. It is probable that at some stage one or more of these huts were occupied by the brothers, but these dwellings have long disappeared. The existing Deltroit homestead was not built until 1903, and it is sobering to remember that by then it was almost forty years since William had made his first selection at Deltroit. It had therefore taken him all this time until he felt financially secure enough to build the impressive homestead that stands here today.

View over Deltroit creek flats along the Hillas Creek valley, 2011

CHAPTER 5

The Junction Hotel

*A*t almost the same time as the Richardsons were selecting land at Deltroit, John Alexander Griffiths established the Junction Hotel on what was to become Deltroit's western boundary. Opening first on 13 November 1868, this pub or coaching inn became the focal point of the settlement known as Hillas Creek. Its purpose was to provide food, drink and accommodation for local settlers, workers, drovers and travellers alike on the increasingly busy Great Southern Road, the main arterial route between Sydney and Melbourne, which passed through the centre of the settlement. As its name implied, the hotel stood exactly at the intersection of the Great Southern Road (now known as Mundarlo Road) and the Adelong Road (today called Deltroit Road, but also sometimes referred to as the Monaro Highway).

Geography

Originally little more than a bush track in the 1830s and 'the product of use rather than design,'[1] the Great Southern Road had previously been known as the Port Phillip Road until it was renamed and marginally re-routed in 1858. Its name was to change twice more: first, in 1928, when it became known as the Hume Highway; and second, in about 1940, after the completion of the new Hume Highway further east, when it became Mundarlo Road and little

The Junction Hotel, c. 1900, with licensee Jim Cooper standing centre right by the main door

more than a local thoroughfare. Between the 1860s and early 1880s, the Great Southern Road was the only method by which the major city centres of Sydney and Melbourne could be accessed from the Hillas Creek district.

At the time of the opening of the Junction Hotel, the traffic on the Great Southern Road was increasing, with the 'unlocking' of the surrounding land for conditional purchase by selectors and the continuing rush to the Adelong goldfields. Moreover, it was most propitiously situated at the base of a steep climb over the Tarcutta hill, which included just below its crest a notorious double-hairpin bend known as the 'Devil's Elbow', where many a dray came to grief, especially on the descent to Lower Tarcutta. Plenty of bullockies and teamsters would have wished to give their bullocks or horses a rest before or after embarking on this hazardous route. Even today, the hill is still treacherous and remains an unsealed and slippery

gravel back road, almost unchanged from the time the Junction Hotel first opened.

The block of land on which the hotel was built was well-watered, both by a small creek fed from a spring in the hills above and by the Hillas Creek, which, except in times of drought, flowed constantly and vigorously on the northern boundary. According to surveyor Thomas Scott Townsend, during the 1840s the Hillas Creek was deep and subject to high floods two or three times a year, which, in his view, made the route of the Great Southern Road at this point 'ill-chosen'.[2] For people living in this area today, such a verdict is revealing since, apart from the extensive flooding of the creek in October 2010, no-one can remember the Hillas Creek bursting its banks previously. It is over seventy-five years ago that any record of such serious flooding of the Hillas Creek itself was recorded in the local newspapers.

ABOVE
The former Great
Southern Road,
leading to the
Devil's Elbow,
2010

OPPOSITE
John Griffiths,
founder of the
Junction Hotel

John Alexander Griffiths

On 27 December 1866, two years before turning to inn-keeping at Hillas
Creek, Griffiths had purchased the 200 acres (Portion 18 in the Parish
of Mundarlo)[3] on which the Junction Hotel was subsequently built.
This acquisition was made under the conditional purchase system, in the
same way that the Richardson brothers settled the blocks at Deltroit.
Concurrently, Griffiths took out a pre-emptive lease of 600 acres on the
adjoining blocks to the south and east of Portion 18.[4] These blocks were
probably Portions 25, 47, 48, 56, 57, 78 and 82 (Parish of Yaven), but the
Pre-Emptive Lease and Conditional Purchase Registers are incomplete
and it is impossible to be certain. Nonetheless, all these adjoining portions,

John Griffiths with four of his daughters, c. 1890. From left, back row: Bertha Maud, Grace Edith; front row: Minnie May, Alice Eliza.

which were mostly along the Great Southern Road towards Lower Tarcutta, were subsequently converted to conditional purchases in the 1870s. Further adjoining land, namely Portions 39, 40 and 140 (Parish of Yaven), were also eventually taken up by Griffiths, making a total landholding of about 1200 acres.

Griffiths had arrived in Australia from England between 1857 and 1859 with his wife, Elizabeth ('Eliza') Simpson. They had married in what is presumed to have been his birthplace, Birmingham, on 12 October 1856. The marriage certificate described Griffiths as a 'Merchant's Clerk' and his father as a 'Carpenter'. Griffiths's background has been difficult to ascertain in part because he seems to have been born with the surname of Clarke, which intriguingly, and for unknown reasons, he changed to Griffiths around 1861.[5] On the other hand, Eliza and her family, who have been easier to trace, were from Derbyshire, where her father was a tailor. She had various siblings including a sister, Ann, who married Henry William Upton also in

Birmingham; and two brothers, Amos and Moses. Like Eliza, these three siblings ultimately came to live at Hillas Creek and the neighbouring district of Tumut.

The first clear record of John and Eliza Griffiths living in Australia is on the birth certificate of their eldest child, Clarence Cyrus, born in Adelong on 15 July 1860. How long the couple had been in Adelong by this time is unknown, but it may have been for about three years. Griffiths was then a gold miner and one of the pioneers of the Adelong reef. However, by 1861, the family were living about 30 miles away at Adjungbilly, where a new gold rush had started. Here, Griffiths erected a substantial building called the Clarence Hotel, thought to have been named after his son. After several years at Adjungbilly and the birth of three more children — Clair Cosman, born on 19 December 1861; Blanche Anne, born on 5 April 1863; and Alice Eliza, born on 26 November 1864 — the Griffiths family moved back to Adelong for a short time before settling down at Hillas Creek.

Hotel's characteristics

By 1868, when Griffiths opened the Junction Hotel, he was already an experienced publican. Clearly, he was proud of his new establishment, judging by the advertisement that he placed in the local *Gundagai Times* newspaper on 21 November 1868. No record of the nature of the original building survives, but the construction is likely to have been modest, probably of timber. It was situated 26 miles from Gundagai, 20 miles from Adelong, 29 miles from Wagga Wagga, eight miles from Mundarlo, 11 miles from Upper Tarcutta and three-and-a-half miles from Lower Tarcutta. Importantly, the Junction Hotel was not an isolated watering hole in an empty landscape, but was part of a larger nucleus of settlement developing in the area and one of a chain of similar hotels, each situated roughly every ten miles along the Great Southern Road. These hotels included the Mundarlo Inn to the north, owned by William Bootes, and the Tarcutta Inn to the south at Lower Tarcutta, owned initially by Alexander Bannatyne and from about 1868 by Peter John Hartnett.[6]

Gundagai Times
Saturday 21 November 1868

The Junction Hotel must have been a considerable success, as only a short time later, in 1874, Griffiths built a new hotel out of stone, which still stands today. It seems likely that the new hotel was built in the same place as the original building, with the stone being quarried at a site just a few hundred yards away, where there is evidence of an abandoned quarry of the same granite. The new stone-built hotel was opened on 2 January 1875 and advertised regularly in the *Gundagai Times* between January and April that year. Among other inducements, Griffiths offered 'superior accommodation to parties travelling either on business or pleasure ... luxuriously furnished throughout' and, with his long experience in the trade, claimed to provide wines and spirits of only the best quality, purchased in Sydney. As for the stables, Griffiths stated that they 'will be always found supplied with plenty of forage and those who prefer a good paddock can also be accommodated.'[7]

The new hotel was a single-storey building in an 'L' shape, situated on the corner where the Adelong Road led at a right angle into the Great Southern Road, forming the 'T' junction that gave the hotel its name. There was a central tap room or bar off the corner entrance, with a high panelled dado rail and deep cellar underneath. There were rooms on either side of the main bar, including one that led into a narrow hallway with another entrance door. There appear to have been four small bedrooms, a dining room, a sitting room, a storeroom and a kitchen. The entire front of the building was covered by a verandah supported by plain wooden posts and brackets, with another verandah to the rear (possibly this once joined up to the verandah at the front so that the whole building was encircled). In the yard at the back and also at the front grew white cedar, oak and acacia trees as well as apples and apricots. When standing at the bar and looking out through the main entrance, one could see straight down the Great Southern Road towards Mundarlo for at least a mile in order to keep a lookout for travellers crossing over the Hillas Creek.

In spite of some alterations in the 1970s and 1980s, the hotel building is substantially in its original form. It is a rare example of a nineteenth-century rural inn in the Georgian style, and is a distinctive and picturesque landmark in the area.

Death of Eliza Griffiths

Six more children were born to John and Eliza Griffiths while they were at Hillas Creek. They were: Bertha Maude, born on 18 April 1867; Grace Edith, born on 11 February 1869; Claude Cecil, born on 6 March 1871; Minnie May, born on 20 May 1872; Conrad Cuthbert, born on 15 June 1874; and Clement Clive, born on 31 August 1875. In spite of having to look after so many children, Eliza seems to have been a stalwart support to her husband. She gave evidence in a lawsuit brought against Griffiths in 1868 by an aggrieved employee for outstanding wages that 'the plaintiff used to breakfast about ten o'clock generally and that he never did any work, unless he called nursing the baby by that name'.[8] The baby referred to in this testimony must have been Bertha, who was born less than one year before.

Eliza Griffiths, wife of John Griffiths, founder of the Junction Hotel

No doubt exhausted from bearing ten children in quick succession, Eliza died on 19 September 1876, aged only thirty-eight years old, and was buried in the Church of England cemetery on the outskirts of Wagga Wagga. Griffiths was clearly distraught and wasted no time in summoning help to cope with his large, young family. He wrote to his widowed sister-in-law in England, Ann Upton, who had three children of her own, asking her to come and housekeep for him:

> Here am I, Elizabeth gone and me left with a hotel, the farm and ten children on my hands. There's plenty of room here, bring the children out and take over the management and I will pay your fare.[9]

Apparently pleased to leave the English climate that was detrimental to her health, Ann Upton departed Plymouth and arrived in Sydney aboard the *Corona* on 23 July 1877 together with her children, William, Annie Louisa and Amy. Her brother, Amos Simpson, and his wife, Mary, emigrated at the same time, having also been sponsored by Griffiths.

Activities at the hotel

By this time, Griffiths had built up a flourishing business, with the hotel commanding a good trade. Aside from being a public house, the Junction Hotel was becoming the focus for social activities at Hillas Creek, including that favourite national pastime, horse-racing. A report in the *Wagga Wagga Express* of 17 March 1875 describes the annual Hillas Creek race meeting (which probably took place on the creek flats immediately opposite) as concluding with a free ball and supper afterwards at the Junction Hotel, the arrangements 'being pronounced first class by the visitors'. According to an earlier advertisement in the *Gundagai Times* of 6 March 1875, Griffiths was Secretary and Treasurer of the 'Hillas' [*sic*] Creek Races' and, interestingly, John Richardson was on that occasion acting as Judge. The racing included a Maiden Plate, a Hack Race, a Handicap, a Jerusalem (where no man was to ride his own horse) and a Donkey Race. Tilting at the Ring was also often

Jim Cooper, licensee of the Junction Hotel, between 1895 and 1903

a popular feature on the racing program, and many years later, on 24 May 1892 (the Queen's Birthday), this event was won by William Richardson, who by then would have been in his mid-fifties.[10]

As time went on and the Junction Hotel changed hands and licensees, it was used for parties and weddings. There is a charming description in the *Gundagai Times* of 24 June 1898 of the wedding between Francis Luff of Adelong Crossing and Louisa Phillips, sister-in-law of Jim Cooper who was the licensee of the Junction Hotel at that time. Both the ceremony and the reception took place at the hotel with 'a breakfast of the best things procurable' and 'speeches of congratulation and encouragement'. Moreover, Toby Corbett, a resident in the Adelong district and a great-grandson of Thomas Richardson, remembers being told that his grandparents, Edward and Louisa Corbett (née Richardson), held an Independence Day party at the Junction Hotel in July each year, since Edward Corbett's father was American.

Importantly, the Junction Hotel was as much of a drinking venue for the graziers as it was for their employees. There was nowhere else in the vicinity for men to go to relieve the boredom and isolation of their lives and to unwind after a hard day's work. Although the hotel developed a reputation for being filled with stockmen, shearers and others working at Deltroit, local graziers also frequented the establishment alongside their men and in addition to the many farmers, tobacco growers, miners, contractors, drovers and travellers who were either in or passing through the area. As early as 30 July 1878, there is a reference in the diaries of R. F. Horsley to his taking his adopted son, Frank, to the Junction Hotel before starting for school. Whether this was for a farewell drink or just to catch the coach to Melbourne is unclear. However, his great-grandchildren Fred and Patricia Horsley recall being told by their respective fathers, Lach and Wallace Horsley, that when they were small they would sometimes accompany their own father to the Junction Hotel. There, they would sit on the verandah and be given a special drink of lemonade with sarsaparilla, a native plant that tasted a little like liquorice.

A lawless and uncivilised place

While a centre of local entertainment, the Junction Hotel seems to have been anything but genteel. In the *Gundagai Times* of 14 February 1874, there is a report of a case before the police magistrate in which the prosecution alleged that Allan Paterson used language at the Junction Hotel 'calculated to promote a breach of the peace'. More graphically, in 1881, Daniel Cox, a teacher at the nearby Hillas Creek School, described his appalling experience of being forced to board at the hotel in the absence of any other accommodation in the neighbourhood:

> Nothing but the prospect of a decent school could induce any teacher to remain here. I am no novice to rough living etc but a more lawless, and uncivilised place to be accommodated at I never saw. This is not my opinion alone. I heard so before I saw the place and experience has more than verified [*sic*] as truth.[11]

He also complained about the cost of staying at the hotel, maintaining that the accommodation there was 'of a very inferior sort, though the charge is equal to what one pays in better places'.[12] In fact, the hotel was considered so 'rough' and of such dubious character by the District Schools Inspector that a female teacher at the school who preceded Cox was removed on account of it.[13]

Cattle being moved along former Great Southern Road towards the Junction Hotel, 2008

Things do not seem to have improved as time went on. In 1888, a drover was arrested at the Junction Hotel where he was camped for having a stolen dog in his possession.[14] Then, as late as 1914, it was reported in the *Gundagai Times* of 8 December that a brawl in the bar, witnessed by Frederick Smiles, a stockman employed at Deltroit, ended in one man being charged with grievous bodily harm. Despite these incidents, the Junction Hotel stayed in existence for almost fifty years. According to Fred Horsley, his father used to tell a story about the hotel in its latter years when Michael Carmody, the incumbent licensee, would order his three daughters to dress in their finery on the last day of shearing known as 'Cut Out'. Carmody would dispatch them on foot all the way up a steep hill above the Junction Hotel to the Gundillawah shearing shed, carrying a tray of free beer. Doubtless the beer was warm and flat by the time the young ladies arrived, but it nonetheless enticed the men to the hotel afterwards.

The Richardsons take an interest

Whether William and John Richardson patronised the Junction Hotel is a matter of conjecture, but it seems very likely that they did, since their grazing enterprise was in such close proximity. Moreover, their later prominent role not only in the appointment of Griffiths as the local Postmaster, but also in the affairs of the Hillas Creek Racing Club conducted at the pub, all point to an association with Griffiths and his establishment. It is plausible that the Richardsons knew Griffiths even before he came to Hillas Creek from the time when he was a miner in Adelong. They certainly knew each other well enough for Eliza Griffiths to act as a witness at the wedding of John Richardson to his first wife, Mary Beaver, in 1873, as evidenced by the marriage certificate.

On 20 January 1880,[15] the Richardsons purchased the Junction Hotel from Griffiths, together with the land immediately surrounding it. As second conditional purchasers, they had previously purchased from Griffiths the other adjoining blocks that he held. All of these purchases were a natural choice as Griffiths held some of the better creek flats and undulating country to the north and west of the other Richardson selections at Deltroit. Griffiths had by this time purchased Warregal, a large property of about 15,000 acres near Parkes, and had begun to move his entire family there. His departure was lamented in the local press, which described him as 'one of the oldest and most respected residents of the Gundagai district'.[16] As to the new owners of the Junction Hotel, they were proceeding down a path that fellow graziers had trod before. Other selectors in the area, including William Bootes at Mundarlo, incorporated hotel businesses with their grazing enterprises. Rather uncharitably, it was said that in this way these selectors got back in the sale of alcohol what they paid their men in wages!

By the time the Richardsons bought the Junction Hotel, there had already been two changes of licensee. Almost immediately upon his arrival at Hillas Creek, Amos Simpson, Griffiths's brother-in-law, took over the licence on 31 August 1877. After eighteen months, the licence was transferred to his sister, Ann Upton, on 24 January 1879, who held it until 1 July 1880.

Thereafter, the licensees of the hotel were chosen by the new owners, the Richardsons, who initially appointed two members of their extended family in succession before placing advertisements in the local papers to let the premises and the adjoining 30 acres.[17]

Closure

The Junction Hotel finally ceased trading in November 1916 upon the transfer of the licence of the last publican, Margaret Carmody, to a hotel in Wagga Wagga and the sale of the contents by auction.[18] The hotel's closure had been foreseeable for some time and was caused substantially by the gradual decline of the importance of the Great Southern Road.[19] Problems had already begun in 1883, when the railway from Sydney was joined at Albury (on the border of New South Wales and Victoria) onto the rail line to Melbourne, effectively supplanting the Great Southern Road as the main link between the two major cities. However, the road and the hotel survived for three more decades because of local needs, especially as there was still a reasonable amount of traffic to and from the properties in the area. Likewise, the road was still the main route from Gundagai and Adelong to Wagga Wagga, and was no doubt also partially sustained by the gold-mining activities at Mount Adrah (a short distance from Deltroit towards Adelong) and Lower Tarcutta, which continued into the early 1900s.

In addition to the railway, the advent of the motor car and demise of both foot and horse traffic meant that, ultimately, the hotel could not survive. What had been a refuge for travellers, drovers, miners, stockmen, farmers and graziers in the heat and dust of the Australian bush became accommodation for employees at Deltroit, a function that it still serves today. However, according to family tradition, it was not just extraneous circumstances that led to the hotel's closure. William Richardson had by this time become increasingly dissatisfied with the 'drinking sprees' of his employees, facilitated by the proximity of the hotel to Deltroit. Importantly, the loss of the place where locals and outsiders gathered to drink and converse proved to be more than a mere inconvenience to its customers. As the main attraction in the area for many decades, its closure was not only the death knell of the Hillas Creek settlement, but was also the beginning of the breakdown in regular communications between the different properties in the area. It was also undoubtedly the start of a gulf in understanding between those living in the country and those based in the towns — something that continues to grow today.

Junction Hotel, 2010

CHAPTER 6

The Hillas Creek Post Office

*T*he Junction Hotel was not the only building of significance at Hillas Creek. Within five years of the hotel being established, there was sufficient demand for a post office to be opened next door and, like the Junction Hotel, it became a magnet for both local residents and those travelling on the Great Southern Road. There is no doubt that William and John Richardson used this post office so conveniently situated on Deltroit's western boundary, and that the increasing size and relative prosperity of Hillas Creek led to its inauguration.

Growing populace of Hillas Creek

By the 1870s, Hillas Creek was a thriving community and, between 1871 and 1873, had doubled its population.[1] The exact size of the settlement at that time is unknown, but it was said to be 'ten to one over that of Mundarlo'.[2] As the local MP James Hoskins noted, 'Hillas Creek is a locality that has recently become thickly populated through the facilities afforded by the land laws',[3] a direct reference to the alienation of land from the squatters, as encouraged by the new system of conditional purchase.

The population of the area was to increase again over the next decade, following gold rushes to Hillas Creek itself and to nearby Lower Tarcutta. These rushes were distinct from those associated with Adelong and Mount

86   *D*ELTROIT AND THE VALLEY OF HILLAS CREEK

Adrah and began later, towards the end of the 1870s. Both Hillas Creek and Lower Tarcutta were proclaimed extensions to the Mount Adrah goldfield, a couple of miles east of Deltroit, on 3 September 1880. Richly auriferous country — both as quartz reefs and, to a lesser extent, alluvial deposits — had been discovered near the Great Southern Road, and, although the vein rock initially had to be transported by dray all the way to Adelong for crushing, extraction and grinding, the reefs were still 'payable' because the country was softer than in Adelong and required fewer explosives.[4] So numerous and rich were the finds in the area that mining was successfully carried out at Hillas Creek and Lower Tarcutta until at least 1906.[5]

Hillas Creek Post Office petition

Understandably, the increasing population in the district became anxious to improve communications beyond the immediate vicinity. Seventy-seven Hillas Creek residents signed a petition dated 24 June 1873, headed up by Junction Hotel owner John Griffiths and addressed to the Postmaster General of New South Wales. Those people whose names appeared on the document comprised twenty-six farmers, sixteen labourers, nine graziers (including William and John Richardson and R. F. Horsley), three women described as 'domestics' or 'spinsters', two carpenters, two sawyers, a miner, a blacksmith, a mason and a variety of other men with occupations mostly connected to the land. Their need for a post office was pressing, especially as the one at Mundarlo, eight miles away and opened by William Bootes on 1 February 1872, had closed less than a year later, in January 1873. Reasons for the closure, as cited by Bootes, were: 'Attention to my private affairs which compels my frequent absence from home coupled with the recent marriage of my daughter by whom the business of the Post Office here was principally conducted.'[6] This closure obliged the residents of Hillas Creek to travel long distances for their post, either 11 miles to Upper Tarcutta, 19 miles to Tumblong (known then as Adelong Crossing) or as much as 20 miles to Adelong.

Memorial
for
Post Office at Hillas Creek
County Wynyard

To The Honorable
The Post Master General
of New South Wales.

The memorial of the undersigned respectfully
sheweth, that your memorialists while praying
for a Post Office, may now justly lay claim to
some consideration for a large thriving and
populous district which has within the last
2 years nearly doubled its population

That your memorialist beg to refer you
to the closing of the Mundarloo Post Office
and the inconvenience arising in having
no Post Office near the Upper Tarcutta distant
11 miles and the Adelong Crossing Place 19 miles

That your memorialists therefore respectfully
request that you will be pleased to grant their
application for a Post Office for the purpose
thereinto and deposited at Hillas Creek as
being a central position, and where suitable
premises are procurable, the same being on the
main Southern Road where the mail
Coach passes daily

And your Memorialists will
ever pray

Names	Occupation	Residence
John A Griffiths	Tollman	Hillis Creek
James Scott	Captstoner	Hillis Creek
Edward Beaver	Labourer	Hillis Creek
Lucy Glascock	Spinster	Hillis Creek

Name	Occupation	Residence
John Dunne	Labourer	Hillis Creek
Thos Doyle	Sawyer	Hillis Creek
Edward Doyle	Sawyer	Hillis Creek
John Hodge	Carpenter	Hillis Creek
John Lamont	Labourer	Hillis Creek
John McDonald	Labourer	Hillis Creek
James Rice	Labourer	Hillis Creek
Willm Chalmers	Labourer	Hillis Creek
Willm Smith	Labourer	Hillis Creek
Hy Eli Collins	Sawyer	Hillas Creek
John Hunter	Sawyer	Hillas Creek
James Campbell	Labourer	Hillas Creek
Henry Garth	Labourer	Hillas Creek
Robert Bean	Farmer	Hillas Creek
Mrs Thomas	Domestic	Hillas Creek
James Watson	Labour	Hillas Creek
James Stoth	Mason	Hillas Creek
James Plows	contractor	Hillas Creek
James Hately	carrier	Hillas Creek
Thomas Christian	Christop	Hillas Creek
Wm Conley	farmer	Hillas Creek
Christopher Sullivan	Farmer	Hillas Creek
Mrs Williams	Labourer	Hillas Creek
John G Trevihan	Grazier	Hillas Creek
Fred Bartholomew	Grazier	Hillas Creek
John Gillespie	Grazier	Hillas Creek
Thomas Moore	Grazier	Hillas Creek
Mrs Trevihan	Grazier	Hillas Creek
M Head	farmer	Hillas Creek
Sion Hunt	farmer	Hillas Creek
Thomas Doyle	Stock man	Hillis Creek
Donald McInnes	Labourer	Hillis Creek
William Richardson	grazier	Hillas Creek
William Beaver	Farmer	Hillis Creek

Name	Occupation	Residence
Edwin Moore	Grazier	
Robert Penfold	Labourer	Hillas Creek
John Richardson	Grazier	Hillas Creek
Michel Calnan	Stockman	Hillis Creek
Hans Hanson	Labourer	Hillis Creek
R H Harley	Grazier	Yabtree
W Harby	Farmer	Yabtree
H S Sherwin	Overseer	Yabtree
Thomas Butlin	Labour	Yabtree
W Cook	farmer	Yabtree
Wm T Jacob	Contractor	Rileys Creek
Nappy Harris	Contractor	Riley's Creek
Charles Carter	farmer	Riley's Creek
James McHack	Free Selector	Riley's Creek
Charles Smith	Labourer	Riley's Creek
B Slade	farmer	Killius court
Robert Beaver Junr	farmer	Hillis Creek
George Dennis	Farmer	Hillis Creek
John Cogan	Farmer	Hillis Creek
George W Last	farmer	Hillis Creek
Clarence O Griffiths	farmer	Hillis Creek
D Connor	Overseer	Hillis Creek
James Beaver	Farm	Hillis Creek
Charles King	farmer	Hillis Creek
Benjamin Beaver	Farmer	Hillis Creek
John Bowrin	farmer	Hillis Creek
Clar C Griffiths	farmer	Hillis Creek
Thomas Powell	Miner	Lukes Creek
James Munro		Adelong
John Wright	Blacksmith	Lower Tarcutta
Henry Staggs	farmer	Lower Tarcutta
John Larkin	Farmer	Lower Tarcutta
James Watkins	farmer	Lower Tarcutta
Moses Larkson	dealer	Hillas Creek

Name	Occupation	Residence
Miss Lewght	Dorpester	Hillas Creek
George King	Farmer	Hillis Creek
Isaac Larkins	Farmer	Hillas Creek
Isaac Staggs	Farmer	Lower Tarcutta
Aaron Johnson	Farmer	Hillas Creek
Fred Larkins	Selector	Hillis Creek

88

However, at the same time that the Hillas Creek Post Office petition was submitted, a flurry of correspondence ensued from the residents of Mundarlo, who sought to have their post office reinstated. They argued that the reopening of their post office would be more logical, since the Mundarlo Inn was the place where the mail coach changed horses. Fortunately for the inhabitants of Hillas Creek, no suitable candidate for the role of Postmaster could be found at Mundarlo, and as the mail coach between Yass (to the north) and Albury (to the south) travelled along the Great Southern Road, directly past the Junction Hotel, the request for a post office at Hillas Creek was granted. Nonetheless, this was only after two further pleading letters by Griffiths, sent subsequently to the Hillas Creek petition, pointing out that a post office there would not only be at the centre of its population — which by now had spread over a distance of 12 miles — but would also be convenient to the inhabitants of Mundarlo and Lower Tarcutta as well as those at Mount Adrah and further up the Adelong Road. As for the argument that any post office should be where the mail coach harnessed fresh horses, in all likelihood, once the post office opened at Hillas Creek, the horses were changed at the Junction Hotel instead of at the Mundarlo Inn. Not only had Griffiths built an extensive wooden stable block on the eastern side of his hotel building, but there was also a blacksmith nearby in Lower Tarcutta who was one of the signatories on the petition.

Within eight weeks of this petition being presented, Griffiths, the literate and respected licensee of the Junction Hotel, was officially appointed Postmaster in the Hillas Creek locality on 12 August 1873. Apparently, he was already well prepared for the event. In anticipation of his appointment, he had earlier begun to erect next to his hotel a wooden post office building, which opened a few weeks later on 1 September. Although the weatherboard building has not survived, the post office continued in various forms until the closure of the Junction Hotel in 1916.[7] The wooden stables that serviced the needs of both the mail coach and other patrons survived into the 1940s, but have since disappeared.

A wilderness no more

It would be hard to overstate the enormous importance of the arrival of a post office at Hillas Creek. During a time of no telephones or internet services, a postal service was virtually the only means of communication with the world beyond the immediate district. Post offices were so important in colonial social and economic life that they were under the control of a cabinet minister, the Postmaster General (to whom the Hillas Creek petition was addressed). By the time of the opening of the Hillas Creek Post Office, postal services in New South Wales had become regular and post offices were handling not only letters and parcels, but also banknotes and gold due to the gold rushes.[8] They began to offer banking facilities and, perhaps even more significantly, telegraph services.

The telegraph provided a means of sending messages between the distant cities and towns of Australia, often thousands of miles apart, in the space of a mere few minutes. By 1858, Sydney, Melbourne and Adelaide were all connected to the telegraph line, and Tasmania followed in 1859. Then, on 22 August 1872, just one year before the opening of the Hillas Creek Post Office, the Australian Overland Telegraph was completed, connecting Australia to the rest of the world for the first time. This was such a major event that it is often referred to as one of the great milestones in Australian history. Suddenly, news from Europe arrived in Australia the day it happened, whereas a letter at that time typically took forty days by sea. Gundagai, Adelong and Wagga Wagga all had telegraph facilities by the 1870s, and although there was no telegraph at Hillas Creek, telegrams could now be sent to the post office there via the mail coach.

The psychological impact on the residents of Hillas Creek when they were granted a post office would have been immense. Undoubtedly, the post office became a centre for social interaction, as well as a symbol of the presence of civilisation in the Hillas Creek community. For the Richardsons especially, not only would a post office have facilitated the more efficient conduct of their grazing business, but they would also have been able to look forward to more frequent and regular communications with their family and friends still living in England. Newspapers and information generally would have been more accessible to them, and, being men of entrepreneurial spirit with interests beyond their own immediate concerns, they would have been overjoyed at the ability to keep abreast of all important events both within Australia and beyond.

Mail and coach services

In its lifetime, the Hillas Creek Post Office also gave the Junction Hotel an additional customer base. It drew residents from surrounding areas, including those along the Adelong Road at Mount Adrah and beyond, who had previously travelled twice the distance to the post office in Adelong. Importantly, it also captured the passengers travelling on the mail coaches run by Cobb & Co. In 1863, this firm of coach transporters became the official carriers of mail in both New South Wales and Victoria, as well as being the first to provide regular, reliable and more comfortable coach services in these areas. Every day except Sunday, a mail coach would stop at the Junction Hotel and disgorge its post and passengers. By 1870, Cobb & Co. were harnessing 6000 horses per day, travelling 28,000 miles per week and receiving £95,000 in mail subsidies. Jim Conroy, a driver on the Great Southern Road, asserted that 'the horses used in those days were of the best ... I generally used to handle 4 or 5 but when the roads were bad, I often harnessed up 6'.[9]

To what extent the mail and coach services to Hillas Creek were interrupted by the varying state of the Great Southern Road is unknown. Although it was the main highway between Sydney and Melbourne, the road was poorly maintained, and, from as early as the 1850s, frequent complaints were made in the local press about its parlous state of repair and its almost impassability in certain places, especially in wet weather. One observer described the road as a 'scarcely formed bullock track with its tottering bridges, rugged steeps and treacherous passes',[10] while another as 'a dust heap in summer and a mud pond in winter'.[11] Surveyor Thomas Townsend wrote of the Tarcutta hill just south of the Junction Hotel and the post office that 'a team seldom passes without some serious accident'.[12] Notwithstanding gradual improvements in the 1860s, accidents on the road were common due to its poor surface, and even little Clarence Griffiths, the son of the publican, was thrown from his horse and fractured his skull on this dangerous thoroughfare (although, on this occasion, it was unclear whether road, horse or rider was to blame).[13]

Apparently prone to regular flooding from the Hillas Creek, a succession of bridges was also washed away, notably in the 1840s (as well as much later in the early 1930s and most likely at other times in between). It was not until 1938 — when the road had been diverted between Tumblong and Tarcutta (known locally as the Tumblong Deviation) — that a bridge of any permanence was built. As part of the deviation and about a mile from Deltroit's eastern boundary, the Department of Main Roads erected a reinforced-concrete bowstring arch bridge, one of only two in the whole of New South Wales. This highly unusual structure has become known to locals as the 'Little Sydney Harbour Bridge' in view of its close resemblance to its much grander namesake. As the bridge was bypassed in 1986 by the new Hume Highway, it is now just an architectural curiosity in the landscape.

Hillas Creek bridge, 2008, about a mile from where the Hillas Creek Post Office once stood

Things go awry

At first, the Hillas Creek Post Office seems to have been tolerably well run as there were no complaints. But its fortunes were very much linked to those of the Junction Hotel and the vicissitudes of the licensees. When Griffiths began to be absent from the hotel, favouring instead his selections near Parkes and leaving his sister-in-law, Ann Upton, in charge, the business of the post office was said to have been 'very carelessly conducted'.[14] It was this neglect that prompted William and John Richardson to write to the Postmaster General of New South Wales on 15 July 1880, asking for Ann Upton to be removed as Postmistress and for William Beaver, the new licensee of the Junction Hotel, to be appointed Postmaster. The letter is the only complete document of any length written by either William or John Richardson to have survived to the present day. It reads as follows:

> Hon. Saul Samuel Esq
> Hillas Creek
> Postmaster-General
> 15th July 1880
>
> Sir-
> We beg to draw your attention to a case of mal-administration, nay culpable negligence, on the part of the Postmistress of Hillas Creek. The Post Office is situated at the Junction Hotel, which was kept by Mrs Upton up to the 1st July. After this date she gave up all connection with the Hotel and went to reside about (1¼) one mile and a quarter distant from the post office.
>
> On the arrival and departure of mails, she comes down and keeps the office open for a short time, somewhere about 5 or 10 minutes, then locks it up and returns home. Any person wanting letters must of necessity, excepting the few minutes she is there, go to her house, when, in most instances, she sends a child to attend to our wants, who is not competent to understand the nature and importance of such onerous duties.

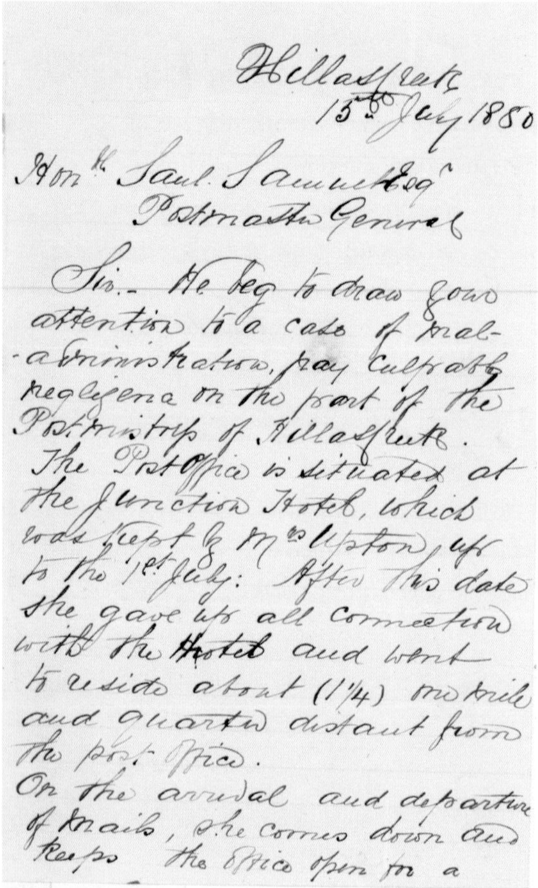

Hillas Creek
15th July 1880

Hon'ble Saul Samuel Esq'
Postmaster General

Sir,— We beg to draw your attention to a case of mal-administration, pay culpable negligence on the part of the Postmistress of Hillas Creek.

The Post Office is situated at the Junction Hotel, which was kept by Mrs Upton, up to the 1st July: After this date she gave up all connection with the Hotel and went to reside about (1¼) one mile and quarter distant from the post Office.

On the arrival and departure of Mails, she comes down and keeps the Office open for a short time, somewhere about 5 or 10 minutes then locks it up and returns home.

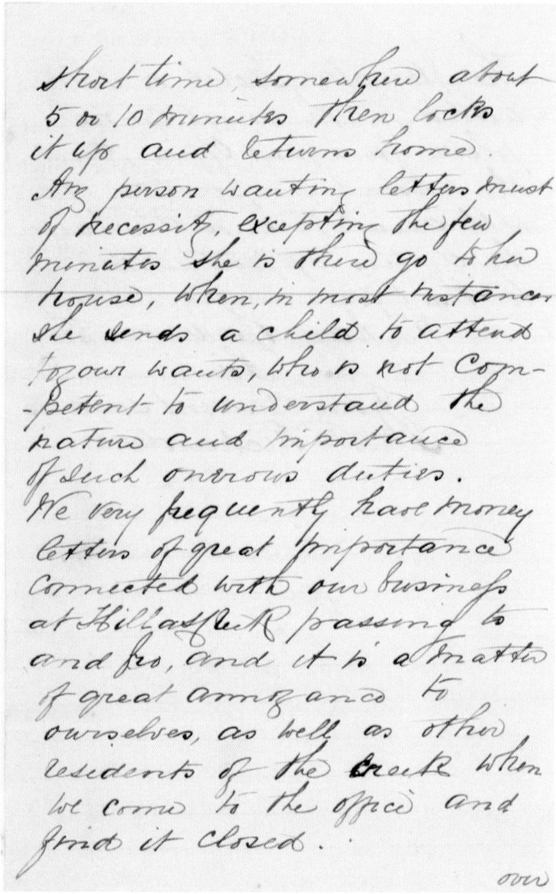

Any person wanting letters must of necessity, excepting the few minutes she is there go to her house, when, in most instances she sends a child to attend to our wants, who is not competent to understand the nature and importance of such onerous duties.

We very frequently have money letters of great importance connected with our business at Hillas Creek passing to and fro, and it is a matter of great annoyance to ourselves, as well as other residents of the Creek when we come to the office and find it closed.

over

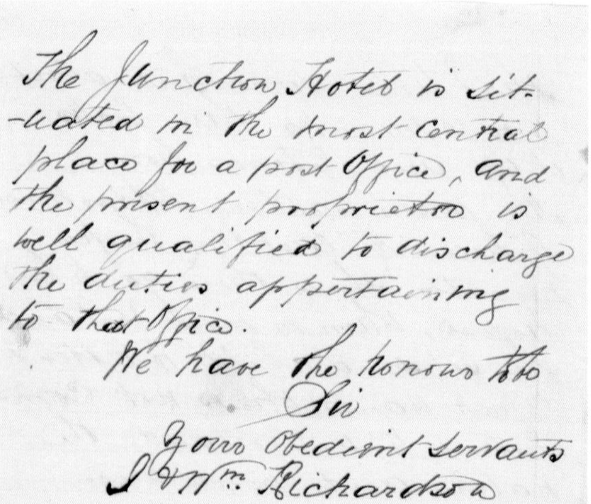

The Junction Hotel is situated in the most central place for a post Office, and the present proprietor is well qualified to discharge the duties appertaining to that Office.

We have the honour to be
Sir
Your Obedient Servants
J & Wm Richardson

Letter written by John
and William Richardson
to the Postmaster
General, 1880

We very frequently have many letters of great importance connected with our business at Hillas Creek passing to and fro, and it is a matter of great annoyance to ourselves, as well as other residents of the creek, when we come to the office and find it closed.

The Junction Hotel is situated in the most central place for a post office, and the present proprietor is well qualified to discharge the duties appertaining to that office.

We have the honour to be, Sir
Your obedient servants
J & Wm Richardson

This letter, in a beautiful hand, is well written and supports the view that both brothers were literate, educated men and among the most prominent members of the Hillas Creek community at the time.

A few weeks later, the Richardsons joined several other Hillas Creek residents in signing another letter to the Postmaster General, dated 9 August 1880, drawing his attention to 'the gross irregularities, and unjustifiable conduct of the Postmistress of Hillas Creek'. They alleged that Ann Upton was using her house, one-and-a-quarter miles away, to sort mail and that she only attended the post office once a day when the mail coach was due at 5pm. They went on to say that 'After taking the bags she mounts the coach and rides home with them', and that 'such arbitrary proceedings on the part of any Civil Servant of the Crown, we never witnessed before'. These complaints were taken very seriously by the Postmaster General and an enquiry was launched, revealing the Richardsons and their neighbours to have been justified in their annoyance. Ann Upton, who claimed that she was, in any event, moving to Parkes with her new husband, Jack Bunt, to join the Griffiths family, was forced to resign, with William Beaver installed as Postmaster in her place.

Since the Hillas Creek Post Office was in 'a detached building, near the Inn',[15] it was logical for whoever was licensee of the Junction Hotel to be put in charge of postal duties, provided he or she was literate. This is, in fact, what happened after the debacle with Ann Upton. However, there

was supposed to be a certain amount of paperwork upon each handover and official stamping of the new post office incumbent, but this did not always occur, with resignations and appointments being frequently out of step with actual events.[16] A small salary could also be claimed by the Postmaster or Postmistress, which in the case of Hillas Creek in 1890 was only £5 per annum for two daily mail bags, one for Tumblong and one for Upper Tarcutta.[17] Each post office was supplied with materials including twine, sealing wax and brass seal, requisitions for postage stamps, labels and envelopes. The Postmaster or Postmistress was required to submit a fortnightly record of the number of letters, cards, newspapers, packets and parcels received and dispatched, along with the postage value of every item.

Decline and fall

Perhaps as a result of the figures in such postal records and the lax behaviour of Ann Upton, it was found that, ultimately, the amount of business at Hillas Creek did not warrant a full post office after all, and it was downgraded to a Receiving Office on 1 October 1880. In spite of various requests, a full post office at Hillas Creek was never reinstated, but the Receiving Office was busy enough in 1912 for the Receiving Office Keeper to be able to claim the maximum allowance permitted of £8 per annum.[18]

The Receiving Office at Hillas Creek finally shut with the closure of the Junction Hotel on 13 November 1916. Alternative arrangements in the district could not be made, as no suitable person with centrally situated premises was put forward as a Receiving Office Keeper. By this time, however, residents in the Hillas Creek locality were receiving regular roadside deliveries, and there were also mail facilities at Mount Adrah, Tarcutta and Tumblong. Nonetheless, with the demise of their own postal facility, another focal point for the Hillas Creek community was lost. Not only was its isolation from other centres increased again, but its ultimate disappearance as a settlement was also ensured.

Hillas Creek after heavy rain, 2011

CHAPTER 7

Developing the Enterprise

$\mathcal{O}$nce William and John Richardson had selected land on Hillas Creek under the conditional purchase system, they began the task of converting into a viable business what was — to their eyes, at least — a wilderness. Like every European settler, it is likely they assumed that because the landscape was empty, it was unmanaged, thereby failing to recognise both the previous interaction between the Aboriginals and the landscape, which had taken place over thousands of years, as well as the fragility of the environment.[1] This misreading of the landscape would, in future years, create difficulties not just for the Richardsons but subsequent occupiers as well, in terms of the grazing capacity, productivity and water resources of the new selections. Purchasing more land was a partial solution, but created the problem of finding yet more capital. Financial burdens became almost intolerable when family tragedy struck at the heart of the Richardson partnership.

'Improving' the land

The first two blocks of land on Hillas Creek that the Richardsons purchased in the 1860s were unsurveyed and unimproved. Although previously part of the vast squatting run of Yabtree, the pasture on these blocks was largely untouched, save for the fire and other practices utilised in the area during earlier Aboriginal occupation. The Crown Plans that were subsequently

Deltroit Road
and Deltroit creek
flats, 2011

drawn up for these blocks and for those that the Richardsons purchased later described the landscape as being 'undulating' and having an aspect of 'open forest'. The many references to gum, box, stringybark, ironbark, oak and apple indicate that the trees were numerous, though not dense, and it would have been possible to gallop a horse through the landscape without fear of injury. The Hillas Creek itself was described as a 'permanent' or 'unfailing' water supply, and the soil as being suitable for grazing or, in some areas, cultivation.

In true European tradition, the priority for the Richardsons would have been to fence their land so as to protect their boundaries, obviate the need for shepherding, facilitate the better management of their stock, and protect the animals from theft and disease. Inevitably, fencing also meant that the land would become more intensively grazed than it had ever been before. Nonetheless, fencing was regarded as an 'improvement' under the Robertson Land Acts. While this legislation specified the work to be carried out on all new selections or conditional purchases and controlled the uses for which the land could be acquired in the first place, it did not regulate how the pasture itself was to be managed. This important and now controversial issue was left to the individual selector, thereby permitting the implementation of many inappropriate land practices.

In spite of its potentially negative impact on native pastures, fencing was one of the most important technological revolutions in Australian pastoral development.[2] Prior to the new land legislation, fence erection by squatters was sporadic, due in part to their lack of security of tenure and also to the cost; however, with the introduction of conditional purchases in 1861, fencing became extensive. Initially, fences were made of brush or the more advanced post-and-rail, with two or three split logs placed horizontally into vertical posts. However, from about 1870, the use of wire and timber fences grew rapidly, as these were less laborious and expensive to build.[3]

Ringbarking was another 'improvement' embarked on by the Richardsons, and which is documented on the Crown Plans of their various land portions. This now much-lamented practice of removing timber by cutting a continuous ring of chips around the trunk avoided the labour of felling the tree and grubbing the stump. At the time, it was widely believed that trees sucked up the moisture and goodness in the soil, while also hindering sunlight falling on the pasture. Thus, it was thought that tree removal would encourage the more vigorous growth of native grasses, thereby increasing productivity.

It is an unhappy irony that nowadays, since trees have become recognised as important in maintaining biodiversity as well as managing soil erosion and salinity, local government subsidies are available for any property owner in the Hillas Creek district prepared to plant them, especially around gullies and along the creek itself. On Deltroit alone, over 130,000 trees have been planted since 1990.

Signatures of William and John Richardson in the Conditional Purchase Registers relating to land at Deltroit, 1885

View over
Deltroit, 2010

Wool and livestock

As regards the utilisation of their new land selections at Deltroit, the
Richardsons grazed sheep and cattle, building up a flock of fine wool Merino
and a herd of Shorthorn. These were the respective sheep and cattle breeds
for which William was 'considered to be one of the best judges in Australia',
according to his obituaries.[4] There were pros and cons in both operations.
Sheep required shearing and more management generally, but their wool
was in high demand abroad and relatively easy to transport. They were also
usually more drought-tolerant, but had the disadvantage of grazing pasture

down closer to the ground than cattle, thereby potentially doing more damage to emerging grasses and vegetation. Cattle required less labour and could be moved faster than sheep over long distances to markets further afield; however, there was only a domestic meat market for both beef and lamb until refrigeration was developed about 1875.

Droving was always an important consideration before sheep and cattle trucks, and it is interesting to note that, at about the same time as buying their earliest blocks at Deltroit, the Richardsons purchased approximately 700 acres at Kyeamba Creek,[5] near the current township of Forest Hill, on the stock route between Deltroit and Wagga Wagga. It is likely that this land was purchased as a resting place in order to feed and water stock on their journey to market. It would have also been particularly useful once the railway from Sydney to Wagga Wagga was completed in 1881 and then linked in 1883 to the Victorian railway line at Albury, which went through to Melbourne. Markets in both major centres would then have become much more easily accessible for the Richardsons, and, with the block at Kyeamba Creek, their stock stood a better chance of being in good condition before being transported by rail.

In running sheep and cattle, the Richardsons were sensibly taking advantage of the buoyant markets for both wool and meat in the first decade of Deltroit's existence. If they had needed to employ any men in the early years, labour was becoming available once again as the gold rushes were abating and disappointed miners were drifting back to the land. Life at Deltroit would have been very similar to that on neighbouring properties, with the diaries of settlers, such as R. F. Horsley at Yabtree, attesting to the arduous and seemingly endless round of chores. Checking and moving stock, building and mending fences, clearing and ringbarking, lambing, calving, weaning, drafting, shearing and even sheep-washing were just a few of the routine activities that filled the grazier's calendar. The old Scottish practice of sheep-washing, now long forgotten, was to rid the fleece of lanolin and dirt, thereby reducing freight on the wool.[6] Until at least the 1950s, there was a paddock at Deltroit called 'Sheepwash',[7] situated on the Adelong Road by the Junction Hotel, indicating that in the past this practice was as much a part of life at Deltroit as anywhere else in the district.

Pasture management and land degradation

As for pasture management, the Richardsons applied the practices that they had learnt back home, in common with most selectors. Unfortunately, rural experiences in England could prove irrelevant or positively misleading under Australian conditions. Not only was the climate of this part of New South Wales entirely different from Westmorland, with lower and unpredictable rainfall, but the native pasture was also much more fragile.[8] Apart from growing in a more arid environment, these grasslands had never been heavily or continuously grazed by domestic animals and had therefore always had ample recovery time in between periods of dry. Managed by the Aboriginals largely with the use of fire, their level of resilience and productive capacity was in stark contrast to the pastures of the more forgiving English landscape.[9]

When white settlement first began in the Murrumbidgee district, grasses grew tall in clumps or tussocks, with a valuable understorey of shorter varieties that protected the often limited moisture in the soil. Cattle favoured the longer grasses, popularly known as 'kangaroo grass', while sheep grazed both, eating the grass down to the surface of the paddock and in drought years, dragging up the roots in their hunger. Such rough usage, exacerbated by the sharp hooves of the stock treading on the delicate ground cover, encouraged weeds and inferior pasture to grow while also loosening the topsoil, which blew away in the wind. In good seasons with plenty of steady rain, graziers coped well enough with the impact of their cattle, sheep and even horses on the native vegetation. However, in times of drought, their properties became eaten out or ravaged and were invariably overstocked.

Billapalap in the 1920s and view of the Yaven Yaven Creek valley

The fragility of the land was not foreseen by either the squatters or the selectors because they did not recognise that the Aboriginals had followed ancient practices to manage it, nor did they take into account that large numbers of cattle, sheep and horses would, in all likelihood, have a very different effect on the land than native wildlife. Animals such as kangaroo, wallaby and wombat trod delicately and grazed lightly compared to the introduced livestock, which stamped hard on the ground in large mobs. From about the 1880s, this damage was increased with the proliferation of rabbits until their numbers were successfully restricted through hunting, rabbit-proof fencing, poisoning and, later, disease.

Not only was the pasture spoiled, but the watercourses too were adversely affected. Trampling by stock on already denuded pasture hardened the ground to such an extent that the run-off rain was accelerated into rivers and creeks, which became silted up with topsoil.[10] Only after heavy rain did those watercourses flow freely again, but they became deeply incised drains instead of wide, gentle glides of water. Nowhere is this phenomenon more evident than on the Hillas Creek, which now flows between high banks scoured and narrowed by run-off and erosion. Successive periods of steady rain are the only times when the creek reaches its full width and gains any depth.

It would be surprising if practical men like the Richardsons failed to observe the deterioration of their pasture and main water course at Deltroit, but it is tempting to conclude that they marched on with their traditional grazing methods regardless. These standard stocking practices, combined with three or four years of drought at Deltroit between 1866 and 1869 and a further dry period in the mid-1870s, would have been enough to wreak havoc on the newly acquired pastures that had only been lightly grazed before. Allowing their paddocks insufficient rest and filling them with too much stock, it would not be long before the pastures failed to regenerate properly. In the Richardsons' defence, there was little material on soil science available at the time;[11] therefore, they would not have been able to fully understand the effect of their operating modes. However, from later measures that the Richardsons took to renovate the pastures at Deltroit, it seems that, as time went on, they began to realise the need to counteract the negative impact their livestock and grazing patterns had on the environment.

Nonetheless, the Richardsons were under constant pressure to capitalise on the strong and growing markets for both wool and meat as well as to pay off their conditional purchases. There was an almost insatiable demand overseas for Australian wool, including from manufacturers in England, especially the highly industrialised Yorkshire mills. Later, when refrigeration of meat for export abroad was introduced in the mid-1870s, meat producers, too, seemed assured of good sales, especially as meat in England was four or five times the price of its Australian counterpart.[12] Understandably eager to produce as much wool and meat as possible given the market conditions, it is likely that this aim would have outweighed all the Richardsons' other considerations. Without realising it perhaps, long-term sustainability was exchanged for short-term productivity.

Although, in some quarters, the degradation of land was beginning to be noticed from at least the 1870s,[13] many still only saw the change in the landscape as a positive one. The rapid transition from a 'wilderness' into a land of plenty, progress and prosperity was remarked on by a journalist in the *Gundagai Times* in a series of articles on the early settlement of the Murrumbidgee district:

One hundred years is not a long period in the cycle of time, but it seems little short of a miracle when we witness the vast change that has been effected in this Great South Land since the date of the Hume expedition. It was no easy task to lay the foundation of a nation ... Pioneers with brave hearts and sturdy strength responded to the call, and like Caesar of old — they came, they saw and they conquered.[14]

William and John Richardson belonged very much in this pioneering category.

Purchase of Billapalap

The Richardsons' primary response to the deterioration of grass and water at Deltroit after the drought of the late 1860s was to buy more land elsewhere. This was a common reaction by settlers to the decline of pastures that had been overstocked. Soon after the drought broke, and probably with the renewed confidence that rain always brings, the Richardsons expanded their landholdings, which would not only alleviate any problems of pasture

Last remaining original building at Billapalap

degradation at Deltroit, but also enable them to take further advantage of the strong market conditions and to achieve economy of scale. The property that they purchased was further up the Hillas Creek towards Adelong, and was known as Billapalap (but sometimes called 'Dutzon' before being included in the parish of that name). Since first being recorded officially as a squatting run in 1848,[15] Billapalap had acquired a considerable reputation and, most importantly, had been improved in the 1850s by the sowing of clover,[16] a very innovative practice for the times.

Billapalap appears to have originally been occupied by Thomas Griffiths, who was no relation to the Griffiths family of the Junction Hotel at Hillas Creek. In 1848, when the run was first gazetted, Billapalap was estimated

TOP
View of drive at
Billapalap, 1928

BOTTOM
Old road to Adelong
from Billapalap, now
abandoned

to be 16,000 acres, with a grazing capacity of 4000 sheep.[17] Historically, the area around Billapalap had a higher rainfall than at Deltroit and, being hilly, lightly timbered country, was ideal for wool-growing. The property also had a double frontage onto the Hillas Creek, which at Billapalap is known by the name of the Yaven Yaven. Rising in the hills near Tumbarumba, the Yaven Yaven becomes the Hillas Creek at Mount Adrah, four miles east of Deltroit, at the junction with the Nacki Nacki Creek.

The purchase of Billapalap was made on or before 7 March 1873 from Thomas Usher Elliott, who lent the Richardsons £5000 at the extraordinarily advantageous interest rate of £7 10s per annum, payable half-yearly.[18] The amount of land covered by this mortgage was 1800 acres, but it is likely that further land was purchased about the same time. Unfortunately, the title documents are incomplete, and neither the full extent of the purchases by the Richardsons at Billapalap nor the pattern of acquisition can be ascertained with any accuracy. Nonetheless, according to a probate valuation in 1886, the brothers' joint assets included land at Billapalap comprising 1210 acres of freehold and 3900 acres under conditional purchase, plus a further 16,000 acres under lease.[19] The leasehold area had another three years to run and at some stage was mostly converted to freehold. A year later, the combined acreage at Deltroit and Billapalap was reported as being 13,000 acres freehold and 9795 acres held under conditional purchase.[20] By 1900, Billapalap alone was reported as comprising 20,000 acres.[21]

In borrowing to expand their operations, the Richardsons were no doubt counting on some good seasons and on the continuing strength of the wool and meat markets. Presumably, they hoped to be able to accumulate sufficient income to pay off the advance of so much capital, but although the mortgage from Elliott was discharged in full on 27 February 1878, another mortgage, this time for £6000, was taken out the same day from the Bank of New South Wales.[22] This cycle of borrowing, both to expand and maintain the existing pastoral enterprise, continued throughout most of the history of Billapalap and Deltroit while they were owned by the Richardsons.

Aside from purchasing the land, the Richardsons bought all houses, huts and buildings at Billapalap, of which there were several, since the property had been previously occupied by at least three families. Thomas Griffiths had

lived there with his family; followed by his brother, George, and his children; before the property was taken over by Thomas Elliott, with five children. The Richardsons not only acquired all this infrastructure, but also bought 1500 head of cattle and 90 horses branded with a simple circle.[23] It seems clear that the brothers were horse breeders and dealers as a sideline to their main sheep and cattle business. In 1886, the brothers jointly owned 145 horses — far more than would have been necessary for stock work. All horses, sheep and cattle would be branded and the circle used by Thomas Elliott was continued by the Richardsons, remaining in use by the family until William's grandson, Jack Fraser, sold Deltroit in the 1960s.[24]

Strategically, the purchase of Billapalap proved to be a good move and no doubt provided some drought-proofing for Deltroit during the recurrence of dry conditions in the mid-1870s. Billapalap was reasonably close to Deltroit, being about 20 miles south and only a two-day drove with sheep,[25] so that operations at both places could easily be combined. It is not clear how the stock on both properties were managed initially. Sheep and cattle appear to always have been grazed at both places; however, by 1900, only the store cattle were run at Billapalap before being moved to Deltroit for 'finishing' and then sent to market.[26] Ultimately, it seems that the income from Billapalap came to pay for the lifestyle of William's daughter, Florence, and her husband, Charles Fraser, and later for that of their son, Jack.[27]

Whether the Richardsons tried to purchase more land adjoining Deltroit before acquiring Billlapalap is uncertain. In 1873, much of Deltroit was surrounded by land either owned by R. F. Horsley or taken up by third parties on his behalf, or held by various other selectors. Ironically, Horsley was to try and sell Yabtree in 1876 and had it on the market for £20,500 including stock.[28] Unfortunately, the timing would have been too late for the Richardsons, who, had they been able to afford it, might have preferred the beautiful Yabtree over Billapalap, with its frontage onto the mighty Murrumbidgee River and its wonderful river flats. While Horsley's diaries make it clear that another grazier by the name of Jenkins, the owner of Nangus Station, was very interested in acquiring Yabtree, there is no mention of the Richardsons ever being considered potential purchasers.

An unexpected death

The need to pay off their conditional purchases and the borrowings on Billapalap, acquired to drought-proof Deltroit and to keep up with market demand, was not the sole problem facing the Richardsons. In a dramatic and wholly unforeseen turn of events, John died prematurely in 1886 from dysentery at the age of only forty-nine. His unexpected death unquestionably placed the whole Richardson grazing enterprise at risk. Suddenly, William, who had been in full partnership with John, was faced with buying out his late brother's widow in order to retain ownership of his by now extensive landholdings. In the absence of sufficient capital of his own, William was obliged to resort to further, much more significant borrowings than ever before.[29]

The financial consequences of John's premature death in relation to the outstanding conditional purchases was threefold. Firstly, William was obliged to pay his sister-in-law the sums that John had already paid to the Crown, as part payment for the land held jointly by the brothers under the conditional purchase system. Secondly, William would, in future, also have to pay the whole of the balance owing to the Crown, instead of only his half share under the partnership arrangement with John. Thirdly, William had to buy, presumably at market value, the other half of all land that had already been paid off under the conditional purchase scheme or acquired as freehold, but which was in the joint names of the two brothers. The borrowings that William needed in order to do all this would have been crushing for him, especially in times of drought. At best, they must have caused him considerable anguish and, at worst, made him fear financial ruin. The miracle that William was able to keep both Deltroit and Billapalap at all is proof of his good management and business skills, the high standing with which he was regarded in the rural and financial community that appear to have stood by him and, last but not least, his tenacity.

With the twin pressures of debt and the desire to take advantage of strong markets in wool and meat, stock numbers on both properties were very high. It therefore seems doubtful that William learned many lessons about the true carrying capacity of either Deltroit or Billapalap. Early figures are no longer available but huge stock numbers were recorded for the properties' combined operations between 1893 and 1901, and there is every likelihood that the numbers were just as high, proportionately to the amount of land held, in the preceding two decades. According to the Australasian Federal Pastoral Directory, William Richardson owned 14,928 sheep and 2312 cattle in 1893; 16,000 sheep and 3228 cattle in 1895; and an astonishing 18,400 sheep and 2200 cattle in 1903, at the end of the devastating Federation Drought that lasted eight years. These figures tend to support the average joint stockholdings at Deltroit and Billapalap, which were given in the *Tumut & Adelong Times* of 4 May 1900 as being between 14,000 and 16,000 sheep (though there were actually 20,000 when the article was written) and 2000 cattle.

Diversification

While grazing livestock was the focus of their business, the Richardsons also engaged in other commercial activities on their land. Horses were one such example and would have contributed even more to the problems of land degradation. The Richardsons may also have planted crops of corn, wheat, barley and oats at various times, as these were known to have been grown at Yabtree.[30] Growing crops to maximise the production capacity of fertile river and creek flats was a common practice among selectors. After John's untimely death in 1886, William further diversified the pastoral enterprise at Deltroit by planting tobacco along the banks of the Hillas Creek. It is plausible that he was looking for additional sources of income to supplement the existing business of which he had become sole owner, and to fund the cost of borrowings necessitated by the sudden death of his brother and partner.

From the mid-1880s to the beginning of the 1890s, the cultivation of tobacco was popular along the Hillas Creek valley, all the way from Mundarlo and Hillas Creek to Adelong.[31] Selectors sublet portions of their land, usually to Chinese farmers who grew Virginia Light and other varieties on the rich alluvial flats by the creek. In return for the use of his choicest land, William took a quarter share in the tobacco crop in part payment of rent.[32] R. F. Horsley came to a similar arrangement with a tobacco grower, Ah Poo, who took prizes at the Wagga Wagga Show for the quality of his crop.[33] Long sheds, roughly constructed of either galvanised iron or saplings with bark roofs, were used to cultivate the seedlings and as drying sheds. The contents of just one of these buildings could be as much as 40 tons of tobacco worth £3000.[34]

The need to diversify into other income-producing activities was also fuelled by the depression of the early 1890s. A financial crash in 1890 in Argentina, which had become a centre of world speculation, caused repercussions throughout the global economy. In Australia, several banks failed, interest rates remained high and prices of all agricultural products fell by up to 50 percent. Those with a diversified business were believed to be best able to cope with the changed economic conditions. There was huge pressure on most graziers, no doubt including William Richardson, who would have had little or no return after financing his borrowings and whose land, against which these loans were secured, was depreciating in value.

Nonetheless, William appears to have weathered this particular storm, and there is no evidence that his grazing business ever teetered on the edge of collapse. On the contrary, by the end of the 1890s, William was still planning ahead and planting barley grass[35] in the belief that this would improve his pastures. While barley grass provides good feed in winter and early spring, it dies off quickly in the heat and provides no further nutrition. Its use has declined since it was proven to be detrimental to the regeneration of native grasses, and its brittle spikes, a hazard to the eyes and gums of livestock and horses. Yet these problems were unknown when William planted the species at Deltroit and saw, doubtless with excitement, how quickly it spread. Moreover, both he and John may have made earlier pasture improvements that were more beneficial in the long-term by sowing rye grass, clover or lucerne. These highly nutritious grass varieties began to be used widely in pasture improvement from the mid-1870s.[36]

A 'model' station

By 1900, in spite of some adverse changes wrought on the landscape by settlement and the vagaries of economic and climatic conditions, especially the prevailing Federation Drought, Deltroit was described by one observer as being a 'model' sheep and cattle station.[37] This fulsome praise for and vivid description of the property is one of only two contemporary accounts of Deltroit that have been found (the other, which is three years later, relates to the homestead after its completion in 1903). The earlier account continues:

> The Deltroit property is one of the finest in the district. Mr Richardson settled on it in 1866 and has added to it ever since. On Deltroit, there are 7,000 acres of land, well cleared and rung. A great proportion borders upon the Hillas' [*sic*] Creek, being beautiful rich flats, averaging half a mile in width. The remainder of the estate is of an undulating nature. The road subdivides the property, which is subdivided into conveniently-sized paddocks. The pasture is knee-deep in places, being mainly rich barley grass, which is fresh to the locality, having only made its appearance in quantity last year … An up-to-date shearing shed, replete with every necessary appliance is built upon the high land. The station is without doubt, of the class which can be truthfully termed "model". No surplus timber is allowed to remain on the land and the fences are kept in first class order.

Certainly, William (and, until his death, John) Richardson had achieved a great deal, establishing a prime grazing property with most, if not all, the 'improvements' considered desirable at the time. It is very unlikely that the brothers could have done so much had they stayed in England. They were perfect examples of the men celebrated in a verse by George Clout: 'The manly yeoman settles on the soil, / And wins its wilderness with hopeful toil'.[38] Their achievements were all the more remarkable in a country that had such an unpredictable climate and rainfall pattern compared to their own. The fact that Deltroit was described as a 'model' property when the whole of New South Wales was in the midst of the most serious drought since white settlement in the colony suggests that William was a better farmer than most, and not a man to be easily defeated.

CHAPTER 8

Early Droughts, Fires and Floods

While the Richardsons were establishing a combined grazing operation at Deltroit and Billapalap on a scale beyond most European dreams of wealth and position, they were doing so in one of the least hospitable climates on earth. The extraordinary intensity of the Australian sun, coupled with unpredictable rainfall patterns, ensured that, in common with the rest of the country, Hillas Creek was as much prone to periodic drought of varying degrees of severity as any other part of the continent. This was in spite of being in a relatively high area of rainfall, which, in itself, did not preclude recurring cycles of drought and disappointing or even disastrous seasons. Before recent developments in the understanding of the sustainability of the Australian landscape and the building of large dams, the rural community was often more or less helpless in the face of such periods of severe dry weather. Neither the Richardsons nor their properties at Deltroit and Billapalap escaped these episodes, which were a test of endurance for all living things. Other natural disasters, namely fire and flood, were also part of the history of Hillas Creek as well as nearby townships and settlements, bringing people together from all sections of the rural community in a mutual desire for self-preservation and out of compassion for their fellow man.

Hillas Creek at Deltroit, 2006

Droughts and devastation

Serious drought conditions prevailed in the Hillas Creek district from the beginning of the Richardsons' arrival in the mid-1860s to the end of the decade, and again in the mid-1870s and mid-1880s. In that era, the cycle seemed to start about every ten years, but there was no knowing how long it would last. On 22 January 1866, a journalist for the *Tumut & Adelong Times* lamented, 'That we may be relieved from this drought is earnestly desired. Even in our favoured district things are beginning to look bad; our creeks are all but dry ...' James Gormly, a resident at Nangus, located about 15 miles north of Hillas Creek, noted on 9 December 1868 that 'the drought is very bad in Wagga, many stock are going to the mountains for grass and there are many dead sheep and cattle on the roads'.[1]

In view of these reports, it seems a little curious that the Richardsons purchased their first blocks of land at Deltroit during this period. Perhaps they believed that the much-vaunted reliability of the Hillas Creek was security enough, or it may simply highlight the optimism that they felt about the new environment in which they were operating. Nonetheless, the drought conditions may explain why their original conditional purchases were cancelled as being within a water reserve and then reinstated a year later. It was shortly after the drought of the 1860s broke that the Richardsons purchased the much larger property of Billapalap. Quite possibly, the pastures at Deltroit had been slow to regenerate after the reappearance of rain because they had been grazed too intensively during the previous three years. It does not take more than two or three poor seasons for even well-managed pastures to be undone by lack of rain, so that the Richardsons' need to find more grass was probably as much of a concern then as their desire to capitalise on the strong markets for meat and wool.

Another very dry period occurred in the mid-1870s, recorded again by James Gormly, who wrote on 10 February 1875 that 'the drought in Wagga district is very serious'. This was reinforced by George Seymour, a stockman at Wantabadgery, a property about 12 miles north of Deltroit, who wrote that 1875 was a 'time of tribulation' during which 'thousands of beautiful bullocks perished in droves, and all hands were kept busy skinning and burning the carcases'.[2] In 1876, local conditions were so dry that it seems R. F. Horsley even contemplated selling Yabtree and moving his operations to his property Gunningbland, near Forbes in central New South Wales.[3] Horsley ultimately withdrew Yabtree from the market, but the episode illustrates the pressures that a series of dry seasons could exert on everyone, including the most established grazier. Aside from the purely commercial consequences on income, there was also the psychological cost: it would have been devastating for Horsley and the Richardsons to witness their prime grazing country succumbing to drought, with years of effort slipping away through lack of rain.

Although these droughts were damaging, and even devastating in some quarters, by far the most pernicious in the early history of Deltroit was the great drought of the 1890s. Unfolding slowly and inexorably from about 1895, this eight-year ordeal that became known as the Federation Drought left the whole colony of New South Wales, with few exceptions, in a desperate condition. In many parts, there was neither a blade of grass nor a running water course, and stock were perishing daily.[4] Aside from sheep and cattle, vast tracts of country were lost by settlers to the banks and other financial institutions that had lent the necessary capital for these pastoral ventures, some on an almost epic scale. An agricultural depression of tragic proportions took hold and lasted into the early 1900s. However, it seems that, in the immediate district of Hillas Creek, conditions may not have been serious until later in the decade. On 30 March 1897, it was reported in the *Gundagai Times* that in spite of the whole country being parched:

> There is plenty of water in the district and there appears to be no scarcity of grass in the neighbourhood of Mundarlo, Yabtree and Hillas Creek. Stock too are in excellent condition. But the outlook for the winter is not encouraging and graziers are getting rid of as much stock as possible.

On 25 January 1898, the first known report of the Hillas Creek itself failing to run appeared in the *Gundagai Times*. The journalist wrote, 'We are having our fair share of the weather glass from 100 deg. to 109 in the

Florence and Isabel Richardson with the Horsley children by Hillas Creek, c. 1895

shade, with no signs of change. Hillas' [*sic*] Creek this summer has ceased to run.' He then added ruefully, 'When Hillas' [*sic*] Creek fails running, I almost imagine that it is not impossible for the famous Murrumbidgee to go likewise on strike.' It is almost certain that the Hillas Creek dried up again in January 1900 and 1903. According to the diaries of John Joseph Pearce, a selector and neighbour of the Richardsons at Billapalap, the Yaven Yaven Creek (of which the Hillas Creek was a continuation) ceased to flow in both these years, and he was forced to dig holes in the sand to find water for stock.[5] It has not been possible to ascertain exactly how long the creek stopped running on any of these occasions, but it is plain from Pearce's diaries that it was certainly for several weeks.

It is not known what measures William Richardson took to overcome these difficult periods, especially the Federation Drought. In common with other selectors, he had probably taken some steps towards water maintenance and conservation, especially in the light of previous droughts. Dams would have been sunk on Deltroit, and one or more wells might also have been dug with a windmill to access underground water. These self-regulating windmills, used to pump water for livestock, began to appear in Australia from about the mid-1860s and were at first imported from

Hillas Creek bone-dry at Deltroit, 2008

Hillas Creek at Deltroit just before the flood, 2010

TOP
Pastures at
Deltroit in
drought,
early 2010

BOTTOM
Cattle at Deltroit
in drought,
early 2010

America.[6] They could be set up so as to pump water into a tank, which was then gravity-fed into troughs. Fortunately, there were also underground springs in the hills on the south side of Deltroit, and these used to be a reliable water source, feeding a series of small creeks that wound their way through the paddocks. Aside from these, there was always the option of reducing stock numbers, transferring stock to Billapalap or sending stock away to pasture in the nearby Snowy Mountains. Drought took its toll on several of Deltroit's neighbours, including the selectors John Beaver and Henry Staggs, who, unable to hold out any longer, sold their land to the Horsleys and to the Richardsons.[7]

The land ablaze

In the Hillas Creek locality, bushfires are an ever-present threat in summer, especially after long periods of dry, as temperatures frequently hover around 40 degrees Celsius in the shade and more in the sun. Violent thunderstorms are a feature of the region and easily spark the first flames, with conditions becoming extremely dangerous if the heat is accompanied by hot, searing winds (usually from the west), which dry out the land further and fan any flames. A destructive bushfire raged for some days around Hillas Creek in early January 1875, leaving nine miles of fencing destroyed and sheep burnt alive.[8] Another extensive fire in the district was in January 1892, stretching all the way from Wagga Wagga.[9] Smaller fires also happened regularly in the district during the summer months throughout the first three decades of Richardson occupation.

Unfortunately, the area around Billapalap appears to have been especially fire-prone. The Pearce diaries make for sombre reading with their many references to excessively dry conditions and the regular outbreak of fires both large and small. During the Federation Drought, the country was particularly inflammable. On 20 February 1900, Pearce wrote that 'a bush fire had started at Billapalap appears close to the station told the boys to get their horses have some dinner and go to help at the fire ...' It seems that the men worked through the night until 4am before they had the fire under control. They were all firefighting again on 22 December later that year, and were described by Pearce as 'thoroughly knocked up' after forty hours' work at the fire front. Another fire burned next door to Billapalap on 27 February 1901, and there were further fires nearby between 3 and 8 February 1902. A fire in November 1904 completely destroyed the stable, loose boxes and cart sheds at Billapalap, containing several vehicles, a great deal of harness, a chaff cutter and several tons of hay.[10] However, it seems that, on this occasion, the fire was man-made and not the result of spontaneous combustion.

The most disastrous fire in the early history of the Hillas Creek district was undoubtedly in January 1905, when local residents fought flames for nine days.[11] Starting on Christmas Day, separate fires in Mundarlo, Tarcutta and Nangus spread in one direction to Tumblong and in another to Mount Adrah, swallowing up thousands of acres of grass, orchards, crops, homesteads, livestock and fences. All station hands were required to fight the fire, and while the men were away trying to save paddocks and livestock, the women donned male attire 'in order that the troublesome skirts would be out of the way', working desperately to save the horses and the homesteads.

Although it was initially thought that Deltroit would not be touched, immense damage was done to considerable areas of grass and fencing. Over 3000 sheep and 100 head of cattle were reported missing at Deltroit,[12] though there is no record of the final losses after inspections were completed. By an extraordinary stroke of good luck, and perhaps through the brave work of the women at Deltroit, the new homestead, less than two years old, was spared. Fortunately, there was also no loss of life at Deltroit, though an elderly miner at nearby Mount Adrah was killed and another was severely burnt.

The fire of 1905 was just as fierce around Billapalap. There is a moving account by Pearce of several days of firefighting, beginning on 1 January. He recorded that the day began with a 'very hot wind strong and increasing to very strong at sunset'. Two separate fires from the direction of Tarcutta joined together and 'the united fires swept everything before them the showers of burning bark and leaves resembling a very heavy snow storm'. The Pearce family narrowly managed to save their homestead but not their stable

Bore by Hillas Creek at Deltroit, 2009

and hay shed, which were completely destroyed along with harness and tack. A stock inspection revealed considerable losses and, while the episode would have been heartbreaking, Pearce adopted an uncomplaining and philosophical tone, wondering to himself, 'what can be done with the stock left alive as all the country appears to be a desert?' These fires were physically exhausting and debilitating for the men fighting them, and 'they suffered greatly from their eyes through the hot ashes being blown into them'. It often took several days before the men could go out into the light again.

Flooding

Between fire and drought, there were sometimes floods, notably in April 1870. This was the greatest inundation to take place in the locality since the disastrous flood of 1852, which swept away the old township of Gundagai, situated on the river flats. According to the *Gundagai Times*,[13] the Murrumbidgee rose from 15 to 37 feet at the Albert Bridge in Gundagai and the local inhabitants could hear 'the river roaring like a stormy sea'. For almost a week, rain fell with 'steady persistency' and 'the hills were enveloped in dense mist and vapour, through which their blurred outlines were only

Hillas Creek in flood, October 2010

Hillas Creek in flood immediately prior to Deltroit bridge being washed away, October 2010

dimly visible'. A mother and her two children were drowned, and many cattle, sheep and horses were swept away, though some managed to come ashore and were ultimately recovered by their owners.

No account has been found of what occurred at Hillas Creek on this occasion. However, it is likely that the residents there would have been seriously affected by the torrential rain and consequential run-off from the broad catchment area of the Murrumbidgee, which had not, as yet, been harnessed by any dam or reservoir schemes (these came much later in the twentieth century). The weather remained wet for the rest of the autumn and early winter of 1870, culminating in another smaller flood in June. It was reported that 'Wagga, in due course, received the flood waters that passed this place, augmented by the swollen streams of the Adelong, Hillas, Kyeamba, Tarcutta, Nangus and other creeks'.[14]

In June 1891, the Murrumbidgee was again in flood, with disastrous consequences.[15] Men at Kimo, near Gundagai, were stranded in trees while trying to rescue stock from the floodwaters, but their attempts were largely in vain and over 4000 sheep were lost.[16] Two of the Kimo men were likewise drowned during a rescue attempt that saved six lives. Aside from sheep, hundreds of bullocks were washed down to Wagga Wagga,[17] and there was extensive damage to crops. Once again, no reports can be traced of how the Hillas Creek was affected by this deluge. Although its water level may have risen dramatically, it is possible that the creek itself did not burst its banks. However, flood conditions returned to the region in 1892, when it was clearly reported that a week of heavy rain made the Hillas Creek impassable.[18] This brings to mind the reports of surveyor Thomas Townsend in the 1840s that in times of heavy rain, the creek was a hazard on the Great Southern Road that ran along Deltroit's western boundary.

In July 1900, there was a further major flood in Gundagai, resulting in significant property damage. This latter flood came right in the midst of the Federation Drought and, in spite of its ill effects, must have been an agreeable change from the intense period of dry. As on previous occasions, the Murrumbidgee became a huge inland sea and 'a boisterous, fretful, seething torrent, laden with timber fragments and tumbling debris, rushing and eddying against the bridges and other obstructions'.[19] With so much water around, it is very likely that the Hillas and Yaven Yaven creeks would have risen to such an extent so as to burst their banks, causing much of the frontage country at Deltroit and Billapalap to be underwater.

Finally, there is a clear report of flooding along the Hillas Creek in the Gundagai Independent of 25 October 1917. After fourteen days of heavy rain, the Hillas Creek was described as coming down a 'double banker', flooding all the low-lying land at Deltroit, especially the lucerne paddocks to the rear of the homestead and partly washing away the Hillas Creek bridge. Two miles of fencing was destroyed at Deltroit alone and the creek was said to be at its highest level in fifty years, presumably a reference to the floods of 1870.

Community spirit

In spite of all these natural disasters, which continued to appear throughout the twentieth century with varying degrees of severity, it was claimed by some that by far the worst scourge of the selector were the rabbits. George Seymour wrote that rabbits introduced by the early settlers

> did more damage than all the fires, floods, droughts and pests put together. They ruined many people and put others on the financial rocks, and they not only cleared thousands of acres of grass, but destroyed trees by ringing them. I've seen them like mobs of sheep on my place waiting for the leaves to fall off the trees.[20]

At Billapalap, rabbits were particularly bad, and it was said that the rabbit warrens there went the whole length and breadth of the property.[21] Plagues of locusts were also a regular feature of rural life and could destroy pastures and crops in a single day.

During such trials and tribulations, the settlers in the Hillas Creek valley relied heavily on each other as they did in other rural communities in the colony. They stood side by side through thick and thin and willingly gave help to their neighbours in times of adversity. There was, of course, no government assistance in the nineteenth century to help those on the land in crisis and, therefore, support from within the community was especially important.

Such support could also be relied on during family troubles. Those afflicted by the death or disappearance of one or more parents and the orphaning of children was an example when people willingly stepped in, especially if they had a prior relationship with the victims' families. Any familial ties or connections with others in the district or the wider colony were usually fostered by the settlers, especially as many were so far from their birthplace. Similarly, the bonds of friendship forged with neighbours were dearly held. In the case of the Richardsons, family ties and friendships were ultimately to prove as essential to their wellbeing as the rain that was often so elusive.

CHAPTER 9

Marriage and Family

*N*ow the joint owner of several thousand acres at Deltroit and also of the extensive Billapalap run, William Richardson felt sufficiently well established to support a wife and family. He was also by then in his mid-thirties and mature enough (for a serious-minded person such as himself) to embark on marriage. Two of his brothers had already married: Thomas had taken a wife soon after his arrival in Orange, whereas John had wed more recently though his wife died in childbirth a short time later.

No information remains about William's personal life before his marriage or whether he had been involved with anyone previously. The first woman known to have attracted his attention was Mary Lysaght, who was living at Hillas Creek and was one of the petitioners for the post office. Her name appears as 'Mary Lisaght' in the petition and her occupation is described as 'domestic'. This could mean that she was working as a servant at the Junction Hotel or at one of the nearby homesteads, or that she was simply living and helping at the home of her married sister, Jane Larkin, who also resided in the area.

William's marriage

Mary, who was Catholic, was brought up in her birthplace of Fairy Meadow near Wollongong, a rural area of open meadow lands noted for

OPPOSITE
William
Richardson,
c. 1910, in
Masonic dress
wearing Royal
Arch regalia

their 'fairy-like' beauty. Subsequently, while still a child, she moved with her family to Taralga, a small community further west in the Southern Tablelands of New South Wales. This background made her a country woman, accustomed to a simpler and more isolated life than if she had been brought up in one of the major centres of the colony. She was four years older than William and almost thirty-nine years of age when the couple married on 3 October 1874 by special licence at St Paul's Church in Geelong, Victoria. Notwithstanding that the marriage was solemnised in a Protestant ceremony, Mary remained a practising Catholic until her death.

It is the greatest mystery as to why William and Mary travelled over 300 miles to Geelong to marry when they were both residents at Hillas Creek. No family stories have been handed down to shed light on this intriguing fact. Neither party appears to have had any family connections in Geelong, but it is possible that William had business to attend to there, either as a result of his carrying days in the Victorian goldfields or connected to his current wool-producing activities. Geelong, after all, was a major port, and wool was exported from there to every part of the globe.

Another reason — and probably the most likely — is that the couple could not easily find a vicar prepared to carry out a mixed marriage between a Protestant and a Catholic. It is possible that, during his time in Victoria, William had become acquainted with Ralph Barker, the vicar who eventually officiated at the wedding, and knew that he would be amenable to arranging such an unorthodox union. The vicar's family, Matilda and Mary Ann Barker, acted as witnesses, which, though not unusual, may also indicate that the whole family were known to William before his marriage.

A further or alternative explanation for the couple's marriage in Geelong is that Mary was pregnant and was trying to conceal the fact from the small community at Hillas Creek. If this was the case, Mary must have lost the baby, as her first child was not born until eighteen months later. Marrying by special licence, as William and Mary did, was indeed more exclusive. Nonetheless, it often implied haste, since it dispensed with the need for banns to be read over a one-month period.

Whatever the reasons for choosing Geelong, it appears that Mary was economical with the truth about her age, claiming in the marriage certificate that she was only thirty-one — eight years younger than she actually was. She was to maintain this fiction all her life, as her obituaries[1] and death certificate stated variously that she was either sixty-eight, seventy or seventy-one, even though she was, in fact, seventy-five when she died. Seemingly, Mary felt insecure about her marriage prospects and had a number of valid reasons for this, aside from the fact that, by nineteenth-century standards, she was already old compared to most other brides.

Mary Lysaght's background

Contrary to what might be supposed, Mary was not from the prominent Lysaght family that pioneered galvanised steel and established a highly successful business in Lithgow. Rather, she was the daughter of Patrick Lysaght, a ploughman and convict who had been transported for seven years to New South Wales from Limerick, Ireland.[2] He was found guilty of insurrection after taking part in the Rockite Rebellion, a particularly violent agrarian movement that began as a reaction against the absolute power wielded by the English and Anglo-Irish feudal landlords in Ireland. Arriving in Sydney on the *Mangles* on 8 November 1822, Patrick Lysaght was eventually granted his freedom in 1829 and, a few years later, became a landholder at Fairy Meadow with several convicts assigned to him as servants or labourers.

Mary's mother was Johanna Elliott, the daughter of Edward Elliott, a dancing master from Limerick and another agitator against the English.[3] He had also been transported to New South Wales in 1822, and his family, including the twenty-year-old Johanna, had been allowed to join him in 1828. Johanna married Patrick Lysaght about the time that Patrick was pardoned, and the couple subsequently had four children: Ellen Theresa, born on 4 August 1830; Jane Elizabeth, born on 14 November 1831; Andrew, born on 1 October 1832; and Mary, born on 28 October 1835. Tragedy was to strike this young family when Mary was only a few months old. At that time, Patrick Lysaght appears to have been a passenger on the *Swan*, a cutter that sank without trace off Botany Bay on or around

27 February 1836 while on a voyage from Wollongong to Sydney.[4] Three years later, Mary's widowed mother remarried, becoming the wife of James Barry, with whom she had another nine children.

Mary not only bore the stain of convict blood, but she was also Irish and Catholic during a time in Australia when both these things were regarded as a social liability. It is not surprising that she hid her true age from the apparently irreproachable William Richardson, who she might have feared would not have been able to overlook yet one more shortcoming in her background. Sadly, nothing at all is known of their relationship and whether they shared a passion for the land that William obviously possessed. Similarly, there are no photographs of Mary to ascertain her appearance, and only very little is known of her character and disposition or why William was likely to have been attracted to her.

According to one of Mary's obituaries, she was of 'an exceedingly kind and generous nature' and 'endeared herself to the whole of her acquaintances and friends by her sterling worth and unostentatious manner'.[5] This description of her lack of pretensions is borne out by the fact that, although she would have had opportunities to take part in the many social activities held in Adelong and Gundagai — including annual agricultural shows and races, regular meetings of literary and debating societies and frequent theatrical and musical evenings — not a single reference to 'Mrs William Richardson' has been found in any contemporary newspaper report or gossip column recounting these events. Mary seems to have been a modest woman, keeping a low profile in spite of her husband's success.

The Larkins

Mary was probably drawn to Hillas Creek by her elder sister, Jane, who had married John Larkin in Wollongong in 1859 and moved first to Nangus, before settling in the Hillas Creek district. The first trace of Mary in the area is on the birth certificate of Jane's fourth child, Emily Edith Ellen, who was born on 30 January 1870. Mary, who was then thirty-four years old, appears on the certificate as the nurse or witness at Emily's birth. By this stage, Mary would no doubt have tired of being at home with her mother, stepfather and nine half siblings, all of whom had, for some years, been living on a property called Bloomfield at Taralga.[6] Since Jane was married and Mary's other full sister, Ellen, had died of scarlatina on 31 October 1848, aged only eighteen, Mary would have been the eldest daughter at home, probably required to help look after her younger half brothers and sisters. Seeking a little more independence perhaps, she appears to have sought out her elder sister and her Larkin family connections.

Unfortunately, John Larkin did not prove to be the most reliable of husbands to Jane. Whatever he may have been when he married her, the evidence suggests that he wound up a dishonest and desperate man. Born about 1836 in West Dapto, New South Wales, he had nine siblings and, like his wife, was of convict descent, though only on his mother's side.[7] His father, Martin Larkin, had a sister, Bridget Ryder, who came to Australia from Ireland in the mid-1850s as an assisted immigrant and whose husband, Edmund, died during the voyage.[8] Although John Larkin was in the area long before, it was his aunt Bridget Ryder who, in about 1873, settled with her son, Bartholomew, on the confusingly named Delatroy Station, Tarcutta, only a few miles from Deltroit, Hillas Creek.[9]

While married to Jane, Larkin fathered her six children: John Edward, born on 1 September 1861; Francis ('Frank'), born on 24 July 1863; Alexander ('Al'), born on 17 June 1865; Emily Edith Ellen, born on 30 January 1870; Joanna Maria Theresa ('Tess'), born on 28 July 1872; and Patrick Henry ('Harry'), born on 26 January 1878. Larkin also had a chequered employment history and ran up a criminal record. According to his children's birth certificates, he was at various times a stockman, a drover and a farmer in and around the Gundagai and Hillas Creek districts. It seems he had a small selection firstly at Nangus and then on the Wagga Road near Deltroit,[10] but it has not been possible to verify this or identify the exact location of either holding. The land near Deltroit may have even been held for R. F. Horsley under a dummying arrangement,[11] since Larkin had known Horsley from at least 1856 and had been employed by him and his partner, Richard Whittaker, as a stockman for two years at Yabtree and also as overseer at another property, Merool Station.[12]

John Larkin's gaol photograph, c. 1878

Notwithstanding these employment opportunities and, later on, the potentially useful Richardson and Ryder family connections close by, Larkin fell into a life of petty crime and was found guilty of cattle stealing on at least two occasions. The first case that has been discovered was reported on 17 May 1865, when he was charged with stealing nine head of cattle belonging to Thomas Mate of Tarcutta.[13] He was convicted, in spite of evidence of good character, while he had been in the employ of Horsley and Whittaker. The sentence that he received after this conviction is unknown, but the trial took place when his eldest child, John, was only three years old.

The next occasion of Larkin cattle stealing that has been identified was reported on 20 December 1878, when he was found guilty of taking about 39 head of cattle from Charles Bardwell of Adelong and, even more brazenly, four bullocks belonging to his own brother-in-law, William Richardson.[14] For this offence, Larkin was sentenced to a term in Berrima Gaol and three years' work on the roads. His gaol records[15] are incomplete but include a photograph of him with a thick, untidy beard. He is recorded as being 5 feet 9¾ inches tall, with grey hair, blue eyes and a burn scar on his upper left arm. It is possible that after Larkin went to prison, Jane never saw her feckless husband again, as she died less than one year later on 14 November 1879, after being diagnosed with haemoptysis, the coughing up of blood frequently associated with pneumonia. She was exactly forty-eight years old, since she died on her birthday.

Susannah Barry

In spite of losing Jane, Mary Richardson had other family close by, whom she would have seen from time to time. Her half sister Susannah Barry appears to have followed her and Jane to Hillas Creek in the mid-1870s, having married (apparently against the wishes of her family[16]) Edward Donnelly on Christmas Day 1873 in Taralga. Ten years later, Edward, who was at one time a labourer, became one of the licensees of the Junction Hotel at Hillas Creek after it had been purchased by William and John Richardson.

Alexander Barry

Another of Mary's half siblings, Alexander Barry, was also in the district from about 1874. As verified by the birth certificates of his first two children, Teresa and Joseph, he was a police constable stationed in Gundagai until he resigned on 14 May 1882.[17] Having enlisted in the New South Wales police force in the 1860s, he was described on the Police Register as being '5' 8½" with grey eyes, a fresh complexion, brown hair and smart appearance'. He was clearly a popular fellow, as the Wagga Wagga press reported with some sympathy in June 1874 that he had been bucked off his horse in the main street and suffered a severe injury to his right knee.[18] In spite of his popularity and professional appearance, he was not above getting into trouble himself. On 25 July 1874, the *Gundagai Times* reported that he had been involved in a fight at the Commercial Hotel in Gundagai. Upon refusing to drink with William Paine, a local resident, Paine assaulted Barry and received 'a fine black eye' in return.

However, Barry's finest hour came the night of the death of his half sister Jane Larkin. Coincidentally, she died on the night of the famous hold-up of Wantabadgery Station by 'Captain Moonlite', an episode that has entered into Australian history as one of the more extreme examples of bushranging violence ever perpetrated. Moonlite, whose real name was Andrew George Scott, was the leader of a gang of five other men who bailed up nineteen people at gunpoint for two days in the small dining room of the

Capturers of the Moonlite Gang, 1879. Alexander Barry, half brother of Mary Richardson, is standing far right.

homestead at Wantabadgery, not more than 12 miles from Deltroit. One prisoner managed to escape and call the police, but they had to move warily with so many innocent people being held hostage.

After many hours, the bushrangers escaped with extra firearms, clothing and supplies, but were later apprehended by both the Wagga Wagga and Gundagai police at another nearby property. During that encounter, in which a hail of bullets were fired on both sides, killing one of the bushrangers and a policeman, another of the gang members, Gus Wreneckie, was mortally wounded by Barry, after the latter's horse was shot from under him. Some sources claim incorrectly that it was Mary's other half brother, John Barry, who was involved in this incident. However, although he too was a police constable, he left the police force on 15 November 1866, thirteen years before this incident.[19]

Moonlite and the three other bushrangers were eventually taken prisoner, and the gallant action of the police was met with 'universal commendation'.[20] Although not generally reported, a story has been handed down for several generations in the Horsley family that Moonlite and his gang called in at Yabtree only a few miles from Deltroit the day before the hold-up at Wantabadgery. The bushrangers were not violent on this occasion, and upon receiving food and hospitality at the hands of Eliza Horsley, whose husband was away, they left quietly and without incident.[21]

Andrew Lysaght

Although not living in the vicinity, Mary had another very colourful relative, her full brother, Andrew Lysaght. He was living in Wollongong, where he had become a publican and Member of Parliament. To what extent he and Mary were in touch is unknown, but he was exceptionally good-looking, with strong, dark features as well as being over six feet tall and solidly built.[22] An imposing and sometimes controversial character, Lysaght established in 1856, at the age of twenty-four, the Fairy Meadow Hotel on a 60-acre block of land that had belonged to his father, Patrick. After his father drowned at sea, the entitlement to the property was transferred to him and his mother on 20 September 1837.[23]

Lysaght hosted the inn at Fairy Meadow for thirteen years, during which time he had a mistress, Ann Goodwin, with whom he had an illegitimate son, also called Andrew. He never married Ann, but instead took as his wife Johanna Mary Lucy Carroll, the daughter of a local squatter, on 6 September 1860 at St Bede's Church, Appin. The wedding was less than three months after the birth of baby Andrew, born on 22 June 1860. Perhaps out of spite, the spurned mistress had her son baptised at the church in Fairy Meadow just two days after her lover's wedding. Presumably, Lysaght was not present at the baptism, but the paternity of the child recorded in the church records would have been widely known in the district, resulting in acute embarrassment for him.

Johanna and Andrew Lysaght had seven children: Ellen Ursula, born on 10 November 1861; Alice Teresa, born on 1 August 1863; Patrick, born on 6 October 1865; Michael, born on 26 June 1867; Angela Florence, born

Andrew Augustus Lysaght, known as 'Ironbark Andy', first cousin of Florence and Isabel Richardson, c. 1920

on 20 December 1870; Andrew Augustus, born on 8 August 1873; and Catherine Mary Maude, born on 4 November 1875. None of the children married, except for Andrew Augustus, but, ironically, it was the illegitimate line through the 'other' Andrew that flourished and produced many descendants.

Becoming a local magistrate in 1870, Lysaght was successfully sued in 1876 for slandering a policeman and calling him 'a flabby old woman', after

Andrew Lysaght's hotel at Fairy Meadow, c. 1954

an incident in Wollongong involving some drunken miners.[24] Subsequently resigning as a magistrate, he became the licensee of the Queen's Hotel in Wollongong and 'identified himself with every movement calculated to advance the interests of the town'.[25] Lysaght became a Member of Parliament for the Illawarra district in 1885 and was additionally involved in local government, holding the office of Mayor several times.

The Richardsons at Billapalap

In the early years of their marriage, William and Mary Richardson lived at Billapalap[26] together with their two daughters: Florence Johanna Dorothy, born on 7 March 1876, and Mary Isabella Teresa ('Isabel'), born on 28 November 1877. It is not known whether the Richardsons had built themselves a new homestead there or if they were living in one of the buildings that existed when the property was purchased in 1873. None of the early buildings at the property have survived, though there is still a beautiful semi-circular drive lined with elm trees that would have partially surrounded the main homestead.

Also living at Billapalap was William's brother and partner, John Richardson. He had married Mary Beaver, the daughter of Robert Beaver, a local selector and himself a former convict, and sister of William Beaver, who became the first licensee of the Junction Hotel after it was sold by Griffiths to the Richardsons. John and Mary married locally at Billapalap on 6 May 1873, in an interesting contrast to William's own marriage the following year, several hundred miles away in Geelong. Mary Beaver Richardson died about three months after her marriage while expecting her first baby; however, John married again five years later on 22 May 1878, this time to Catherine Kiley, who came from a well-known and respected Catholic family. She was the daughter of William Kiley, the owner of Spring Creek and the sister of Patrick Kiley from Red Hill Station near Tumut, the latter known as 'Kiley's Run' and immortalised in a famous poem of the same name by Banjo Paterson. John and Catherine Richardson had four daughters: Maria Isabel ('Mary'), born on 11 April 1879; Margaret Agnes ('Agnes'), born on 15 February 1882; Kathleen Smith, born on 5 April 1883; and Amy Rosina, born on 1 November 1885.

Once again, little information is available about the marriage of John and Catherine Richardson. It is known, though, that aside from their own children they had living with them Thomas Wilkinson Richardson, very much as a member of their family. He was the eldest son of John's first cousin Robert Richardson, who had been a struggling miner in Adelong. Thomas Wilkinson and his younger siblings, Arthur Camplin and Elizabeth Ann, had been orphaned in 1865 and taken back to England by John Richardson to live with family in Westmorland.[27] Their elder sister, Selina Ann, had already died in 1860 at the age of only six. Having been educated at Appleby Grammar School, Thomas Wilkinson returned to Australia in the mid-1870s as a young man. Working initially on Barnawartha near Wodonga, Victoria,[28] a property owned by his uncle, Henry Richardson, he subsequently joined John Richardson at Billapalap. As John only had daughters, it is not surprising that an extremely close relationship akin to father and son developed between the two men, and Thomas remained at Billapalap until John's sudden death in 1886.[29]

This tightly knit group of Richardsons at Billapalap was dispersed shortly before the tragedy of Jane Larkin's death in November 1879. Apparently deciding that it would be more convenient to be closer to the amenities of Gundagai and Wagga Wagga,[30] William and Mary moved with their children from Billapalap to Deltroit at some stage between the birth of their second daughter, Isabel, in late 1877 and that of a third child, Edith Amy Henrietta, born on 9 September 1879 at Deltroit (but who died an infant on 31 January 1881 from 'teething and convulsions'). Jane's unexpected death, coupled with the fact that her husband was in gaol, doubtless caused anguish not just among her children, but also throughout her wider family.

Despite having children of their own, William and Mary rose to the occasion when Jane died, providing a combination of work and refuge for those of Jane's children who needed support. It seems that the Richardsons held no grudge against the Larkin offspring for the wrongdoings of their father, even though he had shamelessly robbed them of livestock. John, the eldest child, was eighteen years old and appears to have been employed at Deltroit. When he himself died from heart failure ten years later, it was William Richardson who acted as informant on the death certificate, which states the young man's occupation as that of 'stockman' and his place of death as Hillas Creek. The third child, Al, who was only fourteen when his mother died, went to live at Billapalap, where he stayed until at least the mid-1940s. For most of those sixty years, he was employed by the Richardson family and their descendants initially under the overseer, Joseph Lambert,[31] before becoming overseer himself.[32]

The two Larkin girls, Emily and Tess, who were only nine and seven respectively, were also taken in by the Richardsons to live at Deltroit. As evidenced by a postcard collection belonging to Tess, which is now in the hands of her descendants,[33] Tess in particular developed a very close relationship with her Richardson cousins, Florence and Isabel. It is not known who brought up the youngest child, Harry, who was only a baby at

On the bank of the Hillas Creek at Deltroit.
From left: Tess Larkin, Isabel Richardson, Miss Curtiss,
Emily Larkin and Florence Richardson, c. 1895

the time of his mother's death, but he subsequently worked at Billapalap with his eldest brother before moving to Nangus. Much later, he appeared as a pallbearer at the funeral of his father's first cousin, Bartholomew Ryder, of Delatroy Station, Tarcutta, in 1914.[34]

Frank Larkin Horsley

Probably the most fortunate of all Jane's children was her second child, Frank. He was no longer living at home when his mother died, having been adopted by R. F. Horsley and his wife, Eliza, in about 1865, probably around the time of his father's first court case for cattle stealing. At that time, Frank would have been just under two years old and his mother, expecting her third child. Perhaps the fear that Larkin could be gaoled if found guilty, and the inevitable financial hardship that would ensue, persuaded the couple to give Frank away. As for the Horsleys, they were anxious for a healthy child, having failed to raise any surviving children together and suffering the loss of twins in 1862 at only a few weeks old. Nonetheless, their adoption of Frank was an act of considerable charity that gave Frank a future that his own parents would never have been able to provide.

The Horsleys were exceptionally generous to Frank, educating him privately at Geelong College, setting him up on a property, and treating him like their own flesh and blood. He officially became Frank Horsley, and even though R. F. Horsley and his wife subsequently had a son of their own, the two boys were given equal opportunities and advantages. When he was back from school, Frank had an idyllic, adventure-filled life on Yabtree, helping on the property with stock work and fencing, riding his colt, and hunting kangaroos and rabbits. The many entries in R. F. Horsley's diaries between 1878 and 1883 describing these activities are written with obvious pride and suggest that the boy gave considerable pleasure to his adoptive father. Frank was also encouraged to keep up with his Richardson relations and sometimes went to Deltroit to help inoculate cattle or brand the calves.[35]

In July 1883, together with a third party, R. F. Horsley bought a 40,000-acre property in central New South Wales called Coobang, near

Frank Larkin Horsley driving his hansom cab in Sydney

Parkes, that bordered another of his landholdings. His intention was to leave Frank his interest in Coobang on his death, but in the meantime he installed Frank there as manager at the age of twenty-one.[36] At first, Frank appeared to rise to this new responsibility. A note on Coobang in the back of R. F. Horsley's diary for 1884 states: 'Frank is getting the works done very fairly. Ringing mostly well done. [...] Dams too very well done, all much better than I expected from one so young.' However, as time went on, Frank seemed to be less interested in the property and more concerned with diversions in nearby Parkes. He neglected Coobang and failed to keep the books up to date. In 1886, he married the daughter of a local publican, Ada Fletcher, but by 1888, he had fallen into debt. Asking R. F. Horsley for an advance of £100, he elicited an angry refusal.[37] Subsequently, Horsley complained that the couple 'both seem frivolous'[38] and that although Frank would inherit Coobang, 'I think he will fool it away'.[39] Sadly, Horsley's prediction came true and Frank ended his days driving a hansom cab in Sydney.[40]

Gathering at Yabtree, c. 1896. From left: Arthur Elworthy,
R. F. L. Horsley (seated), Frank Larkin Horsley (standing left),
Bob White, Netty Menlove (sitting on verandah), Isabel Richardson,
Mr Phillips (standing behind), Fanny Menlove nursing Ivy Horsley,
Florence Richardson nursing Lach Horsley, Mary Agnes Horsley
and Mabel Horsley.

Growing prosperity

By the late 1870s, William and John Richardson were probably both working less on the properties themselves and, instead, were employing others to do most of the physical work for them. Doubtless, they were pleased to have two Larkin boys to bring on as well as the slightly older Thomas Wilkinson Richardson, and to be able to spend more time on management rather than roaming the paddocks while chasing stock. John and William Richardson were becoming men of substance and developing suitable interests commensurate with their positions in the community. Apart from judging livestock at agricultural shows, William became a local magistrate in 1881,[41] a service that he performed more or less continuously for thirty years. He also became a Freemason, ascending the different levels of this organisation to the senior role of First Principal of the Royal Arch Chapter. He probably attended meetings in Gundagai, where a Royal Arch Chapter was established in 1886, and, like many country people, rode to these events in his tails on horseback. Masonic meetings in rural Australia were deliberately arranged around the full moon so that anyone walking or riding a long distance was able to see their way.[42]

William and John had become well established in the neighbourhood, both because of their more entrenched positions in the community as well as the large amount of family around them. Their eldest brother, Thomas, was living in Adelong once again, having returned with his family around 1875. After an absence of roughly fifteen years in Orange, Thomas was now back mining and farming in the district, though neither the name nor the exact location of his property is known. While in Orange, Thomas had married the fifteen-year-old Harriet Betteridge in nearby Chain of Ponds on 3 September 1860. They lived and worked on the goldfields for some years, eventually turning to farming at Kerr's Creek (or Carr's Creek), 20 miles north of Orange.[43]

Thomas and Harriet had fifteen children together, some born in Orange, the others in Adelong. Their third child, an unnamed boy, died after only one day, but the others who survived were: Eliza, born on 24 May 1861; Hellen, born on 27 September 1862; Harriet Isabel, born on 10 November

1865; William Thomas, born on 12 September 1867; Albert George, born on 16 July 1869; Agnes Ann, born on 19 June 1871; Alice Rebecca, born on 10 April 1873; Louisa Dorothy, born on 5 March 1875; Caroline Matilda, born on 27 January 1877; Lucy Emily Court, born on 5 December 1878; Laura Sophia Constance, born on 9 October 1880; John Ernest Edward, born on 20 June 1882; Arthur Henry, born on 1 March 1884; and Charles Walter Smith, born on 27 April 1886. In about 1893, it seems there was a rupture in the family, and Harriet went to live in Albury, taking three of her daughters with her.[44] It is not known which ones she took, but a diary note made much later by one of her granddaughters, Eva Waters, states that sixteen-year-old Caroline Matilda was left behind and put in charge of her younger brothers, whom she continued to care for even after her own marriage.

While Thomas was not as conspicuously successful as William, he was nevertheless prosperous and able to assist at least one of his sons-in-law in a business venture. When his daughter Lucy became engaged to George Henry Figtree of Wollongong, Thomas provided the necessary capital for the young man to begin a coking operation there.[45] The couple married after Lucy had already fallen pregnant, and Thomas stipulated that it was a condition of his financial support that their children be educated at the best schools available. Whether Thomas provided for any of his other children in this way is not known. All of them except the youngest boy married, and several remained in the district, including Louisa, who married miner Edward Corbett, and Harriet, who married local selector Robert Crain. Thomas died in Adelong on 28 July 1901, aged only sixty-six, from chronic bronchitis and heart failure. Judging by the very affectionate epitaph on his tomb, he was much loved by his children and suffered painfully in his final days:

> Father is gone but not forgotten,
> Nor is the good advice he gave,
> Sweetest thoughts shall ever linger
> Around our darling father's grave.

Long days and nights he bore in pain,
To wait for cure was all in vain,
But God alone, who thought it best,
Did ease his pain and give him rest.

Thomas was survived by his wife, who died on 10 October 1911 in Albury, but nothing has been recorded about her life there after their separation and her departure from Adelong.

Henry Richardson, the youngest of the four brothers that came from Westmorland originally, had also settled in the Adelong district, but little is known about his activities. On 3 July 1878, Henry married Mary Ann Todd and was described in the marriage certificate as a 'grazier'. The couple had five children: Ethel Mary Louisa, born on 7 May 1880; Lily Maud, born on 7 June 1881; William Henry, born on 22 September 1884; Daisy, born on 23 May 1890; and Violet May Bell, born on 12 April 1895. None of the children married and there are no descendants. The son, William, died young, aged only thirty, after a brain haemorrhage. At this time, Henry and Mary were living at Wattle Bank on Lower Bago, just south of Adelong at the top of the Yaven Yaven Creek valley. Henry's wife had a younger sister, Amelia, who married Thomas Wilkinson Richardson in 1888, two years after John Richardson's death. No doubt devastated by the death of his unofficial guardian, Thomas Wilkinson was glad to have the comfort of a woman whose family were already closely connected to his own. Henry himself died at Wattle Bank on 26 December 1922.

All the Richardson families in the district appear to have been in contact with each other to a lesser or greater degree. This is clear not only from their various business arrangements, but also from the numerous passing references in the local press to various family members from different branches attending or taking part in social events together, ranging from tennis and cricket matches to agricultural shows. They were a close family whose fraternal bonds held firm in the strange country to which they had emigrated.

Death of John Richardson

While surrounded by a large family on both sides, William and Mary's greatest contact was undoubtedly with John Richardson. He was in full partnership with William in all their pastoral enterprises, holding a 50-percent interest in both Deltroit and Billapalap.[46] His sudden death on 16 March 1886 from dysentery, allegedly 'brought on by eating unripe tomatoes',[47] would have been calamitous for William, both emotionally and financially. In order to save the business, William was faced with buying out John's widow, not only on freehold land that the brothers actually owned jointly, but also on all the selections held under conditional purchase that had not yet been fully paid off. Moreover, in future, William would have the sole responsibility of paying off the balance on the conditional purchases, instead of sharing this with his late brother.

A press report in the *Sydney Morning Herald* at the time claimed that William paid £38,938 10s for John's interest in the business.[48] Whether this figure is accurate is hard to say, but it is certain that the buyout and subsequent burden of financing the business alone plunged William into debt. Inevitably, he took out a series of mortgages, including one dated 7 November 1887 from the Bank of New South Wales for the sum of £20,000,[49] a huge sum in those days and equivalent to over £1 million in today's terms. It seems that, from the title documents relating to both Billapalap and Deltroit, there was at least one other mortgage taken out about this time, dated 18 October 1887, but it has not been possible to ascertain the details. William's decision to take on such a heavy debt burden was made at a time of further drought, and just three years before the financial crash of 1890 and the subsequent depression. It was a move from which his finances never fully recovered.

John, who was described in his obituaries as 'an honourable kind-hearted man' and 'always ready to lend a helping hand to a poor neighbour',[50] was buried in the cemetery in Adelong, mourned by a host of friends and family. His widow, Catherine, and their four daughters, all under seven years old, eventually moved to Sydney, where, thanks to the buyout by William of his brother's share in the business, they would have been able to live in considerable comfort. To what extent, if at all, the two families kept up after John's death and whether John's daughters were ever close to William's, who were of similar age, has not been ascertained. Three of John's daughters, Mary, Agnes and Amy, later attended the same school in Sydney as Florence and Isabel. All the cousins were brought up as Catholics, but none of John's daughters married, apparently living sheltered lives with their mother in Petersham until she died in 1916[51] and, thereafter, together in Hunter's Hill. By contrast, Florence and Isabel led an altogether more worldly existence and went on to travel, to marry and to have families and occupations of their own.

CHAPTER 10

Education and the Hillas Creek School

*I*n spite of what must have been a testing time financially in the years immediately following John's death, William Richardson had nonetheless become an established grazier well able to provide for his family and to educate his two daughters, Florence and Isabel. By 1881, the family had been living at Deltroit for three or four years, presumably in the timber homestead that preceded the spacious brick mansion which stands there today. However, although the move from Billapalap brought the Richardsons closer to the centres of Wagga Wagga, Sydney and Melbourne, there was only one school within a reasonable distance, and that was at Hillas Creek.

Although schooling became compulsory in New South Wales in 1880 for all children between the ages of six and fourteen, government schools were basic and the teachers often untrained, especially in the smaller schools in the bush. Moreover, pupil attendance was frequently irregular, as the realities of everyday life meant that, for many, childhood did not last long. At Hillas Creek, as elsewhere, it was common for boys during harvest time to be withdrawn from school to help with farm work, and for girls to be frequently put in charge of younger children or kept at home for simple household chores. Invariably, the demands and vagaries of a rural existence took precedence over a child's education.

OPPOSITE
Isabel Richardson
in riding habit,
c. 1895

The first Hillas Creek School

Founded about 1876, after an application to the Council of Education
headed up once again by John Griffiths of the Junction Hotel, the Hillas
Creek School was a modest and somewhat drab educational establishment
not unlike most other bush schools at the time. It began as a provisional
school, which meant that it was an elementary school for a minimum
of fifteen pupils but fewer than twenty-five. The school originally stood
where the Great Southern Road crossed the Hillas Creek,[1] about a mile
from the Junction Hotel, and, according to an article in the *Gundagai
Times* of 20 April 1880, was 'a somewhat primitive building of wood that
looks as if it would be pretty cold in winter'. Maud Crowe, who taught at
the school between June 1879 and October 1880 as a novice, agreed with
this statement. When interviewed upon her retirement after forty-one
years of teaching,[2] she spoke of the equipment at 'the little bush school' as
comprising only 'a few odd books and slates', one row of desks without backs
and a large fireplace. Moreover, she attributed her own ill health in later years
to the 'difficult surroundings' she had experienced at Hillas Creek, no doubt
a partial reference to her lodgings at the infamous Junction Hotel.

The school records show that, including Miss Crowe, there were eight
teachers during the school's relatively short existence of nine years. At least
two were dismissed for inefficiency, one was dismissed for drunkenness and
deserting his post, and one resigned, probably demoralised by the lack of
discipline, industry and regular attendance of the pupils. An early inspection
report stated that discipline was 'weak', that the average proficiency was only
'tolerable' and that many of the pupils were incompletely attired.[3] Perhaps
the low standards were partly explained by the fact that, according to Miss
Crowe, some children walked four miles daily to the school and back, while
others travelled 11 miles from Upper Tarcutta on the Cobb & Co coach,
rising at 5am and not returning home until 8pm. The weariness of the
children was such that she allowed them to nap during the day and results 'to
go partly by the board'.

Although there was a schoolhouse, no accommodation was provided
for the teacher, who was obliged to live at the nearby Junction Hotel in

the absence of any other suitable lodging in the vicinity. Living conditions were apparently so rough and unsavoury at the hotel that District Schools Inspector Hicks told his superior, 'Its character is such that I cannot approve it.' Having reached this conclusion, he was obliged to remove Miss Crowe and transfer her to the provisional school at Upper Tarcutta.[4] Her successor, Daniel Cox, claimed on his subsequent dismissal for drunkenness and desertion that his behaviour had been due to the 'wretched' circumstances in which he was forced to live at the hotel and 'the conduct carried on there' by its clientele.[5]

The second Hillas Creek School

The problem of accommodation was not resolved until May 1882, when the Hillas Creek School was moved to another site one-and-a-half miles along the road towards Mundarlo, where a new schoolhouse that included living quarters for the teacher was erected.[6] The reason behind moving the school was the dwindling number of pupils. Although the original school had been upgraded to a public school on 1 July 1880, indicating that it now had twenty pupils or more, this small educational outpost seems to have been anything but a success. According to Daniel Cox, attendance 'considerably diminished' a year later, which he attributed to over sixteen of the enrolled children living more than four miles away at Mundarlo. An official enquiry was then carried out to ascertain how many children from each family attended the school on its current site and how many would attend the school on the proposed new site nearer Mundarlo.

According to a letter dated 25 August 1881 from the local selector, Edward Beaver, to the Department of Public Instruction, five families had children at the Hillas Creek School. Among the list is 'W Richardson', and the number of his children given as attending the school is three. Since Isabel would have been too young to attend in 1881, the three children referred to must have been Florence and her two cousins, Emily and Tess Larkin. By this time, the two Larkin girls were living with the Richardsons at Deltroit and would still have been of school age. As the school was only two miles from

Riding party at Yabtree, c. 1900. From left: Ivy Horsley, Miss Calcott (Horsley governess), Tess Larkin, Lach Horsley, Mabel Horsley, Annie Dunne, Gwen Horsley, Isabel Richardson

the homestead at Deltroit, the girls would either have walked there or, as was common, ridden on their ponies, leaving them to graze in an adjoining paddock usually set aside for this purpose .

It is unlikely that Florence and the Larkin girls continued at the Hillas Creek School after it moved. Although the surviving school records do not include any attendance registers, Edward Beaver's letter seems to show that once the school shifted further away from Hillas Creek, the Richardson family would no longer enrol. Futhermore, in Beaver's list of families sending children to the school at its new location, the Richardson name has been crossed off and the District Schools Inspector noted in a later memorandum[7] that 'The only family that would be thrown out by the removal of the school as proposed is Richardson's ...'

Standards at the school did not improve with the new building and location. On the contrary, an inspection carried out on 28 November 1883 stated that 'The whole school bore an aspect of slovenliness and neglect.' Attendances fell once more, until the school was forced to become a half-time school with the Yaven Yaven School in January 1885. The Yaven Yaven School, which originally opened in 1880 with about twenty-five pupils, was situated on the Billapalap run, midway between Darlow's Creek and the Yaven Yaven Creek.[8] Interestingly, Thomas Richardson not only sent his children to the Yaven Yaven School[9] but also stood in as teacher there for one week in February 1883, when the incumbent, George Read, was absent for a few days. Amusingly, Read wrote to the District Schools Inspector explaining 'that, through my wife's adultery, I am compelled to ask for leave of absence ... in order to attend the Divorce Court, Sydney'. In spite of requests from the residents of Hillas Creek for their school to become full-time again, it was closed altogether in 1886.

A governess arrives

Education was clearly important to the Richardsons, and the mixed fortunes of the Hillas Creek School ultimately made it unsuitable for their needs. Instead, once the school moved towards Mundarlo, they decided to have their daughters educated at home by a governess, then a common practice among many grazier families. The person they chose for the task was a young Catholic girl, Mary Agnes McCaig. She was born in Melbourne in 1869 and had lost her mother at eleven years old. Shortly afterwards, in June 1880, she was enrolled as a boarder at the convent school St Joseph's in Albury, known today as Xavier High School. Instruction at St Joseph's included English, arithmetic, history, geography and French, in addition to the 'ornamental arts' of music, drawing, painting and sewing.[10] Mary was about fifteen when she left St Joseph's on 22 December 1883, having completed fourth class, the highest level in the school at that time. Her record there was impeccable, and on her departure she was showered with prizes in English, arithmetic, the catechism and music, obtaining a First Order of Merit in the latter, for which she evidently displayed a precocious talent.[11] Throughout her life, she was known as a gifted and consummate pianist.

Mary McCaig's background

Mary Agnes
McCaig as a
young child,
c. 1879

In spite of her excellent academic record and Catholic faith, which she shared with Mary Richardson, Mary McCaig was in some ways a surprising choice of governess for the Richardson girls. Not only was she very young and inexperienced, probably only fifteen when she took up her position, but she belonged to a family that had, at various times, attracted considerable notoriety. To begin with, Mary was closely related to the well-known, yet controversial, Catholic priest Father Patrick Dunne, being either his great niece[12] or, more probably, his first cousin. The colourful career of this energetic and indefatigable missionary is beyond the scope of this book; however, among other things, he was a vigorous campaigner in Australia for Catholic education in town and country, a tireless supporter of emigration from Ireland as a means of rescuing people from misery and starvation, and a champion of new ecclesiastical buildings and architecture.[13] The great deeds of this illustrious relation may well have impressed the Richardsons and worked in Mary's favour, but Dunne was not without his failings.

Twice virtually banished from Australia by the Catholic Church, Fr Dunne fell out very publicly with Bishop Goold of Melbourne over the control of church funds, in a dispute that was chronicled in the secular press. Moreover, he later became embroiled in the financial troubles of Bishop Quinn, with whom he had promoted Irish immigration to Queensland.

Fr Dunne had himself chartered a vessel from Ireland in 1862 with 400 migrants whom he settled in Brisbane and the area known as Darling Downs, where they became the nucleus of a large Catholic community. Leaving Queensland, Fr Dunne moved to New South Wales, where he initiated and organised the building of both the Goulburn and Wagga Wagga cathedrals. During his life, he was also famous for holding the first ever mass on the Victorian goldfields in a makeshift tented church at Ballarat, and for the establishment of numerous schools in Victoria, New South Wales and Queensland.

Fr Dunne was to have a great influence on the course of Mary McCaig's early years,[14] and it is likely that he was behind her entry into the convent

Mary Agnes Horsley (née McCaig), former governess to Florence and Isabel Richardson

school in Albury. In 1875, he was put in charge of the new mission at Gundagai and, a few years later, succeeded as Vicar-General of the Canberra and Goulburn Diocese, which at that time included Albury and Wagga Wagga. Shortly before this, Mary's father, John McCaig, departed for Fiji on the vessel *Nil Desperandum*; McCaig may have wanted Mary's mother, Bridget, and all of their five children to join him later, or he may have abandoned them. Nevertheless — and no doubt encouraged by Fr Dunne — Bridget and all of her children came to live in Gundagai in 1876, effectively placing themselves under the care and protection of their influential and charismatic relation. Mary was the youngest child, at only seven years old, and her four siblings were Francis, aged seventeen; Catherine, aged sixteen; Dennis, aged fourteen; and Charles, aged twelve.

John McCaig

Aside from Fr Dunne, the other controversial figure in Mary's life was clearly her father. Whether the Richardsons were aware of this elusive and intriguing character or whether the McCaig family and Fr Dunne did their best to conceal his existence and his exploits is unknown. Born about 1825 in County Derry, Ireland, John McCaig came to Australia with his parents and siblings as free settlers. Starting off his business career in 1851 as a storekeeper in Colac, Victoria,[15] he was appointed Postmaster the following year[16] before subsequently embarking on more ambitious schemes. He became, at various times, a miller, a land agent and then a sugar planter, before dying in reduced circumstances in Fiji. All his larger ventures proved in the end to be spectacular failures, perhaps as a result of either incompetence, ill luck or a degree of dishonesty on his part, and seem to have cost poor McCaig his freedom and, ultimately, his marriage.

It is impossible not to have some sympathy for such a character and to speculate about what went wrong with McCaig's affairs. His eventual bankruptcy in Queensland and his own Peter Pan personality must have been unsettling and wearisome for his family. Deeply involved in community affairs in Colac between 1851 and 1862, McCaig led an application to the

John McCaig's
flour mill at Colac,
Victoria, by Robert
Camm, 1884

government for a stipend for a priest and the subscription list for a new school
building (donating £50 together with his brother-in-law),[17] as well as being on
the District Roads Board,[18] a prospective parliamentary candidate[19] and a local
magistrate.[20] In short, he was a pillar of the community and clearly prosperous
when he married the sixteen-year-old Bridget Dunne on 31 March 1857 in
Geelong. The couple, who were both part of a literate group from Northern
Ireland,[21] were married by Fr Bermingham, a close friend and relation of
Fr Dunne who had by this time offended Bishop Goold and recently been
removed from Geelong, where he had established several schools.[22]

McCaig was an attentive husband, arranging a nursemaid for his wife
after the birth of their daughter, Catherine,[23] and, soon after, asking the wife
of a solicitor friend to bring a selection of cloaks from Geelong for her to
choose from.[24] In 1857, McCaig began building the Polworth Flour Mill
at Colac, which was completed in 1859 with the use of a large workforce.[25]
With potential causes ranging from overcapitalisation and poor budgeting,
to the economic slump in Victoria in this period, to local competition
from other millers, letters between McCaig and his solicitor Edward Doyle
indicate that he fell into considerable financial difficulties.[26] By 1861, the
mill was up for sale along with other land and buildings owned by McCaig
in Colac,[27] and the family moved first to Pentridge (now Coburg) near

Melbourne and then to Brisbane, where Fr Dunne was pioneering Irish Catholic settlement. On the way, the preoccupied McCaig lost a carpet bag at the railway station in Geelong,[28] which, in addition to a number of unbanked cheques, included many personal items for his toilette — 'an ivory handled razor ... a gold pin repaired set with deep red carbuncle; a white and yellowish horn comb ... and a bottle of essence'. Most amusingly of all, he mislaid at the same time 'a lady's nightgown'!

Arriving in Queensland in November 1862, McCaig initially set up a store and soap factory before being induced, so he claimed, by Bishop Quinn 'with all the force of his flowery and persuasive eloquence' to become his agent in relation to £15,000 worth of land holdings.[29] The introduction to Bishop Quinn was surely effected by Fr Dunne, who was in Brisbane with his first shipload of migrants recently arrived from Ireland. All went well until early 1865, when McCaig failed to render proper accounts to Quinn, who promptly repudiated the agency arrangement.[30] Unfortunately, a number of innocent people unaware of this disagreement paid McCaig for land that he had no authority to sell and were subsequently forced by Quinn to pay again.[31]

In the end, McCaig, who had once more, to say the least, 'mismanaged' his finances, was not only declared insolvent, but also put on trial for fraud. Although no record can be found of the outcome of these proceedings, he is presumed to have spent some time in gaol.[32] In a letter to the editor of the *Queensland Daily Guardian* that is full of pathos, describing his family as 'entirely dependent for support on the bounty of others' and himself as 'a beggar in this city', McCaig claimed he was duped by the bishop and, moreover, let down by Fr Dunne.[33] It seems that, just at the time his land agency was repudiated, a lease that McCaig had arranged informally with Fr Dunne for land at Kangaroo Point, and upon which he had opened a store, was also cancelled, thereby causing a dual loss of income to the family.

It is unclear what happened to McCaig's family during his troubles, but they may either have stayed on in Brisbane or have gone to live with Bridget's family near Melbourne. Seemingly, they were already there by 1869, as Mary always claimed she was born in Melbourne, though no birth or baptism record for her has ever been found to verify this. Presumably, wherever the family were between McCaig's trial and Mary's birth, McCaig spent some time with his wife and children, before either separating from or abandoning them and leaving for Fiji on 5 December 1872. Reinventing himself, this time as a sugar planter, McCaig built a small mill at Nadroga in south-west Fiji, though, according to his obituary,[34] 'the enterprise proved anything but a success'. Horsley family stories also allege that his youngest boy, Charles, accompanied him to Fiji in 1872; however, these claims appear to be incorrect.[35]

Nonetheless, at some stage after 1872 and before 1888, Charles did join his father in Fiji, where McCaig eventually died, a ruined man, in 1892. Thereafter, it seems that history may have repeated itself. Charles married Harriet Walker in Suva on 14 March 1888 and, after fathering three children, he walked out on his family and left for the Gilbert and Ellice Islands, where he had another family with an islander.[36]

Bridget McCaig

On 2 January 1877, Mary's mother became the principal teacher at the Catholic school in Gundagai (now St Patrick's), with her eldest daughter, Catherine, acting as assistant.[37] There can be little doubt that all of this was arranged by Fr Dunne, who oversaw Catholic education in the area and was patron of the school.[38] The *Gundagai Times* reported that 'Besides the usual course of instruction given in Primary Schools, the girls will be taught Plain and Fancy Needle Work, and the more advanced Plain Dress-Making'. In addition, 'Miss McCaig will give Evening Lessons in Music and French'.[39] Where Mary's mother and sister had learnt these accomplishments is unknown, especially as Mary's mother married at only sixteen, presumably having little time to develop either her talents or teaching skills.

Nonetheless, both mother and daughter appear to have made a great success of their respective positions at the Catholic school. On 27 December 1878, the *Gundagai Times* reported on the high proficiency of almost all the pupils in their annual examination, pronouncing, 'The answering was in almost every instance excellent.' When Bridget McCaig died suddenly of heart disease on 18 April 1880, her funeral was reported to have been

Bridget McCaig

'very largely attended',[40] suggesting that she was widely liked and respected in the community where she had worked.

When Catherine left Gundagai a short time after, she was presented by the local Catholic congregation with an English gold watch and chain, engraved with the inscription 'in recognition of her services gratuitously given in the choir and of her zeal and efficiency in the school'.[41] She also received a gold cross and charm in the shape of Cleopatra's Needle. Catherine appears to have left Gundagai for Brisbane, possibly also an initiative of Fr Dunne, who would have been on hand when Bridget died and well-positioned to arrange the welfare of all her 'orphaned' children. Catherine made a new life for herself up north and married Walton Frederick McCarthy in Brisbane on 26 December 1884.

With a family history as colourful as this, Mary McCaig's background may therefore not have been above reproach, though the full details may, of course, not have been known to the Richardsons when they engaged her. Most probably aware of her connections to Fr Dunne, who was after all an important public figure working in the vicinity, they were likely to have also been impressed by the reputation of her late mother, a woman of strength, independence and, presumably, piety, and may have known nothing at all of her father. It would be intriguing to know how Bridget McCaig presented herself to the Gundagai community, who might not have viewed her with such respect if she was indeed an abandoned wife and a Catholic one to boot.

Mary McCaig's influence

Whatever they did or did not know about her, the Richardsons employed Mary for about nine years. Whether they had employed any other governess previously is not known. Mary's family had wanted her to go to Melbourne on leaving school in Albury and to live with relations, but she insisted on being independent and earning her own living.[42] Assuming that Mary began her role of governess in early 1884, Florence would have been eight years old and Isabel would have been six. Precisely how Mary managed her young charges and organised their day is not recorded, but she would have passed on all that she had learnt at the convent. Mary must surely be given credit for Isabel's musicianship and exceptional skills as a pianist, which later earned her a place at one of the most prestigious music academies in Rome. This common love of music is illustrated by a tea and concert held at Mundarlo in aid of St Peter's Church, at which the young governess, Mary, and her charge, Isabel, played a duet that, according to a report in the *Gundagai Times* of 1 May 1891, 'displayed both grace and skill'.

It is not known if Mary also had charge of the two Larkin girls, Emily and Tess, who were part of the Richardson family at Deltroit when she arrived. They were then fourteen and twelve respectively, and almost as old as Mary herself. Conceivably, Emily and Tess were sent away to school, but it has not been possible to identify any school records confirming that this was the case.

Formal schooling

The luxury of a private boarding school education may have been reserved by the Richardsons for their own daughters, Florence and Isabel, who were sent to the prestigious Convent of The Sacred Heart of Jesus in Rose Bay, Sydney (now known as Kincoppal-Rose Bay), for formal secondary schooling. The two girls entered there at the same time on 23 February 1892; however, Florence, being older, left after only two-and-a-half years in September 1894, whereas Isabel stayed until June 1895. Both girls won prizes while there, but Isabel always seemed to do just a little better than her older sister.

The timing of the Richardson girls being sent away to school coincided almost exactly with the marriage of their governess to Fred ('R. F. L.') Horsley on 25 January 1892. Mary's fairytale marriage to the heir of Yabtree (and Frank Larkin's brother by adoption) is reminiscent of the famous Charlotte Brontë novel *Jane Eyre*, which was first published in 1847. Whether or not Mary had read the book, she would have known how incredibly lucky she was to find love and marriage with a charming and well-to-do landowner (three years her junior), while she herself was a governess, occupying the ambiguous social position of neither servant nor family. Without such a match, she would probably have been destined for a frugal and lonely life — a poorly paid governess and a spinster.

According to the Horsley family, the couple courted while Mary was employed at Deltroit, meeting regularly beneath the wide-spreading boughs of a river red gum on Yabtree's boundary near the Hillas Creek bridge.[43] The 'tryst tree', as it is known, still stands, and Mary threatened anyone who dared knock it down with dire consequences. Mary herself grew to be one of the most remarkable, popular and widely loved figures in the area, remembered fondly by those who worked at Yabtree and in the Hillas Creek district during her lifetime and, even today, by her many grandchildren.

Debutantes

As for Florence and Isabel, they both left school at seventeen and returned home to Deltroit. By now, they would have been among the most eligible young women in the area, with their accomplishments and their background. No doubt there were parties and entertainments for them to attend in the surrounding area, and it is known that their friend, the new Mrs Horsley, and her husband often entertained at home.[44] Moreover, there were picnics as well as riding and tennis parties at Yabtree and even afternoons floating down the Murrumbidgee River in a rowing boat. Several Horsley family photographs of these activities include both the Richardson girls and Tess Larkin.

Florence herself had a 'Coming Out' ball, and there is a photograph of her, taken in 1894, looking whippet-thin in a lace gown, very tall and

Picnic at Yabtree on the Murrumbidgee, c. 1900. From left: Isabel
Richardson, Tess Larkin, Lach Horsley, Mrs W. Oliver, Mr W. Oliver
(manager of Yabtree), unidentified woman, Mabel Horsley,
Florence Richardson, Mary Agnes Horsley, Fanny Ryan nursing
Ivy Horsley, unidentified child, Mrs James Beveridge, Miss Beveridge
and Tessie Menlove.

striking with dark hair and eyes and the distinctive long, oval face of her father. There was probably a similar event for Isabel the following year, but no photographs or reports survive. These young women were leading a life of more refinement and leisure than the one that their parents had led at the same age. Money and position, together with the benefits of a full-time governess and later an elite boarding-school education, had taken them along an easier path. Nonetheless, judging from subsequent events, both girls were encouraged not to restrict their lives solely to the domestic sphere, but to be independent women, to use their minds and to exploit their talents. Feminism was just coming to the fore in New South Wales in this period, with women granted the right to vote as early as 1902.

Furthermore, both Florence and Isabel had strong personalities,[45] and this, coupled with their height, gave them both a formidable presence. In addition, Isabel was reserved and, like her father, very enterprising in spirit.[46] She also became devoutly Catholic, though it is not clear whether she was particularly religious as a young woman. Nonetheless, it is easy to imagine that prospective husbands might have been more than a little intimidated by the two girls. Florence and Isabel took their time in finding suitable partners but, compared to their mother, married early, in their twenties. They each chose very different men as husbands and went on to lead completely contrasting lives on opposite sides of the world.

CHAPTER 11

Florence and Isabel Richardson

*O*n the afternoon of Wednesday 30 May 1900, Florence Richardson married the prominent local solicitor Charles John ('Charlie') Fraser in a Roman Catholic ceremony at St Mary's Cathedral in Sydney. Florence was twenty-four years old (though the marriage certificate wrongly states her age as thirty-four) and her groom was thirty-one. Nothing is known of their courtship or how the couple first met, though they would have moved in the same affluent social group of graziers, business people and professionals that prevailed in the vicinity of Deltroit.

Described in the press as a 'fashionable' wedding,[1] reports differ as to whether it was a small affair attended only by 'the relatives and intimate friends of the parties'[2] or a larger gathering. Certainly, Florence, with her height and bearing, looked regal in white lace, a plain veil fastened to her dark hair by a headdress of small flowers, and a tumbling bouquet of poppies and roses. She towered above her diminutive[3] bridegroom, who, by all accounts, made up for his lack of height by having the most outgoing and dynamic personality. The wedding breakfast was held at Needs' Rooms, Nithsdale House, an establishment in Liverpool Street that could be hired for private functions and that was located amid the offices and consulting rooms of many professional people. No mention is made in any reports of a honeymoon.

Charlie Fraser

There can be little doubt that Florence's parents, William and Mary Richardson, would have been delighted at their daughter's match. Clearly a serious-minded and extremely hard-working individual, Fraser's numerous interests and activities during his lifetime were often reported extensively in the local press. These articles are remarkable for being unanimous in their description of him as one of the most exceptional, widely respected and popular men in the whole of the Riverina district.

At the time of his marriage, Fraser was practising as a solicitor in Tumut, where he had spent most of his childhood. Born on 10 June 1869 at Reedy Flat (now Batlow), near the Upper Adelong goldfields, his father was Charles Daniel Fraser, a well-known miner in the district who had been born in New York. His mother was Mary Ann Kelly, an Irish immigrant also living in the Upper Adelong area. Charles Daniel Fraser played a prominent part in extracting gold from the bed of the Adelong Creek, before making sufficient money to take over the Miner's Rest Hotel in Reedy Flat. Subsequently, about 1874, he established the highly successful Royal Hotel in Tumut, a building that was said to be both 'fine' and 'commodious' as well as a rarity outside the city.[4]

Fraser was the second of the six surviving children of Charles and Mary Fraser, all of whom were educated to the highest standards available. Attending St Patrick's College in Goulburn (incidentally founded by Fr Dunne), Fraser was always known at school as 'the brightest of scholars' who also excelled at sport.[5] Studying first to become a surveyor, he switched to law before joining a legal practice in Tumut around 1887 as an articled clerk. He was subsequently made a partner there in 1893, and the firm became known as Fraser and Emanuel. After an association of approximately fifteen years and three years since his marriage to Florence, Fraser left the partnership in Tumut in 1903 to set up his own legal practice in Gundagai with his younger brother, Walter. The residents of Tumut were so saddened by Fraser's departure that they held a farewell banquet in his honour, attended by the mayor and the local Member of Parliament. The press report of the occasion, the attendance of which exceeded all expectations, filled almost four columns of the *Adelong Argus*.[6]

Florence and Charles Fraser's house in Gundagai

Among the many tributes paid to Fraser during the course of the evening were descriptions of him as being 'generous and kind hearted ... calculated to make friends wherever he went' and a 'straightforward, genial and energetic member of the community'. Above all, the mayor himself declared that Fraser's good qualities were such that even 'if he tried, he could not speak as well of the young man as he was deserving of'. The mayor continued that not only was Fraser 'one of the brightest young men in the district', but he was admired for 'his courage and true grit which had made him the sterling man that he is'. In reply, Fraser was overwhelmed with the warmth and gratitude displayed towards him. He spoke of his 'great regret' at leaving Tumut, explaining that the only reason for doing so was his having embarked on married life. He said that now 'he could see it was essential for him to do more in the future, and he felt that one of the ways for gaining that end was to launch out on his own account'.

Early years of marriage

Moving to Gundagai, Charlie and Florence Fraser bought a large house at the top end of First Avenue: number forty-five, also called 'Trangby'. The house had been built by the father of a friend of Fraser's, William Paine, who was a well-known local builder.[7] Presumably, the couple had lived previously in Tumut, since Fraser could not reasonably have travelled there without a motor car on a daily basis from Gundagai, 20 miles away. Precisely when the Frasers moved from Tumut is unclear, since the purchase of Trangby was not until March 1905,[8] two years after Fraser retired from the legal practice of Fraser and Emanuel. Possibly, they stayed on for a time in Tumut, or they lived somewhere else in Gundagai before Trangby was purchased.

Trangby, which still stands today but in a considerable state of dilapidation, was a spacious, single-storey, classic Victorian house of brick, surrounded on three sides by a bullnose verandah, fenced with decorative cast-iron panels in a lace design. A flight of steep stone steps led up to the front door as the house was built into the side of a hill overlooking the town. At the back, there was a two-storey stable block and, on the western side, a shady garden. In Gundagai, the Frasers had the advantage of being closer to Deltroit than if they had remained in Tumut.

It was while they were living at Trangby that the couple's five children were born. The eldest, Charles William John ('Jack') was born on 18 July 1902. The siblings who followed were: Mary Isobel ('Isobel'), born on 3 April 1904; Harry Francis, born on 2 December 1905; Robert Michael Grant ('Bobbie'), born on 4 March 1908; and Dorothy Clare ('Poppy'), born on 9 November 1909. Bobbie died from gastroenteritis and whooping cough at the age of only two on 14 December 1910 and was buried in the cemetery at Gundagai. This was a particularly sobering time for Florence, who had buried her mother only five months before. In the important photographic collection of Dr Gabriel of Gundagai,[9] there are several pictures of the Frasers' nursemaid in uniform, and another of Jack and Isobel playing on the stone steps at Trangby.

Jack and Isobel Fraser at the family home in Gundagai, c. 1908

In the fifteen years after moving to Gundagai, Fraser built up a thriving legal practice with his brother, Walter, and became a conspicuous figure in the town. Apart from being 'an able and careful lawyer, competent to hold his own against any up country solicitors', Fraser involved himself in a large number of community interests and causes. The fact that he was 'a good and entertaining public speaker, able to impart information on any subject (being exceedingly well read)'[10] and also had a strong sense of humour made him an invaluable committee member and campaigner for any public cause he chose to support. He was known to be fearless and independent and a townsman of unequalled merit.

Among other things, Fraser was a founding member of the Gundagai Hospital and held the unique distinction of being, at different times, not only mayor (between 1910 and 1912), but also the first president of the Gundagai Shire (1924)[11] and chairman of the Pastures Protection Board (between 1922 and 1934). He was undoubtedly the most effective manager that the local Pastures Protection Board had ever had and one of the best in the state, as he was also elected chairman of the Council of Advice for Pastures Protection Boards for the whole of New South Wales in 1930.[12] Through his work for Pastures Protection, he identified himself closely with the man on the land and fought tirelessly for the interests of stockowners, including the control of livestock disease and pests such as rabbits and dingoes, and the maintenance of travelling stock routes and reserves.

On a more low-key level, Fraser was also responsible for a multitude of good deeds, many of which were never publicised. Ever ready to extend a helping hand to the underdog, he was also an unfailing friend to all that knew him.[13] Being charitably minded, Fraser was prone to giving his numerous friends and acquaintances free legal advice, which was not always in the best interests of his firm,[14] and personally gave generously to the wounded soldiers in the First World War.[15] He initiated and funded the planting of trees along Sheridan Street, the main thoroughfare in Gundagai, and was behind many other schemes to make the town more attractive. As one commentator wrote, 'Though Fraser was small in stature, he was a big man who did big things and did them properly.'[16]

In the sporting arena, Fraser was an excellent cricketer for the Gundagai Cricket Team and inaugurated the Gundagai Golf Club. He was also heavily

Nursemaid and Jack Fraser in the garden of the Fraser family home in Gundagai, c. 1908

Sheridan Street, Gundagai, in front of the post office. Charles Fraser is standing second from right.

involved in horseracing, a passion that he shared with his wife, who was a keen rider. Fraser became one of the first presidents of the Southern District Racing Association, as well as being an early member of the Gundagai Race Club. Later, when the couple were living at Deltroit, Florence bred race horses and polo ponies, aiming to breed a horse that would win the prestigious Wagga Wagga Gold Cup. While she never achieved this triumph, Florence nonetheless bred a famous race horse, Silver Billy, who had a record of three wins in three starts at Gundagai, Yass and Cootamundra and was nominated for the Caulfield and Melbourne Cups in 1929.

Both Florence and her sister were keen attendees of the Picnic Races and would meet up with friends there, including their former governess,

Mary Horsley, herself an excellent horsewoman. From the turn of the century, Picnic Races became an important event in the social calendar of the country, bringing families together from miles around. It was one of the few opportunities for people who lived long distances apart to see each other. Racegoers would dress up in their finest clothes, regardless of whether the day was one of intense heat, and enjoy refreshments they had brought themselves or purchased in the tea tent. Beer and ice-cream were on sale, too, and often there was a brass band to entertain the crowd before and after the races. It may have been at one of these occasions that Florence first met Fraser, possibly introduced by his younger sister Clare, a contemporary of Florence's from school in Rose Bay and an outstanding student like her brother.[17]

A talented pianist

In the early years of Florence's marriage, Isabel was concentrating on her music. By her talent and motivation, she obtained a place at one of the four prestigious music academies in Rome, probably the Liceo di Roma (subsequently renamed the Conservatorio di Santa Cecilia). This was an extraordinary achievement for a girl from the Australian bush who had received only three years of formal education at a convent school in Sydney and who presumably had minimal experience of hearing music being played at a professional level. Attempts have been made to ascertain whether, after leaving school, Isabel had ever attended one of the handful of private music academies in Sydney at the time, but insufficient records remain. A great deal of Isabel's skill, application and determination to succeed must surely be attributed to her remarkable governess, Mary Horsley, who was not only an excellent pianist herself, but had made a considerable success of her life notwithstanding her difficult and impoverished childhood.

With some style and no doubt pride, Isabel's father took her to Europe. Six months before, he had managed to pay off a substantial portion of his debts. He must have been both relieved and excited that he was at last financially secure enough to be able to absent himself from Deltroit and take his daughter on an extended trip abroad. Leaving Australia on the *RMS India* on 15 March 1902,[18] William and Isabel travelled together to England, Scotland and Ireland before reaching the Continent. In the course of their travels, it is likely that they saw family in Westmorland, and it seems that they also witnessed the coronation of Edward VII.[19] It is not known which European countries the pair visited other than Italy, but it appears that William stayed with Isabel in Rome for three months, presumably to settle his daughter into her new environment. They also reportedly had a private audience with the Pope in this period.

Regrettably, the records of the Liceo going back to the early 1900s are incomplete, but Isabel's grandchildren believe that she was in Rome for about one year. One thing is certain, however: Isabel studied under Giovanni Sgambati,[20] a virtuoso pianist of international repute who was also a composer and a favourite pupil of Franz Liszt. Since Sgambati not only co-founded the Liceo in 1877, but also taught there for the remainder of his life, it seems likely that it was the Liceo rather than any of Rome's other music academies that Isabel attended. Isabel's leather-bound music folder embossed with her initials in gold is still in the hands of her descendants and contains a number of Sgambati's scores, with pencilled annotations believed to be by him. By all accounts, Isabel was so proficient a musician that she had a career as a concert pianist ahead of her had she wished to pursue this as a profession.

While in Rome, Isabel may have stayed at the Trinità dei Monti, the convent associated with her school in Rose Bay as both were run by the Society of the Sacred Heart. Unfortunately, no records were kept of the young women who, having finished their schooling, came to Rome, usually to study art, and stayed at the convent as a 'Grande Pensionnaire'. The location of the Trinità dei Monti would probably have suited Isabel well, being at the top of the Spanish steps close to the Liceo in the Via dei Greci.

During her time in Rome, it seems that Isabel also missed seeing her first cousin, Andrew Augustus Lysaght, the sixth child of her uncle and aunt, Andrew and Johanna Lysaght. Andrew Augustus had become a qualified solicitor practising in Sydney, recognised for his expertise in mining and industrial legislation, but travelled to Rome in 1905 in order to study art.[21]

Later, he became a Member of Parliament, like his father. Having a very strong personality and artistic interests as well as being far from home, he would have found plenty in common with his cousin Isabel, had they met up.

In the last quarter of 1902, William left Isabel in Rome and returned to Deltroit. Having been away for at least six months, he was no doubt itching to get back to his properties, his sheep and his cows. His first grandchild, Jack Fraser, had also been born in his absence, and he was probably missing his wife and eldest daughter, too. Most important of all, however, William, now a wealthy man, had commissioned a new homestead to be built at Deltroit, one worthy of his status as a significant livestock holder in the Riverina and of the beautiful property that he had taken almost forty years to establish. This mansion was due for completion around March 1903[22] and, in all likelihood, work had already begun while he was away.

Isabel's engagement

John Brook as a young man

It was around the early 1900s that Isabel appears to have met her future husband, John Grant Brook. His family had been successful and prominent woollen manufacturers in Yorkshire for three generations. Brook himself had effectively inherited his father's Larchfield Mill in Huddersfield in 1888, but had sold it and retired early from business in 1901. Isabel most likely first met Brook while she was travelling in England with her father, since they could easily have stayed in Yorkshire on their way north to visit family in Westmorland. Alternatively, it is conceivable, though less plausible, that at some time prior to 1901, Brook visited Australia to source wool for his mill and that Isabel met him during that period. However the couple met,

So sorry to have missed mail last week but I think there is some excuse, don't you? Love. I. R.

POST CARD.
THE ADDRESS TO BE WRITTEN ON THIS SIDE.

Miss T. Larkin
Deltroit
Gundagai
N.S.W. Australia

Scarborough from the Valley Bridge. *Aug. 17th '05.*
Mum says she will write next week so don't be anxious. Love I. R.

I.—"Does it taste?"
DRINKING THE WATERS AT HARROGATE.

At Dinis Island, Killarney. *Isn't this a pretty spot? I wonder if Dad remembers it. I. R. Oct 16th*

Royal Victoria Hotel. *where we are staying - Oct 16th* Killarney
I. R.

R. C. Cathedral, Killarney. *Here I went to Church this morning - All on my own on a jaunting car. I. R.*

A selection of the many postcards written by
Isabel Richardson to Tess Larkin at Deltroit

Had neither time nor news for a separate letter for you this week Judith. Had a grand day at Ardgate on Wednesday - It was a clear day and the King was there of course. Hope you are well. I. R.

2—Here goes!

DRINKING THE WATERS AT HARROGATE.   Dec 15th

[handwritten]

3—Good———!

DRINKING THE WATERS AT HARROGATE.

Dec. 15th 1905.   J. R.

[handwritten across top] I wonder if you are starting shearing today as we usually intend to do, but don't until altogether prepared. Love. J. R.

Buttermere

4—Shop 'uns!   Dec 18th

DRINKING THE WATERS AT HARROGATE.

[handwritten] Had lunch with Miss Totally. She's charming. J. R.

5—"Nothing, when you're used to it!"

DRINKING THE WATERS AT HARROGATE.   Dec 18th

[handwritten] Motored over on Saturday. Had a very jolly time. J. R.

6—"Don't waste it!"   Dec 18th

DRINKING THE WATERS AT HARROGATE.

[handwritten] Very few people at Harrogate (I do wish no longer) J. R.

Carte postale. Postkarte. Cartolina postale.
Dopisnice. Correspondenzkarte. Levelező-Lap.
Post card. Weltpostverein. Briefkaart.
Union postale universelle. Unione postale universale.
Всемірный почтовый союзъ. Poczta. Открытое письмо.
Karta korespondencyjna. Korespondenční lístek.
Cartão postal. Brefkort. Brevkort. Tarjeta postal.

Adresse:

Miss Jessie Larkin
Delroit
Gundagai
N. S. Wales
Australia

[handwritten along side] Sorry my letters were so short last week. Hope all well. Days are so warm — no rain. Very little shearing yet — these will soon be a drought in Queensland if — Love. J. R. June 17th

Isabel returned from Europe to Australia in June 1903, but left for England again, this time with her mother, on 15 March 1905 on the *SS Marmora*. According to a series of postcards[23] recording her second visit to Europe and written by Isabel to her cousin, Tess Larkin, at Deltroit, Isabel was in Huddersfield by June 1905.

Regrettably, although there are several dozen of these postcards, they contain only the briefest of messages and give tantalisingly few details of what was actually happening in Isabel's life in this period. It appears that she spent the remainder of 1905 in and around Huddersfield, making excursions to tourist attractions all over Yorkshire and also travelling to Ireland, Scotland and London. Although Brook is not specifically mentioned in any of the postcards, no other reason has emerged to explain why Isabel chose to base herself in Huddersfield for so long. By the end of the year, things between Isabel and Brook were clearly becoming very serious. William himself returned to England in November 1905 (in the company of Jock Mason, the son of the local Tumut doctor),[24] presumably to look over his prospective son-in-law and the Brook family.

By March 1906, there seems to have been an engagement. A postcard from Isabel to Tess with an obscured postmark, but sent from somewhere in France, says simply and enigmatically: 'So sorry to have missed mail last week but I think there is some cause don't you?' Clearly, Isabel had fallen for Brook and, with her artistic leanings, was doubtless now reluctant to exchange the sophistication and stimulation of Europe for the isolation of an Australian sheep and cattle station. A woman of adventurous spirit, Isabel determined to live in England, far away from her parents, sister and Larkin cousins, and to relinquish the possibility of a career as a concert pianist in favour of the more conventional path of marriage and family. At that time, even if Isabel had wanted to become a professional pianist, it would have been most unusual — if not, impossible — for her to do so while married to someone of the social standing of John Brook.

The Brooks of Huddersfield

Isabel's beau was charming, urbane, extremely good-looking and a gentleman. He was also wealthy. His father, a man of socialist tendencies and politically active, had built the Larchfield Mill to the south of the town of Huddersfield and beside the canal tow path in about 1866, the same year that William Richardson bought his first block of land at Deltroit. Employing at least 200 people,[25] the factory complex grew to include a main five-storey mill, four three-storey buildings, a two-storey weaving shed, warehousing and office space, as well as an engine house, boiler rooms and a 130-foot square stone chimney.[26] By the time Brook's father died, the mill had become the sixth largest in Huddersfield.

Taking over from his father and managing the business for thirteen years, Brook was in charge during a period of upheaval that saw increased competition from foreign textiles, the introduction of tariffs in the United States to protect their own industry, and a significant increase in the price of coal.[27] There exist anecdotal but unsubstantiated stories in the Brook

Larchfield Mill, Huddersfield, which belonged to the Brook family

ABOVE
Fernbrook,
Huddersfield,
where John Brook
grew up

OPPOSITE
Grace Brook, an
ardent suffragette,
c. 1900

family of a dishonest bookkeeper and large company debts that were personally discharged by Brook himself. However, it seems that when the mill was finally sold in 1901, it was, in fact, a going concern at a time when many other similar mills were in serious difficulties.[28] There is no record of how much the mill was sold for, but Brook was also a joint beneficiary under his father's will of a trust fund of £118,000 (equivalent to approximately £7 million in today's terms). Clearly, he had sufficient funds, both from the sale of the mill and from other assets in his father's estate, to retire from business at the age of only thirty-four and to never work again.[29] Brook seems to have been the antithesis not only of Isabel's father but also of her brother-in-law, Charlie Fraser, both of whom were self-made men working tirelessly in their respective occupations all their lives.

Aside from his wealth and social position, it is easy to see why Isabel might have been attracted to Brook and his family. Here was a man who was socially Isabel's equal but whose life and background were intriguingly different to the one she had known. Apparently, after the sale of the mill, Brook was leading the life of an English gentleman, shooting and fishing like his late father and generally enjoying the spacious Victorian family home, Fernbrook, on the outskirts of Huddersfield. How refined this must have seemed to the young Isabel compared to her father's much more rigorous life in the Australian bush! Moreover, while Huddersfield itself was in the heart of industrial Britain, it was nevertheless within easy reach of many other interesting places such as Harrogate and York. These towns offered a range of social and cultural activities a great deal wider and no doubt more sophisticated than Isabel would have been used to at Hillas Creek

ABOVE
John Brook as
a child

OPPOSITE
Isabel
Richardson in
her wedding
gown, 1906

or in nearby Adelong and Gundagai. Nor had living in a manufacturing town prevented the Brook family from pursuing some of life's more exotic pleasures. Before he died, Brook's father had owned a sailing yacht, the *Dotterell*, which had been used to cruise the British Isles, the Mediterranean and Scandinavia.[30]

Brook and his family were unusual and unconventional in ways that surely piqued Isabel's curiosity. For one thing, the family was secularist; for another, Brook's widowed mother, Grace, and one of his two sisters, Agnes, were ardent suffragettes. There is even a photograph of Grace Brook with a copy of *The Vote* on her lap, presumably indicating how strongly she felt about the emancipation of women. Agnes, who never married, was also a keen pianist like Isabel, and both women lived with Brook at the family home in Huddersfield. Brook also had an older brother, George, who had died prematurely, but not before becoming a well-known naturalist specialising in marine life and coral. He is recorded as having visited the home of Charles Darwin in Kent in 1880 in his capacity of secretary for the Yorkshire Naturalist Union.[31] Among his many achievements, George constructed, with his father, one of the best aquariums in the UK, which he used to house the marine creatures he was studying, and installed a special pumping and aerating apparatus he designed himself.[32]

Isabel marries

As for Brook's attraction to Isabel, her intelligence, pronounced musical gifts and by now well-heeled Australian background were doubtless a little different to most of the girls he had met. She would have been refreshing to him, especially after his experience of running the mill and living in the bleak north of England. Whether her Catholicism and his secularism were ever an obstacle to the union is unknown. Nevertheless, the couple were married according to the rites of the Roman Catholic Church on 18 July

Isabel Brook in her
going-away outfit
after her wedding,
1906

1906 at St Mary's Cathedral, Sydney, where Florence had married six years earlier.

The wedding was reported at length in the press and was about as grand and as costly as could be arranged; nonetheless, it seems to have been a quiet affair. The beautiful photograph of the bride in her wedding dress is matched by the fulsome description given in the *Daily Telegraph* of 21 July 1906. According to this report, the bridal gown

was of ivory Duchesse satin, the skirt made over a petticoat of chiffon, and draped with Brussels lace, silver and orange blossom. Brussels lace also draped the bodice made with a corselet belt, and her veil of exquisite lace was caught up with a diamond ornament. Her diamond pendant and shower bouquet were the gifts of the bridegroom.

There were three bridesmaids — namely, Tess Larkin, Violet Turner and 'little Miss Ivy Horsley', who was Mary Horsley's youngest daughter. All three were reported as having received expensive gifts of jewellery from Brook. Mary Richardson, the bride's mother, was also gorgeously attired in 'black lace over white chiffon glace, with a black and white bonnet', while Florence wore 'a gown of hydrangea-blue silk, trimmed with Paris-tinted lace, and a hat in the same shade, trimmed with mauve and pink shade flowers'. Florence's husband, Charlie, acted as best man.

After the ceremony, a reception was held at the Hotel Australia, before the newlyweds departed for a honeymoon spent initially in Medlow Bath in the Blue Mountains north of Sydney and then in Northern Queensland. In December 1906, the couple returned to England to live initially at Fernbrook until 1907, when they bought a house in the more congenial and fashionable spa town of Harrogate nearby. They called their new house 'Wahroonga', an Aboriginal word meaning 'happy home'. Even though she had visited Huddersfield before, the possibility that Isabel experienced something of a culture shock once she actually began living there is high,

Christening of
Marjorie Brook in
Harrogate, c. 1908.
Isabel Brook is
seated far right.

especially with its smoke-filled air and crowded streets. It was a world apart
from the serenity, expansive landscape and seasonal rhythms that she was
used to at Deltroit.

John and Isabel Brook had four children, all of them daughters:
Marjorie, born on 8 July 1907; Dorothy Helen ('Helen'), born 3 July 1909;
Mary ('Bonnie'), born on 29 August 1913; and Margaret ('Peggy'), born on
25 April 1917. All the children were born in Harrogate except for Helen,
who was born in Gundagai during a family visit to Deltroit. Interestingly,
the birth certificate describes Brook's occupation as 'Independent Means',
confirming not only that he was a 'gentleman', but also that he had by now
left business behind him. Another point to note is that in attendance was
Dr Gabriel, the man whose famous photographs of Gundagai at the turn of
the century, including pictures of the Fraser family, are now in the National
Library in Canberra.

OPPOSITE TOP
Tennis party at
Yabtree, c. 1910.
From left, front row:
Janet Kidd, John
Brook, Tess Larkin,
Wattis Beveridge;
middle row: Emily
Larkin, Isabel Brook,
R. F. L. Horsley,
Miss Calcott
(governess),
unidentified man;
back row:
James Kidd.

OPPOSITE
BOTTOM
Outside Yabtree
homestead, c. 1910.
From left: John
Brook, Isabel Brook,
Emily Larkin, Wattis
Beveridge, R. F.
L. Horsley, Miss
Calcott (Horsley
governess), Janet
Kidd, Tess
Larkin, James
Kidd and
unidentified
man.

RIGHT
Isabel Brook
with her four
children. From
left: Marjorie,
Peggy (sitting on
lap), Helen and
Bonnie (behind).

After her marriage to Brook, it seems that Isabel barely played the piano, devoting herself to her family and taking up bridge, which she played very seriously. Having exceptionally high standards in all things,[33] it is possible that she preferred not to play the piano at all rather than to play at a level below that which she had reached before her marriage. Although Isabel remained in England all her life except for some extended visits to Australia early on in her marriage, she was always a great supporter of the Australian Cricket Team and other sporting heroes from her native land. Apparently, in spite of the charms of Europe, she never quite cut her ties with the colonial background of her youth.

Deltroit homestead (formerly Deltroit House), 2011

CHAPTER 12

Deltroit House

On his return from Europe in late 1902, William finally realised a dream that he had no doubt cherished for many years: namely, the building of an impressive homestead at Deltroit. Having lived under the shadow of extensive debt since the untimely death of his brother, John, over fifteen years ago, William had at last been able to pay off in full the large mortgage of £20,000 in favour of the Bank of New South Wales on 13 September 1901.[1] The discharge of the mortgage was witnessed by his son-in-law, Charlie Fraser, who was at that time still practising as a solicitor in Tumut.

The timing of the discharge is remarkable, falling as it did in the midst of one of the worst droughts that New South Wales had experienced since white settlement. While no doubt a great relief, the removal of this mortgage may nonetheless have only released William from some of his indebtedness. It seems that there were other mortgages over land at both Deltroit and Billapalap that may still have been outstanding in 1901, including a mortgage for £6000 taken out on 27 February 1878, but it has not been possible to identify their full extent nor if and when they were discharged.[2]

Before the new homestead

It had taken William almost forty years since first acquiring land at Deltroit to be able to afford the luxury of a large brick homestead, in keeping not only

OPPOSITE TOP
Earliest known
photograph of
Deltroit House,
probably taken in
1903 when it was
completed

OPPOSITE
BOTTOM
Deltroit
homestead, 2010

with his position as an important Riverina stockowner, but also with the other major properties in the area, including Yabtree, Jelingroo and Toonga. Both the difficulties of farming in the Australian bush and some unexpected turns that life had taken in the preceding years had forced William to postpone the construction of the magnificent mansion at Deltroit, which stands here today. It seems that William was also prudent and cautious by nature, otherwise he might have embarked on a major building project much earlier, maintaining all his existing borrowings or borrowing further to finance the works.

Instead, it appears that he and his family had contented themselves by living in a more modest homestead built of large slabs of timber, a design that was common in the mid to late nineteenth century. Unfortunately, no descriptions survive of this original building, which was probably built just prior to the family moving from Billapalap to Deltroit shortly after Isabel was born. It was, however, in this old timber homestead and not the grand brick mansion at Deltroit that Florence and Isabel Richardson were brought up, together with their cousins, Tess and Emily Larkin.

The original Deltroit homestead was situated only three feet from the site of its replacement[3] and remained in that position until the works to the new homestead were finished. It is just partially visible in the earliest known photograph of Deltroit House (as it was known then), taken about the time that the new homestead was completed during the first half of 1903. Stories have been handed down over time that the old Deltroit homestead burnt down, but this has not been proved. On the contrary, an article in the *Adelong Argus* states clearly that it was, in fact, removed to a position near the shearing shed 'to act as a home for the station-hands'.[4] Since the structure is no longer in existence, it may have burnt down after it was moved to this new location. However, there are no press reports of the event nor any clear recollections remaining among Richardson descendants or local people, and it may simply have fallen down through neglect or lack of use. Another theory is that the many fires at Billapalap in the early 1900s, which caused so much damage there, may have become confused over time with what occurred at Deltroit.

Design and construction

Contrary to the popular belief in the neighbourhood, Deltroit House
was not designed by the well-known architect William Monks, who
was responsible for a number of important houses in the area, including
Yabtree, and also several of the finest buildings in Wagga Wagga. The
architect of Deltroit House was William Mark Nixon,[5] who, having been
employed in the Colonial Architect's Office and the New South Wales
Railways Department, had commenced independent practice in Sydney
in 1893. At the time of the construction of Deltroit House, Nixon was
in partnership in Pitt Street with John Shedden Adam, having previously
had another partner, Alfred Allen. By 1902, Nixon was an award-winning
architect, becoming increasingly known for many substantial houses
both in Sydney's suburbs and in the country, as well as for designing or
remodelling churches, schools, banks and other public buildings. He
subsequently designed the Gundagai Hospital when this was built in
1904,[6] the introduction to the committee in charge of the new hospital

being no doubt effected by William Richardson and his son-in-law, Charlie Fraser.

The new homestead at Deltroit, described as being of 'noble proportions' and 'a perfection of architectural design', was 'in composite style, being partly old English and partly Gothic'. Features such as small gables used purely for decoration gave the house an English rustic charm, whereas a pentagonal corner bay window with its conical 'candle snuffer' roof and the many tall chimneys throughout the building created a more Gothic feel. It was the mix of these different features that was the hallmark of William Monks, and it is therefore not surprising that the homestead at Deltroit has so often been wrongly attributed to him. Besides the character of its decoration, the homestead was in a single-storey or bungalow style, with a high-pitched roof whose steep gradient was only marginally reduced as it swept over the ten-foot-wide verandahs surrounding most of the building. Above all, it seems that the house was built to be cool in summer, yet, in spite of the many large fireplaces, it remains bitterly cold in winter when temperatures plummet regularly below freezing.

The actual building of the house was carried out by the well-known local builders C. Hardy & Co. of Wagga Wagga and was overseen by Harry Hardy himself,[7] one of the sons of the founder, Charles Hardy, who had established the family business around 1861. The firm had a reputation for very high standards of craftsmanship and used a number of builders trained in England.[8] Always solid and well finished, the many impressive buildings in Wagga Wagga and the Riverina executed by C. Hardy & Co. included court houses, railway stations, schools, churches, mills, breweries and private residences. Apparently, the project at Deltroit was so large and important that Harry Hardy 'never left the job since it started'.[9]

Materials and layout

The quality of the bricks used to build the new homestead was unparalleled.[10] Made by Alfred Emery of Tumut, they were of a 'rich purple' clay found on Deltroit and 'such as a tradesman likes to handle, wanting no cleaning nor tuckpointing'. In short, they were, without exception, 'the handsomest and best made in the whole district'. The roof of the house was made of slate and supported by slender decorative timber posts placed at intervals around the wide verandahs. The house faced east into the morning sun and was positioned on a gentle rise above the Hillas Creek, overlooking the flats. Approached by a 'spacious flight of steps' now long disappeared, the front door, which was embellished by multicoloured sidelights, opened onto an imposing rectangular hall with a wide arch in the high ceiling and small black and white tiles on the floor. In this mosaic was spelled the name 'Deltroit' in capital letters. It was a grand entrance calculated to impress the visitor and announce to the world that William Richardson was now an important and wealthy man.

The archway in the main hall led into a corridor 32 feet long that ran the full length of the house at right angles to the entrance. The straight line of the corridor was broken by two arches of the same design as the one in the entrance, one being identical in size, the other being slightly smaller. At the southern end of the corridor was the drawing room, which was 22 feet

Original tiled
hallway at
Deltroit House

long and 16 feet wide, with a ten-foot bay built out onto the verandah. There
was an ornate, three-tiered, grey marble mantelpiece and, in common with
the rest of the building, the drawing room had a 14-foot-high pressed metal
ceiling by Wunderlich of Sydney.[11] The decoration of the ceiling in this
room was particularly elaborate, being a symmetrical design with arabesques,
cornucopias of fruit and flowers, in addition to acanthus leaves in every
corner. It was probably the first of this pattern to be erected in Australia.[12]

Also at the southern end of the house was the principal bedroom,
20 feet by 16 feet, with a beautiful and unusual pentagonal bay in one
corner divided from the main room by a wide arch. There was a second
large bedroom on the eastern side, with a corner bay and a door into a
comfortable, almost rectangular sitting room. Three further bedrooms were
located along the western side of the house. The bathroom 'with handsome
enamel baths, adapted to having hot or cold water laid on' also had 'every
necessary that can possibly be wanted in a bathroom', including hand basin,

TOP
Deltroit House
between 1910
and 1920

BOTTOM
Deltroit garden,
late 1950s

linen press and 'conveniences'. Finally, in the main house, there was a spacious dining room on the western side, with a black marble mantelpiece, bay window and doorway into the kitchen and next-door laundry. The kitchen was 'fitted up in a most elaborate manner, having gas and water laid on with large range, cupboards, presses, safes etc.' It was intended that the principal rooms of the house would be parquetry and that the walls 'be ornamented with French dadoing'. All these details are given in an article that appeared on 17 March 1903 in the *Adelong Argus*, which is one of only two articles about Deltroit found in contemporary material.

In addition to the main section of the building, it appears that on the north end of the house there was a wing that contained the servant's quarters, pantry, storeroom and a 'commodious office'. A large garden, later planted with many trees of European origin (mainly elm), surrounded the homestead, and there was a tennis court in the far corner to the south, near the Adelong Road. A small creek, fed from a spring in the hills nearby, ran intermittently on the most westerly side of the garden into the Hillas Creek below. On the southern verandah, latticed enclosures were put up in the corners to provide extra shade when sitting outside, and an ornamental arch was erected for climbing roses opposite the drawing room and principal bedroom windows.

Near the house on the northern side, Nixon designed a brick stable block and two-storey coach-house with large tanks for drinking water and a

Aerial view of Deltroit homestead, 2009

pump for washing carriages. This was accessed by a huge circular drive from the Adelong Road, which passed in front of the house before reaching the stables and returning back to the road near the tennis court. Altogether, the new Deltroit homestead was said to be of 'infinite credit to the artisan who planned it, Mr Nixon, and to the enterprising character of the popular squire of Deltroit, Mr Richardson'.[13] The cost of this 'handsome and imposing mansion' was in excess of £3000, with the gas lighting and extras alone amounting to £200. Interestingly, this sum is only a little less than the cost of £3334 9s 10d incurred in building the Gundagai Hospital one year later.[14]

Today, the house is almost fully intact, save that the elegant tiled floor in the hallway was removed in the 1970s. According to Tom and Jenny Barr-Smith, who owned Deltroit at the time, the tiles were badly damaged by previous occupants. The only other major change is that the servants' wing has disappeared and in its place is a modern extension that now houses the

OPPOSITE TOP
Original front
entrance to
Deltroit
homestead,
c. 1950s

OPPOSITE
BOTTOM
The front
entrance today

kitchen and dining room in an open-plan design, along with a comfortable, low-ceiling sitting room with a small bay window to the west and a central fireplace with limestone travertine surround. The original kitchen is used as an office and den, and the dining room as a bedroom. What was once the drawing room is now the main bedroom, and a billiard room has been made out of the original second bedroom on the eastern side. The interconnecting sitting room is now the farm office. All but one of the pressed metal ceilings are in mint condition and have been fully preserved. The front door is no longer used as such, and the house is entered through the extension on the northern side, straight into the kitchen and dining room area.

A family home of sorts

On the whole, Deltroit House was very large for a family whose children had either left home or were about to do so. Florence was married and living in Gundagai, and Isabel was in Europe while the house was being constructed, living at Deltroit only intermittently between her return to Australia in July 1903 and her subsequent marriage in 1906. It must have been strange for Isabel to return from her sojourn in Europe not to her familiar home, but to a stately mansion that bore no resemblance at all to the house in which she had grown up. No doubt the grandeur of Deltroit House struck her forcibly and, after her travels, she may even have thought it a little incongruous, its obvious references to English nineteenth-century architecture looking perhaps a fraction odd in the quintessential Australian landscape of New South Wales.

Florence and Isabel were not the only ones to have left Deltroit by the time of its new homestead. It seems, from several entries in the diaries of John Pearce from Hillside near Adelong, that both Emily and Tess Larkin had been living with their brother, Al Larkin, from at least 1901 and possibly much earlier, probably keeping house for him at Billapalap. Even though Al was briefly married between 1901 and 1902, there are a number of references in the Pearce diaries to social visits between the Pearce women at Hillside and the 'Misses Larkin' taking place between 1901 and 1903, indicating that

OPPOSITE
The Brook and
Fraser children
playing in the
Deltroit garden,
between 1910
and 1920

both Larkin sisters were living at Billapalap. However, it seems that, when Al remarried in 1904, Tess and probably Emily moved back to Deltroit. The various postcards to Tess from Isabel, sent while the latter was in Europe during 1905 and early 1906, were always addressed to her cousin at Deltroit, and Tess continued to receive postcards from Isabel here until at least 1908, after Isabel had married and moved to Huddersfield.

While the precise movements of Emily are not known, both she and Tess were shown on the Electoral Roll of New South Wales for 1908 as living at Deltroit. Emily must therefore have moved back from Billapalap around the same time as Tess, sometime between 1904 and 1905. Reputedly great fun,[15] Emily never married and, at some stage, returned to live again at Billapalap with her brother and his family. Subsequently, she was a frequent and welcome visitor to Deltroit and appears in several family photographs. As for Tess, she may have remained at Deltroit until her own marriage on 6 November 1911 to a clerk, William Joseph Elliott, who was also her first cousin.[16]

Clearly feeling the pangs of separation from family and all that was familiar, Isabel returned to Deltroit within three years of her marriage in 1906, leaving England on 5 February 1909 on the *Asturias* with her husband and their firstborn child, Marjorie, who was then less than two years old.[17] It is not known how long the Brooks stayed in Australia, but it must have been at least six months since their second daughter, Helen, was born in Gundagai in July the same year. The Brooks came back the following year[18] when Isabel's mother, Mary, died unexpectedly on 4 July 1910 from gall stones and heart failure.[19] Mary, whose character and personal appearance remains largely unknown, was buried on a morning of heavy rain in the Roman Catholic portion of the Adelong cemetery next to her third child, Edith Emily, who had died as an infant.

Presumably concerned for her widowed father and no doubt enjoying being back in Australia, Isabel and her family stayed almost two years, eventually leaving Sydney on the *Demosthenes* and arriving back in England on 22 October 1912. Isabel's mother-in-law, Grace Brook, had died a month earlier in Harrogate, and this perhaps finally prompted a return home. Whether the Brooks remained the whole time at Deltroit is unknown, but they probably would have attended the wedding in Sydney

of Tess Larkin, to whom Isabel seems to have been close. After the departure of the Brooks, William was left to inhabit the vast spaces of his mansion by himself, except for the servants and possibly also Emily Larkin. Perhaps it did not matter all that much to William that he had been deprived of the opportunity of enjoying his splendid new house with his wife for more than a handful of years and that the homestead was empty much of the time. He was leaving something enduring for posterity and, of course, for his heirs, Florence and Isabel.

Death of William Richardson

Rather than going into decline, William remained physically strong and continued to take a very active interest in his pastoral enterprise, even though he was seventy-two by the time of the Brooks' departure. An article that appeared two years later in the *Tumut & Adelong Times*[20] described Deltroit as looking 'particularly well just now' and that

> Richardson, the squire of the holding, despite his advanced age can be seen taking his daily walks over the property. These walks are said to run to about 20 miles daily. Mr R can ascend a hill as nimbly and actively as a well-trained footballer.

William was indefatigable and must have agreed with the old adage that the best manager is the farmer's footprint!

How Deltroit fared during the First World War is not clear, but William was perhaps lucky not to have any sons to enlist. It seems, however, that a number of his workers did, as a later obituary mentions that William gave them each a letter saying that they would be put back on their old jobs when they returned.[21] Whatever his thoughts on the war itself, William is likely to have been pleased with the 1916 announcement that the British Government would purchase the entire Australian wool clip for uniforms and other military purposes for a fixed price per bale, which was 55 percent above pre-war levels. This would have been a welcome respite from the difficult years in the 1890s, when climatic and economic conditions had kept wool production and prices down. Perhaps it was this boost to farm income that enabled the installation of electric light at Deltroit in October 1917, not only in the homestead, but also in the men's quarters and shearing shed.[22]

Although evidently a man with a strong constitution, William's mind eventually started to deteriorate, and he would be found wandering on the Adelong Road towards Billapalap, lost and disorientated.[23] It seems that in this final phase of William's life, Florence moved to Deltroit with her husband and children. With Isabel making a new life in England, Florence was going to be the one to take over the running of Deltroit and Billapalap. No doubt she would have been anxious to be near her father in his declining years, also enabling her to keep fully abreast of the current state of the properties and the direction of the business.

On 8 March 1920, William died, aged eighty-one, in the beautiful homestead at Deltroit that had taken almost a lifetime to achieve. The cause of death given was 'senile decay'. It brought to an end the full life of a well-known, deeply respected man who had worked tirelessly to improve his circumstances and those of his many dependents. William was buried next to his wife, but in the Church of England portion of the Adelong cemetery, the funeral cortege being a very large one and the pall bearers, all his employees.[24] Described movingly as 'one of the grand old pioneers who blazed the trail into the wilderness for future civilisation'[25] and as 'highly esteemed by all acquaintances',[26] including those who worked for him, William was admired as much for his loyalty and integrity as for his many achievements. The standing in the community with which he was regarded is perhaps reflected in the massive granite cross that marks his grave.

On his death, William left a will dated 21 April 1910, the effect of which was that, as his wife had predeceased him, his entire estate was to be divided equally between his two daughters. There were no other beneficiaries and, in particular, there were no legacies to any of the Larkins. This was something that clearly caused upset among the Larkin clan as, some years later, there are letters from Emily Larkin to the Probate Registry in Sydney requesting a copy of William's will.[27] Perhaps William felt that he had served them all well in his lifetime, providing work and shelter for

Driveway through the Deltroit garden, 2010

them when their mother had died and continuing to do so up until his own death. Certainly, he must have trusted his daughters to maintain these arrangements as necessary.

Once again, Isabel and her family came out to Australia, this time on the *Orsova*, departing London on 3 April 1920. The purpose of this visit was to mourn her father and to determine the division of William's assets. The total value of the estate was calculated at £55,786 12s 7d, but the schedule of assets showing the separate values and acreages of Deltroit and Billapalap at that time is missing from the probate file. Poignantly, the surviving documents show that, in addition to these significant assets, there were also outstanding debts of £23,758 19s 5d, including one for the sum of £22,569 owing to the Union Bank of Australia. This was almost the same amount as the borrowings that William had paid off in 1901 just before he built Deltroit House. While he had made a huge capital improvement on Deltroit, it seems that William may have continued to shoulder heavy debts incurred prior to the new homestead being built. Alternatively, it could be that William lost grasp of his affairs with advancing age, subjecting himself to fresh financial burdens in the last years of his life. Whatever the true cause, the ultimate effect of these continued significant borrowings would only become apparent in the fullness of time.

CHAPTER 13

The Fraser Years, Part One

*U*pon the death of her father in 1920, it was Florence, now in her forties, and not her husband, Charlie Fraser, who took over the running of Deltroit and Billapalap.[1] Fraser appears to have given up his large legal practice in Gundagai about this time, although he remained extremely active in community affairs, especially through his work on the local Pastures Protection Board, of which he was chairman between 1922 and 1934. It was said that the work he did for the board and the men on the land could never be 'fully estimated', and that he put 'heart and soul' into the job.[2]

Formidable Florence

It seems that Fraser liked nothing better than to don his oldest clothes and work in the Deltroit garden. Swagmen who saw Fraser as they passed by would ask him if there was any work to be had on the place, to which he would reply, 'You'd better go and see Mrs Fraser. I'm only the rouseabout.'[3] It was Fraser who was responsible for the planting

Florence Fraser

Charles Fraser

of over 200 magnificent elm trees in the garden and stable yard at Deltroit and along the Adelong Road. They were grown from cuttings taken from the huge elm in front of the homestead at Yabtree, probably planted in the 1830s by the Hillas brothers.[4] R. F. L. Horsley would come regularly to Deltroit with some cuttings, and over a drink Horsley and Fraser would determine the position of the trees. Since elms are deciduous, with long, spreading branches, they provide shade in summer and light in winter, and are also faster-growing than their rival English import, the oak.

While her husband focused on his own projects, Florence took charge of the grazing enterprise she had inherited. Clearly no fool, she had a formidable personality and stately presence, commanding great respect among her workers, business contacts and friends alike.[5] She also had a feminine side, as evidenced by one report that stated she possessed a 'marvellous personality' and exhibited a 'charming manner' towards everyone.[6] She was known among her workers as 'the boss' and could be either very firm or indulgent, as the occasion demanded.

The abiding impression of Florence is, however, of someone rather grand. Vignettes, such as the one her grandson, Jock Fraser, recalls from his mother, lend support for this view. She vividly described Florence sweeping around a Sydney warehouse, inspecting Deltroit wool bales, with agents from well-known brokers Pitt, Son & Badgery trailing behind. Several locals, including the late Lyle Allen whose father established Allens, the second-largest general store in Adelong, remembered Florence shopping there in the 1920s. The shop assistants would leave the other customers standing as soon as Florence walked in and attend to her needs. She frequently made large purchases that were subsequently delivered to Deltroit by a two-horse cart while she herself returned to Deltroit in her motor car.

The Fraser
family, c. 1915.
From left: Harry,
Florence, Poppy,
Jack (standing
behind), Charles
and Isobel.

Florence's team

Florence was fortunate in that she had a loyal and exceptionally industrious
team of workers. In that period, there were eight full-time men working
at Deltroit and five or six at Billapalap.[7] Some of these workers had been
employed by her father, but there were at least two important employees
at Deltroit that Florence selected herself. Firstly, she employed as overseer
in the mid-1920s, Cyril Leo Crowe, who had grown up on a property,
formerly part of the famous run of Darbalara near Tumut. His first job was
as a shearer in South Australia,[8] but he subsequently returned to the Tumut
district and in 1925 married Annie Isabella Webb, a childhood sweetheart.[9]
The couple came to Deltroit, where they lived in the Junction Hotel, then
being used purely as accommodation for Deltroit workers. They had a
daughter, Helen, born at Deltroit on 25 November 1926.

Crowe was a tall, good-looking man, very fair and with blue eyes, whose impeccable manners, even temper and love of the land earned him the epithet 'Nature's Gentleman'.[10] Devoutly Catholic, he was thoughtful and considerate, never swore or drank, and always raised his hat to a lady. Altogether, he served the Fraser family selflessly for twenty-two years, sometimes based at Billapalap but mostly at Deltroit. Both Florence and, later, her eldest son Jack depended on him for his good sense, ability to motivate and organise the station hands, and for his work ethic.

In addition to Crowe, Florence employed a local resident, Billy Simpson. He was born four miles away at Mount Adrah and worked briefly for his uncle, Ned O'Dwyer, a former licensee of the Junction Hotel and breeder of racehorses in Melbourne.[11] Taken on by Florence in the 1920s as a stockman, Simpson was a great horseman and horse-breaker. He had a wife, Sarah, who worked as a cook at the Deltroit homestead, which at that time had full-time staff of six servants, including maids and gardeners.[12] The Simpsons shared the Junction Hotel with the Crowes, and the two families became very close friends,[13] living in separate halves of the stone-built hotel that had experienced such a colourful past. There were two kitchens in the building at this time, which presumably allowed each couple some independence.

Simpson, like Crowe, was a tall, handsome man. He wore a gold watch on a chain in one pocket and carried a sovereign holder in the other.[14] Stern and blunt, he nonetheless had a stammer that caused him no end of frustration. He had the habit of ending each sentence with 'yer see, yer see?' in a desperate attempt to make himself understood.[15] He was another very hard worker, conscientious and loyal, employed by the Fraser family even longer than Crowe, for a remarkable thirty-five years until 1963. It was rumoured, but never proven, that Simpson hid his savings under the floorboards of the Junction Hotel.[16]

Al Larkin

Also among her most noted employees, Florence had the strong hand of her first cousin, Al Larkin, who had been living and working at Billapalap since he was a boy. Growing to a man of medium build with a small moustache,[17] he was well known about the Adelong district and regarded by some as a difficult character to get along with,[18] though, according to the Pearce diaries, he was also very neighbourly. There are countless entries describing his visits to

Jack Fraser (far left) and Billy Simpson with polo string, Susie, Sally and Roulette

Pearce's property, Hillside, either alone or accompanied by one of his sisters, his wife or even his youngest brother, Harry. On these occasions, Al would sometimes bring a case of pears,[19] some fresh beef[20] or the mail from Adelong.[21] He regularly borrowed some bullocks from Pearce and a wagonette, mostly for farm work and, once, to transport a piano to Billapalap.[22] Before Florence took over, Al also acted as the go-between when two rams Pearce had recently purchased from her father died for no apparent reason.[23]

Al was much older than Crowe and Simpson, being in his early sixties by the time they arrived at Deltroit. Notwithstanding, he remained in charge at Billapalap until the late 1930s. He was an outstanding horseman and an exceptionally good judge of cattle,[24] but he was also a rum drinker, often to excess.[25] Apparently, only his close friend Edward Corbett, who had married Thomas Richardson's daughter, Louisa, could handle Al after one of his wilder bouts of drinking.[26] A popular story is told of Al returning home from Adelong along Black Creek Road one winter's night after 'a spree', whereupon he slid off his horse into a ditch and fell asleep. On being found half frozen the next morning by the station hands, the doctor pronounced that only the alcohol level in his blood had prevented his dying of exposure.[27]

Marrying firstly the sweet-natured Ellen ('Nellie') Hassett on 25 April 1901,[28] who died childless from pneumonia only two years after their marriage, Al subsequently married Edith Hockaday on 10 April 1904. Both of Al's wives were from Adelong, and Nellie was from a prominent landowning family in the district. It is believed that Al's first child was Norman Alfred, born out of wedlock to Edith on 21 April 1896, eight years before Al married her, having wedded Nellie in between. Al had five more children with Edith: Francis Alexander ('Frank'), born on 24 July 1905; Reginald John, born on 1 October 1906; twins Emily and Mary Elizabeth, born 4 October 1907; and Frederick Vincent, born on 3 May 1911. At least two of Al's sons, Norman and Frank, worked with him at Billapalap,[29] with the former also a soldier in the First World War. Additionally, it seems from the Pearce diaries that Al's youngest brother, Harry, was among the Billapalap workers for a time.

In that era, a degree of formality in appearance and speech, which has now disappeared, was retained by the overseers and station hands.

Photographs confirm that the overseer was always dressed, whatever the weather, in a shirt, jacket or waistcoat, a hat and usually a tie. Al especially was noted for always being correctly dressed, often in a three-piece suit and wearing his hat at a jaunty angle.[30] Men referred to the overseer as 'Mister' and to the manager or owner of the property as 'Sir' or 'Madam'. No-one ever thought of being asked to the main homestead for a drink or anything to eat, except during the Christmas party. These codes of conduct helped to keep order where everyone lived together 'above the shop' in a demanding, physical environment, surrounded day and night by the same people and isolated from civilising influences.

Buying out Isabel

Before Florence could fully take charge of Deltroit and Billapalap, she was obliged to confront the difficult question of how to give her sister, Isabel, her half-share of the total estate, as per their late father's will. On paper, this was effectively £16,000, being approximately half of the remaining value of the assets, after taking into account all indebtedness. In reality, it was probably rather more, since the values placed on the land and stock at the time of probate were likely to have been underestimated — as was commonly done — in order to reduce the death duties that were also payable. While Isabel had married a wealthy man, there can be no doubt that dividing up the estate fairly would have been an awkward transition for the two sisters.

By this time, Isabel's life was becoming more established in England. Now the mother of four daughters, the family was living in Harrogate at the house that she and her husband had named Wahroonga. Upon hearing of her father's death, Isabel made arrangements for the whole family to visit Australia. Brook left almost immediately on 20 March 1920 on the *Ormonde*, taking the two eldest girls with him. Isabel followed with the two youngest children and a nanny on 3 April 1920 on the *Orsova*. How long they intended staying when they left is not known, but they did not return to England for at least two years. During this extended stay, the eldest girls, Marjorie and Helen, were sent to their mother's old convent school in Rose Bay, Sydney, until the end of the Australian academic year in December 1922.

LEFT
Isabel Brook

RIGHT
John Brook

The details of the buyout of Isabel's share in her father's estate have been lost over time. However, it seems likely that Florence borrowed to pay off her sister,[31] or possibly that Isabel agreed to defer the settlement of her entitlement. There is no evidence of any land sales at Deltroit or Billapalap in the 1920s, and it was not until much later in 1934 that over half of Billapalap was broken up and sold. Presumably, one of the chief reasons for this sale was either to raise funds for the repayment of borrowings incurred on the division of the estate between the sisters, or to finance the final settlement between them, which may have been postponed to this date. Although never fully articulated, Isabel's descendants remember that there was some feeling in the family that the buyout of Isabel was not quite fair and that she had received less than her due.

Florence the grazier

After years of huge fluctuations in wool prices, especially during the depression of the early 1890s and around the First World War, the 1920s was a promising time for those involved in wool production. The UK was buying about 50 percent of Australia's total wool export — far more than the pre-war figure of 30 percent. Florence would probably have been feeling optimistic about her grazing enterprise and, rather than paying back any of the capital she and her father had borrowed, appears to have made only interest payments up until at least 1934 and the subdivision of Billapalap.[32] This would account for the fact that, upon her death, the indebtedness over Deltroit and what remained of Billapalap had increased to approximately two-thirds of their combined value, notwithstanding a significant rise in land prices.

Whether or not Florence understood the slippery slope on which she had embarked, she appears to have carried on the mix that her father had established of a large flock of Merino sheep with a smaller, select herd of Shorthorn cattle. As the *Gundagai Times* reported on 22 January 1924, Deltroit had 'for very many years ... been renowned for the quality of its wool, mutton and beef products', and this year achieved the season's record

Silver Billy, champion racehorse owned by Florence Fraser and her son Jack

price for its wool clip of 32¼d per pound (or £46 12s 4d per bale). It was further reported in the same article that the wool, comprising 354 bales, was 'attractive, soft, super style and of fine quality' and was a 'feather in the cap of those responsible for its preparation'. No doubt Florence was partly counting on the wool clip to ultimately clear the backlog of debt, but this would only be possible if wool prices remained high.

Grazing sheep and cattle was not, however, all that interested Florence. Being passionate about horseracing, she also bred thoroughbreds and polo ponies, greatly assisted by the skills of Billy Simpson. Several of the racehorses gained notoriety, and one, Silver Billy, was particularly successful. Bred from a stallion called Night Raid, Silver Billy took the coveted Picnic Cup at the Yass Picnic Races in March 1929 and the Geraldra Cup at the Cootamundra Picnic Races in April the same year, as well as almost becoming a runner in the Melbourne Cup. Some of the polo ponies were good enough to be sold to the Ashtons, a famous polo-playing family in New South Wales, but many were kept for Florence's two sons, Jack and Harry, who became keen players. Poppy, the youngest daughter, was also a good rider and took an interest in the horse operation.

Times of plenty

In these seemingly affluent times, Florence provided an enviable lifestyle for her family. After early schooling in Gundagai, all four children were sent to private boarding schools in Sydney — the boys to St Ignatius' College, Riverview, and the girls to their mother's old school, the Convent of the Sacred Heart of Jesus in Rose Bay. Harry was later moved to Sydney Grammar after a disagreement with the Rector over smoking.[33] Jack and Harry were high-spirited and boisterous, and there are many stories of their

ABOVE
Florence and
Charles Fraser
with guests at
the entrance
to the Deltroit
homestead,
c. 1930

RIGHT
Poppy Fraser
riding Harry's
champion polo
pony at the
Dudley Cup,
c. 1930

escapades, some less flattering than others. As young men, they would practice their golf strokes against the fly screen of the verandah at the old weatherboard homestead at Billapalap and were regularly in trouble for rowdy behaviour in the pubs in Wagga Wagga.[34]

While growing up, Jack and Harry became close friends with the Horsley boys, especially the slightly older Lach and Wallace, with whom they were also at school. When any of the eight Horsley children came over to Deltroit on their ponies, Florence stood by the front door with a broom, 'ready to sweep them out with the dirt when it was time to go'.[35] Lach Horsley always remembered coming to Deltroit as a young lad and hearing the first radio transmission in the district.[36] There was so much static that barely a word of the broadcast could be understood.

The children's respective parents were, similarly, good friends, not only as the result of being neighbours, but also because Mary Horsley had previously been Florence's governess. Mary's husband, R. F. L. Horsley (who referred affectionately to his wife as 'Polly' or 'Pol'), had also kept up with Frank Horsley, his brother by adoption and Florence's first cousin. Forced to sell his property, Coobang, due to poor management and debt and after a spell of working unsuccessfully for the Horsley family on another property not far from Yabtree, Frank had moved to Sydney around 1901 and was driving

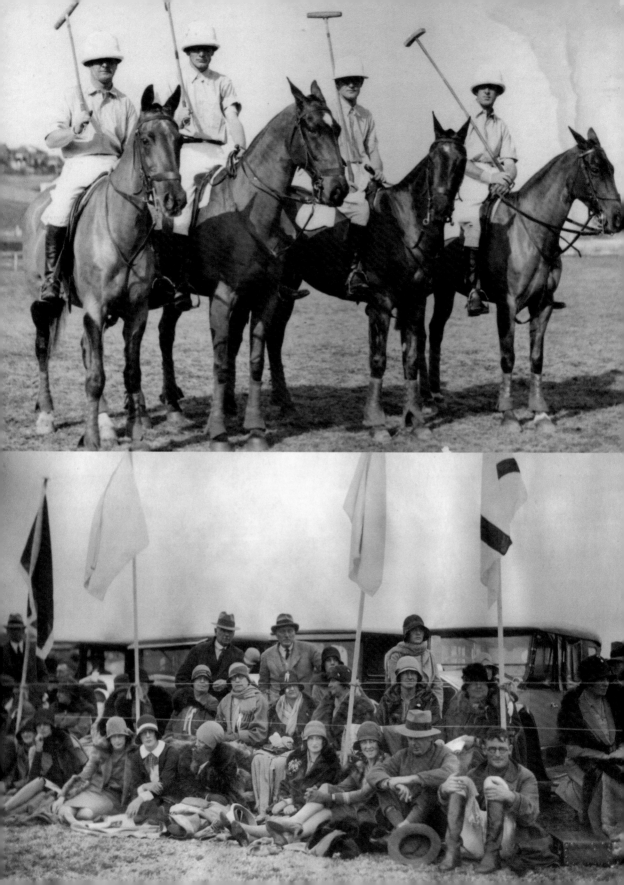

a hansom cab. He had earlier married Ada Mary Fletcher in Parkes on
26 February 1886 and had six children, only two of whom, Hattie Thelma
and Frank Lachlan, survived to adulthood.[37] It is not known how much, if
at all, Florence kept up with Frank, but an undated cutting from the local
Manly paper indicates that she attended his funeral in 1920.

There was a great deal of socialising between the Fraser and Horsley
families, often revolving around sport or race meetings. Picnic Races were
a regular time for the families to meet and took place all around the region
from Wagga Wagga to Holbrook and from Cootamundra to Yass. The horses
were usually of a lighter grade than those in the big races in the cities and
were ridden by amateur jockeys, including Lach and Wallace Horsley.[38] Both
Florence and Jack owned horses, including the highly successful Silver Billy.
Additionally, the Fraser and Horsley boys regularly played polo together,[39]
sometimes joined by Neville Horsley and a neighbour, Fred Beveridge.
At different times and in various combinations of four players, these boys
formed the Gundagai Polo Team during the 1920s and early 1930s. Games
were played either at polo clubs in Sydney, Goulburn, Gundagai, Narrandera

Jack Fraser and friend at a polo match, c. 1930

and Hay (the latter two places being west of Wagga Wagga) or on the polo fields of various properties. At Yabtree, polo was played on the river flats,[40] but no record of Deltroit having any polo grounds has been found. However, at one stage, there appears to have been a polo tournament in the district called the Deltroit Cup.

Difficulties emerge

It seems that for a time, there was little to disturb this privileged life being led by the Frasers. The usual volatility of climate, which frequently threatened to eliminate the profit margin of every grazier in the district, appears to have been largely absent in Florence's era. There were no notable droughts at Hillas Creek in the 1920s or early 1930s, though there was a significant flood at Gundagai in May 1925 and torrential flooding of the Hillas Creek in October 1923, February 1924, mid-June 1931 and late August 1932, with the Hillas Creek Bridge washed away on each occasion.[41] This embattled structure was still positioned on the Great Southern Road (renamed the Hume Highway in 1928), between Mundarlo and the main Hillas Creek settlement, about a mile from the Junction Hotel.

Although there are no reports of any natural bushfires occurring in this period, there was a serious bushfire in December 1926 started by a match or cigarette thrown by a careless traveller. This fire reportedly destroyed 1500 acres of grass at Deltroit, though, due to the quick and efficient work of local men in fighting the blaze, no stock was lost.[42] The fire broke out near the Junction Hotel and had a front of half a mile long. It travelled past the Deltroit woolshed opposite the homestead on the Adelong Road and, fanned by a big wind, spread to the back portions of Yabtree and Mount Adrah. Although not mentioned in the press, it seems that, given the route of the flames, the homestead would have had a narrow escape.

Possibly far more damaging to the wellbeing of Deltroit and its residents than any natural or man-made disasters was the Great Depression of 1929 to 1932. This was a time of extreme hardship for most people in Australia, especially as it was a country heavily dependent on exports. Wool and wheat prices fell sharply, the former to a mere 6d per pound. Export sales dropped dramatically, and almost 32 percent of Australians were out of work. Even the local Gundagai Hospital was threatened with closure because of debts of £2000.[43] For many graziers, it made more economic sense to boil sheep down for tallow and soap than to shear them for wool, and rabbit became the only meat that most people could afford. Florence's bet that she could carry on her grazing business and an expensive lifestyle on borrowed money was about to be proved wrong.

Although wool and meat prices started to rise after 1932 and a gradual economic recovery began, things were very difficult in the rural industry for a long time. Export markets for both wool and meat, especially to the UK, continued depressed in the first half of the 1930s as the determination of the British government to safeguard the future of Britain's own agricultural industries hardened.[44] All markets were becoming generally more competitive, and the outlook for wool consumption in particular was that it would very likely go down with the emergence of new synthetics. Another problem facing all primary producers was the mounting fear in Europe that there would be another war with Germany.

Land sales and subdivisions

It was against this background that Florence took the difficult decision to subdivide Billapalap, held in her family for sixty years, and to sell off the major portion. To what extent she was influenced by prevailing economic and political conditions, the pressure of borrowings inherited from her

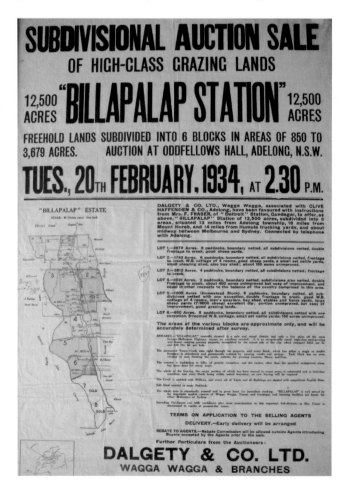

Notice of Billapalap subdivision sale, 1934

father (which, by now, had increased) or the demands of different family members including those of her sister, Isabel, is not known. It seems likely that some or all of these factors played a part, but that the actual trigger may have been the engagement in early 1934 of Harry Fraser to Lorraine MacPherson,[45] the daughter of a grazier from Boorowa, New South Wales, about 75 miles north of Deltroit.

Harry was by now a man of almost thirty who needed a property of his own to manage and on which to bring up a family. Florence's solution was to purchase Riversdale, a property on a sweeping bend of the Murrumbidgee only ten miles from Deltroit along the old Great Southern Road towards Tumblong. About 1200 to 1500 acres in size, with beautiful river flats on which grew millet, corn and pumpkins, the property also had a charming homestead dating from the 1920s. It was here that Harry and Lorraine Fraser, who married on 16 June 1934, had their only child, Jock, born on 19 March 1938.

Shortly before the purchase of Riversdale, Florence enlisted Dalgety & Co. of Wagga Wagga and Clive Haffenden & Co. of Adelong as joint auctioneers to put up for sale on 20 February 1934 six freehold blocks of 'high class grazing lands' at Billapalap. According to the auction notice, these blocks comprised 12,500 acres in total, varying in size from 850 to 3679 acres each. Every block had an area fronting onto the Yaven Yaven

Creek, but Lot 5, on which the homestead stood, had the additional advantage of double creek frontage. It also had various buildings, including the homestead itself, described as a 'good weatherboard cottage of four rooms' as well as 'men's quarters, hay shed, stables and horse yards, large sheep yards (7/8000 sheep) and excellent dip'. None of these have survived to the present day, nor are there any photographs or contemporaneous accounts providing details of their appearance. All that remain are the enormous elm trees that extend along the drive.

Two other blocks put up for sale also had cottages and yards, namely Lots 2 and 6, the former including a small shearing shed. Billapalap itself was described in the auction notice as 'an exceptionally sound, high-class wool-growing and heavy carrying grazing property' of 'undulating to hilly' country. It was also said to be 'abundantly and permanently watered' by the Yaven Yaven Creek, together with other creeks and springs rising in the nearby hills. The fencing on the property was advertised as being in 'first class condition', with every block within a rabbit-proof fence. The final inducement for prospective buyers were the words in the particulars that 'the whole area is abundantly grassed and in great heart for immediate stocking'.

It seems that after the auction notice was printed and just before the auction itself, there was a change of plan and Florence agreed to sell a further 1500 acres. According to a report in the *Adelong & Tumut Express* dated 2 March 1934, a total of 14,000 acres was eventually sold at Billapalap in eight lots, instead of six, as originally advertised. The subdivision seems to have been known in the district as a 'forced sale'[46] and, while it created great interest, the bidding at auction did not reach the vendor's reserves. Instead, all of the 14,000 acres were sold by private treaty before and after the auction. In every case, the buyers were local men, including W. J. Pearce (the son of John Joseph Pearce of Hillside) and Edward Corbett, who had married Louisa Richardson. It is hard not to conclude that the local community decided to carve up the property between them and came to an agreement among themselves as to the highest prices they would pay. Doubtless, it was the failure to reach the reserve prices that forced Florence to sell more land than she had originally intended.

Fancy-dress party on the verandah at Deltroit, c. 1930

After the subdivision, Florence was left with somewhere between a sixth and a third of the total land she had inherited from her father at Billapalap. Testimonies vary considerably as to whether this was only about 3000 acres[47] or as much as 8000 acres[48]. The former estimate is likely to be more accurate, since it is corroborated by documentation on Florence's death only two years later. What is beyond dispute, however, is that the property that had provided such a considerable part of the Richardson and Fraser lifestyle, chiefly through its wool clip, had been substantially dismantled. Precisely what happened to the proceeds of sale is unclear, but some was spent on the purchase of Riversdale for Harry. The rest was probably paid over to the bank in repayment of loans and possibly also to Isabel, as part of a delayed settlement of her inheritance. In any event, Florence had lost considerable economy of scale and a valuable source of income, especially in any future years of strong wool and meat prices. Unquestionably, the confidence with which the Frasers had hitherto led their charmed life at Deltroit was now gone.

CHAPTER 14

The Fraser Years, Part Two

$\mathcal{A}$ few months after the sale of land at Billapalap, Charlie Fraser died unexpectedly on 3 May 1934 at the age of only sixty-five. He had been campaigning hard for re-election on the Pastures Protection Board and, shortly after another victory, collapsed at home at Deltroit, slipping into unconsciousness. He died a few days later in hospital, the cause of death given as atherosclerosis or heart disease. The funeral was at St Michael's Cathedral in Wagga Wagga and attracted a huge number of people from all walks of life, including the Horsley family.[1] Amid a great show of affection, Fraser was buried in the Wagga Wagga cemetery.

In his will, Fraser left almost nothing, suggesting that he had probably placed his entire financial resources at Florence's disposal for the running not only of the family household, but probably also of Deltroit and Billapalap. It is a further indication too that the Frasers were by now 'asset-rich and cash-poor', and had been 'feeling the pinch' for some considerable time. Her husband's death must have been a blow to Florence, who, in spite of being 'the boss', would undoubtedly have consulted him on many matters relating to her grazing enterprise, in addition to those concerning family and other interests that they shared. She became reclusive, rarely leaving her home, and, according to her own obituary two years later, was seen only once in Gundagai after Fraser's death, at the opening of the Memorial Ward at the Gundagai hospital in honour of her husband.

OPPOSITE
Jack Fraser in
uniform, c. 1940

Jack Fraser

By the time of her husband's death, Florence's eldest son, Jack, had been very much involved with the management of Deltroit and what remained of Billapalap. He had developed a good working relationship with both Cyril Crowe and Billy Simpson, the latter sharing his love of horses. As his brother, Harry, had already been given Riversdale, Jack was the heir apparent to the Deltroit and Billapalap properties, subject to the claims of his sisters, Isobel and Poppy. Moreover, his father, always so active and prominent, was now dead and Jack's thoughts would inevitably have turned to the future. It was an appropriate time for him to marry.

The young woman he chose was Dorothy Maud ('Dor') Campbell, one of the three attractive and artistic daughters of Alfred and Edith Campbell who lived at Ellerslie, next door to Billapalap. The sisters had a brother, David, who became a famous poet and writer of short stories. Jack and Dor probably met through the usual social network in the district, either at a Picnic Race or at a private party. Nothing is known about their courtship other than that Dor's parents were apparently concerned about the ten-year age gap and the fact that Jack was Catholic[2] while they were Presbyterians. Nevertheless, Dor became Mrs Jack Fraser on 22 May 1935, when the couple married quietly in a Roman Catholic ceremony at St Canice's

Dor Fraser, c. 1946

Church, Sydney. The bride was twenty-three and her groom was thirty-two.

According to a detailed report a fortnight later in the *Tumut & Adelong Times*,[3] the wedding and reception afterwards at the Macquarie Club were beautiful. The bride wore a cowl-neck gown of pale cameo pink silk that was 'perfectly cut', and a coat of angora fastened at the waist with a 'unique silver buckle'. She had a halo hat of pink silk and a spray of orchids to finish the toilette. About a hundred people attended the reception, including the Horsley family. The reception rooms, where a buffet was arranged, had been 'artistically decorated with tall branches of gladioli, pink roses and carnations while glowing log fires added an extra air of comfort'. When departing for

their honeymoon in Melbourne, the bride wore a nut-brown woollen crepe and matching hat. Unfortunately, there is only one photograph of the event.

On paper, it would appear as if Jack and Dor had little in common other than having grown up in the same district. Dor's father, a medical practitioner, had purchased Ellerslie in early 1912[4] as part of a larger grazing enterprise together with his brothers. The property was 35,000 acres of some of the finest sheep country in the state, and was well managed and maintained.[5] Dor had initially been schooled at home by a governess before being sent away to Abbotsleigh in Sydney.[6] Her childhood at Ellerslie with her siblings was both carefree and gently cultivated, as vividly described by her brother, David Campbell, in his book *Evening Under Lamplight*. In March 1936, shortly after Dor and Jack were married, Ellerslie, including stock, was sold for £200,000 — said to be the largest property transaction in New South Wales for many years.[7] Dor's parents went to live in Sydney, but her mother visited Deltroit occasionally, with two white maltese dogs that she would walk along the dusty Adelong Road — which still remains unsealed today — towards the new Hume Highway.

Dor Campbell on her wedding day, 1935

Death of Florence Fraser

Dor Campbell as a child at Ellerslie in a sulky with her mother, c. 1920

With both her sons recently married and her husband dead, Florence determined on a six-month trip to England to visit her sister and the Brook family. Taking her eldest daughter, Isobel, with her and accompanied on the voyage by Alfred and Edith Campbell and their youngest daughter, Meg, the party left on the *Strathaird* in the second half of April 1936. Florence's youngest daughter, Poppy, did not go on the trip and, by this time, may already have met her future husband, Tom Weigall, whom she married in 1937.

Florence's sister, Isabel, was by now living in a rambling house called Lidwells on the outskirts of Goudhurst, a small village in Kent. The house was purchased by the Brooks around 1924, shortly after their extended stay at Deltroit at the time of William Richardson's death. Originally a large sixteenth-century farmhouse, the building had been expanded further in

Victorian times and was a sixteen-bedroom family home with extensive grounds.[8] During the First World War, the house had been turned into a military hospital between 17 May 1915 and 31 March 1919, where almost 1500 patients were treated.[9] Badly damaged in this period, Lidwells had been partly renovated with government compensation, but required further extensive work by the Brooks after they purchased it.

The gardens at Lidwells were glorious and, in particular, there was a large walled area known as the 'French Garden' that supplied the house with fruit and vegetables, the surplus being sold at Covent Garden in London.[10] There were excellent asparagus beds that were Isabel's pride and joy, and greenhouses in which grew nectarines and peaches. Also in the grounds were two grass tennis courts, a duck pond and a large orchard. Two full-time gardeners maintained this sanctuary, which also included two cottages within its boundaries. The house itself was staffed with maids, a cook and a nanny. Isabel had by then become devoutly Catholic and a keen bridge player, while her husband, John Brook, had grown more remote, drinking quite heavily and spending long periods of time alone in his study.[11] Like her sister, Isabel had a grand manner about her and moved in a smart social set — all of her daughters had been presented at Court, dressed in pink satin and holding pink ostrich feather fans.[12]

It seems that Florence may have seen her sister only briefly, if at all, on her trip and may never have even visited Lidwells, as she was taken ill on the passage over from Australia. Then, on arriving in London, she was told by a Harley Street specialist that she needed an operation for gall stones,[13] the same complaint that had been a cause of her mother's death. There must have been a complication because on 1 July 1936, the day after the operation, Florence died at the London Clinic, Devonshire Place. She was only sixty years old and was buried in the cemetery of St Mary's Church in Goudhurst, the village where the Brook family was living. Only three years later, on 20 October 1939, John Brook himself died and was buried next to Florence. Upon Isabel's death on 6 August 1962, though she had moved to nearby Tunbridge Wells, she too was buried in Goudhurst cemetery next to her husband and sister.

Florence's legacy

In her will, executed just days before her departure for England, Florence left her entire estate (save for insurance policies amounting to about £10,000) divided equally between Jack and his sisters, Isobel and Poppy. The total value of the estate, comprising chiefly Deltroit, Billapalap and livestock, was given as £92,797, almost double what the estate was said to be worth on the death of William Richardson fifteen years before. This was in spite of the sale of most of Billapalap and the purchase of Riversdale for Harry. However, there were also large debts amounting to £59,590, which, proportionately to the value of the whole estate, indicated that indebtedness had risen from about half to two-thirds under Florence's stewardship, notwithstanding capital-raising exercises.

Deltroit was described in the probate valuation as being 'a very good property, well balanced for breeding, wool growing and fattening on the creek frontages'. Improvements were also noted as being in very good order, but the fencing was regarded as needing 'heavy and expensive reconditioning before long'. Rabbits and swampy areas were given as threats to the wellbeing of the property, if not properly managed. At this time, Deltroit comprised 7587 acres (approximately 6182 acres freehold and 1405 acres still held under conditional purchase) and its carrying capacity was estimated at 11,000 sheep.

Also included in the probate file was a valuation for Billapalap, by then comprising only 3277 acres of 'well-improved' and 'very good wool growing country', with a carrying capacity of about 3000 sheep. There were apparently no buildings left, and Billapalap employees were said to have been living on a neighbouring property. The only other real estate was some land at Kiandra in the foothills of the Snowy Mountains, valued at £150, and a leasehold block at Mundarlo of nominal value. The total number of Merino sheep given in the probate documents was 14,393 and of Shorthorn cattle, 560. Interestingly, no horses were mentioned except a few station hacks, draught mares and a stallion. It seems that either the polo ponies and racehorses had been sold by this time, probably in an effort by Florence to retrench and curb expenditure, or they had previously been transferred into Jack's name.

Jack takes over

It was this truncated and heavily mortgaged pastoral business, which had been in the same family for two generations and so carefully put together by William Richardson, that fell to Jack to manage. What his thoughts were on his inheritance is not known, but he was passionate about the land and was not afraid to make changes.[14] He was an innovator and instigated a program not only of land conservation and improvement, but also of genetic-based breeding, especially in his Shorthorn herd. However, he faced the same problem as his mother when her father, William, died. Jack was obliged to buy out his sisters, although this did not occur until some years after Jack had taken over.

The precise details and timing of these buyout arrangements is unclear, but Jack's youngest sister, Poppy, appears to have taken her share first. To raise the necessary capital, about 1800 acres at Deltroit was sold to the Horsleys,[15] consisting of roughly 1300 acres on the eastern side towards Mount Adrah and 500 acres on the road opposite the Junction Hotel. This reduced the size of Deltroit to just under 6000 acres. On the other hand, Isobel, who never married, received some of the income from Deltroit and

Deltroit Shorthorn crossing Hillas Creek, c. 1950

lived in Wagga Wagga, where she had a florist business. After the war, she moved back to Deltroit and lived in a cottage built for Jack and Dor when they were first married. This single-storey bungalow of timber was on the south side of the Adelong Road towards the Junction Hotel and a short walk from the back of the Deltroit garden. It was not until Deltroit was sold many years later that Isobel received a capital sum, which she used to purchase a large flat in Sydney.

Once again, the Larkins were left out of these asset divisions and, as late as 1945, Mary Elizabeth Larkin, one of Al Larkin's twin daughters, wrote to the Registrar of Probate requesting a copy each of Florence's will and that of Florence's mother, Mary Richardson. She would have been disappointed as the latter died intestate, and the former made no provision for nor mentioned any legacies in her will to any member of the Larkin family. Al

Isobel's cottage at Deltroit, c. 1950

was still working at Billapalap, by then in his early seventies, and appears to have been living with his second wife, Edith, his spinster sister, Emily, and those of his children who were unmarried. Their precise whereabouts are unknown, but it seems that the family were in accommodation nearby or in a cottage on the property erected after the subdivision. Al continued to work the remaining 3000 acres at Billapalap with his eldest son, Norman, until the property was sold in the mid-1940s.[16]

Jack's team

Cyril Crowe was still on the Fraser payroll when Jack inherited, but moved to Billapalap about this time. It seems he became overseer, but Al remained active there, the two men working very well together as a team along with Norman.[17] Soon afterwards, in 1939, Crowe lost his wife to cancer but remained at Billapalap until mid-1940, having sent his little daughter, Helen, to live with a maiden aunt. Crowe was a keen and effective rabbiter and at every spare moment went rabbiting on Billapalap, which was infested. It was said at one time that there were so many rabbit warrens on Billapalap that it was possible for these pests to cross from one end of the property to the other without ever going above ground.[18]

Crowe was a conscientious and hard worker on whom Jack relied heavily. He commanded wide respect and years later, after he had moved to Yass, was visited by the Horsley family whenever they drove past on their way from Sydney to Yabtree.[19] He nearly lost his life in a fierce bushfire in February 1940 that spread over 30 miles all the way from Tarcutta, south-east to Batlow and past Billapalap.[20] A total of 200,000 acres was destroyed in this disastrous and petrifying event. Bravely rounding up 1500 sheep on horseback into the yards, Crowe took cover under the table in his cottage and almost suffocated with the smoke that enveloped the house as the fire

Ken Galvin at
Deltroit, 2010

blazed all around.[21] His life was spared, but all the stock in the yards and thousands of other sheep, as well as several hundred head of cattle and horses, were burnt to a cinder.

Once Crowe was installed at Billapalap, Billy Simpson was promoted to overseer at Deltroit. Living with him and his wife, Sarah, in the Junction Hotel was their nephew, Ken Galvin, who had arrived at Deltroit as a six-year-old a short time prior to Florence's departure for England and her subsequent death. Galvin, who was born near Adelong, was a child of the Great Depression. His mother was dead and, through the effects of the economic collapse in the early 1930s, his father had lost his small property on Galvin's Creek granted to him as a soldier-settlement block after the First World War. Life was extremely tough for many years, and Galvin still recalls hundreds of swagmen, sometimes eighteen or more a day, walking along the old Great Southern Road looking for work in the days when he was a young boy. They would call in at the Junction Hotel, asking if there were any jobs to be had at Deltroit, and were always given something to eat, usually bread and jam, by Galvin's aunt and uncle.

Initially, Galvin attended the bush school at Mount Adrah, but when he was fifteen he became a station hand at Deltroit, despite his small build. As a child, he would fish yabbies out of the creek, which, in those days, ran continuously alongside the Junction Hotel, and eat them straight out of a pot of boiling water, sprinkled with salt. He trapped water rats in the Hillas Creek and sold their skins for a guinea to a man in Grahamstown, near Adelong, for ladies' fur coats. Galvin also recalls sleeping on the verandah in a sleep-out while Billy Wylds, an elderly, former hand who had worked for Florence and her father for fifty years, slept inside the hotel in one of the kitchens. Hawkers selling clothes and haberdashery regularly passed by with their waggonettes, including Jimmy Eliza, who was addicted to horseracing, and Inda Singh, an Indian with 'a white turban and face as black as night' who showed the young Galvin how to build a fire from a pyramid of sticks.

Life at Deltroit, however, was not all simple pleasures. The working day started at 7.30am, with an hour's break for lunch, and rarely finished before 6pm. If a man was working out on the boundaries of the property, he took his lunch — usually a meat sandwich with some pickles and a slice of cake or biscuit — in a saddle bag. All workers were expected to work five full days and a half day on Saturdays, though up until the 1920s work did not finish on Saturdays until 4pm. Simpson went every morning at 7am to the Frasers' bedroom door, which led out onto the homestead verandah, and sought his orders from Jack, who received him in his dressing gown.[22] Morning tea would have been brought to the Frasers shortly before, at 6.45am. The same reporting for duty and checking in for orders would occur at lunchtime, except that the meeting would take place at the homestead backdoor.

Jack was widely reputed to be a hard man to work for, but was nonetheless a man of integrity and vision. He was very serious, hated trivia and held strong opinions.[23] He was used to having everything his own way and on his own terms. He had a hot temper, even at school, and developed a reputation for sacking his workers at the drop of a hat.[24] Crowe and Simpson were the only two people who did not take Jack's outbursts literally. On occasion, Jack would ask Simpson where all the workers had gone and, on being reminded that he had sacked them all, Jack would ask Simpson to get them back. No doubt Jack lived under considerable pressure, carrying the weight of maintaining and developing what was left of his family's heritage, in spite of a very different rural economy to the one in which his grandfather had established Deltroit and Billapalap. The size of the indebtedness he had inherited must also have worried him. He is remembered by those who worked at Deltroit in this period as a troubled man who regularly found solace in good whiskey, of which he was very fond.

Jack's innovations

One of Jack's main objectives on taking over Deltroit and Billapalap was to build up a commercial Shorthorn herd of unrivalled quality. It is beyond dispute that this is precisely what he achieved, and the herd became known

in the cattle industry as the finest in Australia, probably even in the world. As one neighbour recalls,[25] the Shorthorn cattle that grazed on the rich lucerne flats at Deltroit were magnificent and he had never seen anything like them before. They were very broad across the hips, square and heavy with a rich roan colouring. Jack was very progressive in his approach to breeding[26] and worked hard on the Shorthorn genetic base, which he did by regularly purchasing all the best Shorthorn bulls at the Royal Sydney Show and using white bulls to cover red heifers to achieve his desired roan-coloured progeny. An excellent judge of cattle like his grandfather William, Jack built up a friendship with Simon Fraser, the fifteenth Baron Lovat[27] (known as 'Shimi'), a distinguished Scottish Shorthorn breeder who often came to Australia to select cattle for stud purposes.[28]

Jack always kept about fifteen bulls, running between thirty and forty females with each one and selling up to 100 young bulls per annum to stations in the Northern Territory.[29] In particular, he sold twenty bulls every year to Brunette Downs,[30] a famous property of over three million acres that remains one of the largest cattle stations in Australia. Having dramatically increased the Shorthorn numbers as well as their quality, there were, at any one time, between 450 and 500 breeding cows in a combined herd at both Deltroit and Billapalap of up to 1200 head.[31]

Although his chief interest were the Shorthorns, Jack also made improvements to his flock of Merino sheep, especially the fat lamb operation. For this part of the enterprise, he introduced cross-breeding,[32] joining Merino ewes first with Romney Marsh rams and then crossing their female progeny with Dorsets. Later, after the war, Jack was one of the first graziers to introduce a spray dip for sheep[33] instead of continuing with the awkward and traditional plunge system. The spray dip was an easier method

New spray dip at Deltroit, c. 1952

of handling stock as, once rounded up into the yard, the spray would go around them in a circle. The arrival of the new dip was quite an event in the locality, and there is even a photograph to commemorate its inauguration.

In addition to the fat lamb enterprise, the wool clip remained an important part of the overall income stream. The entire flock, including the sheep at Billapalap, were shorn in September or October in the large shearing shed at Deltroit. This early timber structure with an iron roof stood on the Adelong Road opposite the Deltroit homestead, but burnt down in the 1980s in obscure circumstances. It had about twenty stands, was wood-panelled inside and, in 1917, had been wired with electricity for machine shearing and lighting.[34] Shearers' quarters had been erected alongside the shed and may even have been a modification of the original Deltroit homestead that had been shifted there in 1903. Using horses and dogs, the sheep from Billapalap took two days to drove through Ellerslie and along the travelling stock route on the western side of the Yaven Yaven and Hillas creeks, all the way to Deltroit.[35] Shearing the mob, which under Jack's auspices grew to about 16,000 sheep, took up to four weeks, and there was a different contractor each year as Jack was difficult to please. Once baled, the

Hay baler demonstration at Deltroit, c. 1950

wool was transported to Tumblong by truck along the new Hume Highway on Deltroit's eastern boundary and then shipped to Sydney by rail.

Aside from his stock, Jack cherished the land on which they grazed, adopting many farming methods that were compatible with land conservation and improvement.[36] At Deltroit, he began to experiment with subterranean clover and other improved pastures, including phalaris, which he planted on the creek flats as well as on some of the lower hills behind. Lucerne was also grown along both sides of the creek and was cut and baled twice a year. In order to stem erosion, Jack adopted, prior to sowing, the contour ploughing method promoted by the Pastures Protection Board. All these initiatives had potential to greatly improve the existing grazing land, increasing the amount and nutritional value of the feed, provided that the paddocks were not overstocked. Later, and in addition to new varieties of pasture, Jack began the practice of spreading large amounts of superphosphate at Deltroit to further increase the carrying capacity of the land.

The Second World War

The implementation of some of these new ideas, particularly the planting of phalaris and the carrying out of contour ploughing, occurred after the Second World War in which Jack enlisted on 4 July 1940. Crowe was summoned back to Deltroit from Billapalap and managed both properties for the period that Jack was away. Simpson and his nephew, Galvin, were sent to Billapalap to replace Crowe and to help Al Larkin. Dor, rising to the occasion, took the place of a man in these difficult times[37] as young men available to work on the land became scarce. Three Italian Prisoners of War were assigned to Deltroit and lived in the shearers' quarters.[38] They were unpaid, receiving board and lodgings in return for work. Crowe, with his impeccable manners and consideration for others, was very kind to these displaced men who, in a gesture of appreciation, cooked spaghetti one evening for the Crowe family. Little Helen Crowe refused to eat it and has never forgotten the novelty of the dish. Although living with an aunt, she visited Deltroit regularly and would sometimes play with the slightly older Galvin in the garden of the Junction Hotel. It was a tight-knit community among the workers, and Crowe was especially good friends with Reg Whiting,[39] the overseer at Wallace Horsley's property, Gundillawah, on Deltroit's western boundary.

Dor Fraser mustering at Deltroit, c. 1940

During the war years, the women in the Hillas Creek district had a genuine fear of being invaded by the Japanese.[40] Dor and Isobel Fraser both had revolvers as protection, and planned with the Horsley women to take to the hills and fight a guerrilla war if need be. Fortunately, they were never in danger in any way, and, although Neville Horsley was tragically killed in the fighting abroad, the war passed relatively quietly for Dor and Isobel, with only limited food shortages and rationing. All the properties in the area (including Deltroit) had their own meat and homegrown fruit and vegetables, as well as milk and eggs. Sugar and clothing were the only things that were in short supply.

Jack returned from the war, having fought in North Africa. He was unharmed and came home in December 1942. He never spoke about his experiences to his family or friends and focused on his grazing pursuits, especially his Shorthorn cattle. Not long after the war was over, he sold in 1945 or 1946 what remained of Billapalap to Jack Mackay, who had a drapery business in Adelong. All the Shorthorn cattle and most of the sheep

Jack Fraser (centre) serving in the Second World War in North Africa

were moved to Deltroit, with some sheep sold, reducing the total flock to about 12,000.[41] It seems that about this time, Al Larkin, now in his eighties, moved to a retirement home. He had been employed in the Richardson and Fraser family operations ever since he was a young man and, in spite of his fondness for rum, had been widely respected and a rock on which they had all relied. He died in July 1949, aged eighty-four, in a nursing home in Young,[42] about 50 miles north of Deltroit. His unmarried sister, Emily, who is remembered by Jock Fraser as a regular visitor to Deltroit during the war, died on 7 June 1948 in a hospital in Sydney.

It is not clear what the reason was behind Jack's sale of Billapalap. Perhaps he wanted to concentrate on consolidating all his new initiatives at Deltroit, or maybe the sale was to settle death duties still outstanding on Florence's estate. Possibly, Jack simply needed to clear some of the debt inherited from his mother. He had also recently become a father, with the

birth of his and Dor's only child, Susanne ('Sue'), on 1 March 1944, which might also have caused the deep-thinking Jack to reflect on how best he might secure the future for his family.

A few staff changes occurred about this time, too. Simpson and Galvin returned to Deltroit from Billapalap, and Crowe moved on to a property of his own in the Bowning district near Yass. In 1947 he had remarried, choosing as his second wife a nursemaid from Yabtree, Thora Wright. She was briefly a cook at the Deltroit homestead and the couple subsequently had three children together.

After the war

Although the war changed society fundamentally, life at Deltroit was still very much as it had been before — comfortable and, for the most part, civilised. There was a full-time cook and a milk-kill gardener, responsible not just for the garden, but also for milking the cows kept for domestic needs and for killing sheep for mutton. The wives of various stockmen would also come regularly and work in the house.[43] There was, in addition, a governess for Sue, including a woman called Enid Keenan who was the longest incumbent of her post. Jack was not above becoming embroiled in arguments with domestic staff and, on one memorable occasion, had a fight with the cook's husband after she had upset Dor by her insolence and inferior cooking.[44] It appears that, on being twice summoned from the shearing shed to intervene between the women, Jack, in exasperation, took on the beefy Scotsman, who got the better of him.

The homestead itself seems not to have been altered since being built by William Richardson. The only changes made by Jack and Dor were that

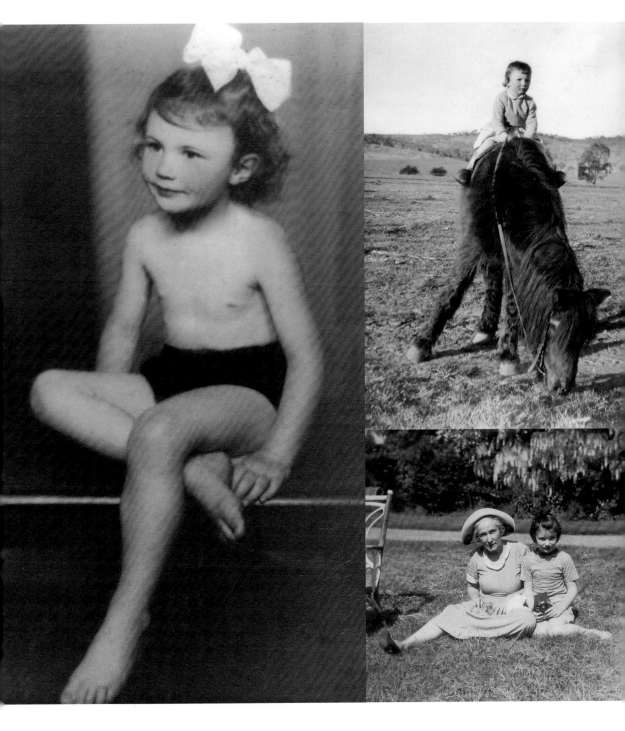

LEFT
Sue Fraser, c. 1948

RIGHT TOP
Sue Fraser on her pony
at Deltroit, c. 1946

RIGHT BOTTOM
Sue Fraser with governess
Enid Keenan in the garden at
Deltroit, c. 1952

Sue Fraser outside the main entrance of Deltroit House, c. 1946

they used the original drawing room as their main bedroom and moved the dining room (on the western side) to the room opposite that faced east into the morning sun. The old dining room then became a spacious sitting room. The servants' quarters were still at the far north end, but a small brick house (since demolished), erected by Florence between the homestead and the Coach House, was used as extra staff accommodation. Sue's bedroom was the small room next to the original main bedroom on the western side of the homestead, where a sleep-out for young visitors was created on the verandah. Large bookcases stood in the far south end of the hall, and stuffed deer heads with antlers that Dor allegedly hated[45] were hung outside on the eastern verandah so that she would not have to look at them.

Outside, the garden had matured and become a sylvan refuge, especially in summer. Not only had the elm trees planted by Charlie Fraser spread, but there were now also two huge deodar trees at the north end of the homestead and a shade garden with high ornamental arches under-planted

Billy Simpson on his favourite mare, Monaro

with hellebores.[46] On the south side of the house there was a shrubbery, including large viburnum bushes, and in the back garden, facing west, there were fragrant white cedars growing close to the house and a profusion of roses. The lawn on this side of the garden stretched to the paddock fence that stood on the homestead side of the small creek that ran a few feet from the tennis court and the orchard. The driveway, lined with an avenue of elm, was still in use and went all the way around the homestead to the front door. This entrance was now fringed by three magnificent wisterias (one white and two blue) that grew on a frame along the entire eastern side of the verandah. A deep herbaceous border ran along the far edge of the lawn opposite the front door and was divided by a steep flight of stone steps, flanked on each side by large urns that led down into a sunken garden paved with flagstones.

As for the outbuildings and surrounds, the Coach House had been modified to accommodate two cars and there remained a vegetable garden, meat house, fowl run and stables. Although Jack's polo playing days were over, more than a dozen stockhorses at Deltroit were kept for pleasure riding and stock work, as well as several ponies for Sue and two old draught horses.[47] They were grazed on the large paddock in front of the homestead and, each morning, the stockhorses were brought into the horse yards for the men to select which they would ride. Some men had their own horses but were allowed to keep no more than two. Simpson had a special mare called Monaro, with a coat that shone like copper and hindquarters that could spin on a sixpence. Even during his spare time, no man could ride any of the Deltroit horses without Jack's express permission.

Social life

While Jack was hard and sometimes acerbic, Dor had an altogether different personality. She was soft and gentle, with a great sense of fun.[48] One day, she invited the Horsley women to stand in the Deltroit kitchen under umbrellas to inspect her failed attempt at making jam in a pressure cooker that had exploded and sprayed the contents all over the kitchen walls and ceiling. Aside from being mischievous, Dor loved art, poetry and music, and regularly held square-dancing parties in the American fashion in the black- and white-tiled hallway of the homestead. Some heavy drinking took place at these parties, with Jack's sister Isobel being a notable culprit. Dor also enjoyed gardening, painting and, in later years, pottery. Although she was a competent rider, she rode little, and only in wartime did she become involved in the daily operations at either Deltroit or Billapalap. As Galvin recalls, Dor was 'one of the loveliest women you could ever meet both in her nature and in her appearance', a view shared by everyone who knew her.

Horses and racing were still a large part of life at Deltroit, and Jack had a couple of racehorses, including 'Mangoplah', that he owned with Ollie Cox, who was married to Ivy Horsley. Mangoplah, named after Cox's property near Wagga Wagga, was tipped one year to be a winner of the coveted Wagga Wagga Gold Cup. However, the famous jockey Athol Mulley, who had ridden the horse to victory in Sydney and Melbourne, pulled out at the last minute and rode another horse so that, in the end, Mangoplah was beaten. Sue remembers that this caused an enormous hullabaloo at home.

Sue Fraser with her dog, Sandy, swimming in Hillas Creek

The same horse often ran against Lach Horsley's Yabtree, and there was some good-natured rivalry between their owners.[49] Picnic races also continued to be big events in the social calendar, with everyone looking forward to them in the same way that weddings would be eagerly anticipated.

The close friendship between Jack and the Horsley brothers, now both married, remained strong; at one time, Jack would telephone Lach every evening for a chat after dinner. Ivy Horsley's husband, Ollie Cox, had also become a close friend of Jack's. He was flamboyant, charismatic and, like Jack, an excellent sportsman. Cox was also chairman of the Murrumbidgee Turf Club and loved horse-racing. In the 1950s, Cox began a liaison with the unmarried Isobel Fraser that went on for many years, causing a great deal of friction and family feeling. Sue remembers that she was not supposed to know about it, but she did. The affair also created some difficulties socially, as people felt they could not ask the Frasers and Lach Horsleys together, only one or the other. The rift was only repaired years later, after the Frasers sold Deltroit and went to live in Queensland.

Christmas was usually a time for family reunions. Harry Fraser, who had served in the war like Jack, rarely returned to Deltroit, having sold Riversdale in 1942 and moved his family to Mudgee. However, his sister, Poppy Weigall, and her three children, Joanna, Catherine and William, would visit from Dubbo and stay with Isobel in her cottage. Dor's sister, Diana, and her husband, Richard Eckersley, often came with their children, Simon and Ann, the former of whom vividly remembers playing 'Bobbies and Bushies' on horseback with his cousin Sue among some tall thistle growing on the Hillas Creek. There were also picnic and swimming excursions for which the draught horses and an old cart were used. Breakfasts, even in the heat of summer, were grand, with polished silverware on the sideboard and dishes laden with eggs, bacon and kidneys. The house was always cool because of the wide verandahs that prevented any sunlight

Jack Fraser fishing in the Snowy Mountains, c. 1955

penetrating and the additional frame that now held up the wisteria.

Every year after the war, there was a big Christmas party on the lawn in front of the homestead for Deltroit workers and other grazier families in the district, together with some of their employees. The highlight for the children was ice-cream brought in from Wagga Wagga in a large, green canvas container packed with dry ice. The smoke that rose out of this contraption added to the excitement of the occasion. For the workers especially, this annual party was much anticipated. A new pub had opened at Tarcutta in the late 1930s and there was occasionally some team sport, including cricket, played at Mundarlo and Deltroit,[50] but otherwise there was little for the workers to do in their free time apart from rabbiting and fishing.

After the war, there were many important visitors at Deltroit, including Dor's erudite brother, David Campbell, who had been to Jesus College, Cambridge, and played Rugby Union for England. More impressively, he had served in the Royal Australian Air Force during the war and earned a Distinguished Flying Cross. He would arrive at Deltroit driving a convertible sports car and wearing his Cambridge University scarf with élan.[51] His visits were always great fun, and he would make up limericks for the family and their friends. Another visitor of significance was Baron Lovat of Beaufort Castle in Inverness, whose herds not only of Shorthorn, but also of Angus, Galloway and Jersey, were widely admired.

Perhaps the most notable and eagerly anticipated visitor of all at Deltroit was Bob Kleberg, the owner of King Ranch in Texas. This organisation was, at the time, the largest privately-held beef-producing operation in the world and had pioneered a new breed of cattle, the Santa Gertrudis, by crossing Shorthorn cows with Brahman bulls. The Santa

Gertrudis were particularly suited to semi-arid or tropical conditions, and Kleberg had begun making overseas property investments to enable him to develop the breed further and extend his herds. In 1951, Kleberg introduced the Santa Gertrudis into Australia for the first time with the importation of several hundred head from his Texan ranch and the simultaneous purchase of Risdon Station in Queensland. During visits to Australia, Kleberg became a huge admirer of the Deltroit Shorthorns and, from the mid-1950s, regularly bought females from Jack for breeding purposes. In this way, a relationship began between the two men, which would ultimately change the destiny of Deltroit itself as well as the Fraser family.

Change on the horizon

Generally, the period from the mid-1940s to the mid-1950s was a good time in Australia to be on the land. For a change, wool prices and exports were climbing steadily towards an all-time high. In 1953, almost four million bales were sold at just under £405 million[52]. Similar figures were recorded in the next three years due to continuing demand from the UK and the USA and the re-emergence of Japan as a major wool buyer. The market for beef was also very positive, rising from a pre-war export value of about £10 million to £27 million by 1954. There were, of course, problems for all primary producers, such as a huge rise in the minimum wage, which affected production costs, and inefficient transport facilities.[53] Prolonged strikes in the wool industry among shearers had also become an issue. However, there was only one significant drought in 1957, with no other natural disasters, unless the rabbit plague could be counted as such. At Deltroit, family life was pleasant, including caravan holidays when Sue returned home from school at Frensham, where she was sent between 1956 and 1960. When Jack could spare the time, he loved to fish in the Snowy Mountains and to play golf. He still had a short fuse and characteristically fired his long-standing station hand, Ken Galvin, in 1957 after a trivial incident in the cattle yards.

However, in the late 1950s, wool prices plummeted due to the growing success of synthetics and the spread of agricultural protectionism in some of

Australia's key export markets. The prospects for beef were equally uncertain because of increased competition from countries such as Argentina. Graziers were receiving the same annual return as they had ten years earlier, but now had to meet costs estimated to have increased over 130 percent in the same period.[54] Clearly, these numbers adversely affected Jack's overall income and his ability to finance the borrowings over Deltroit that were still significant. He carried on for a few years, before asking his daughter, Sue, when she was only nineteen whether she could think of any compelling reasons not to sell up. She remembers feeling disappointed and angry with herself that she could not come up with any. Sue was on the threshold of adulthood and, although she had always had a vague idea of herself at Deltroit at a distant point in the future, she was not ready to settle there now. Unlike her grandmother, Florence, whom she never knew, she wanted to explore the world at that stage, rather than stay on the property.

Jack must have agonised over what he should do. Aside from the weight of family history at Deltroit and the fact that he had lived there all his life, anyone who has ever worked the land would understand the deep and intense connection Jack now had to the place. Nor was his ambition primarily to make money; he was more interested in the science of creating quality Shorthorn cattle and in nurturing the land. Nonetheless, he may have felt that, at sixty, he was getting too old to carry on doggedly and see through yet another downturn in the rural industry. He probably also recognised that he was lucky to have an obvious buyer hovering in the wings — Bob Kleberg of King Ranch. Sensibly, Jack agreed to sell Deltroit to him in 1963, bringing to a close almost thirty years of his own hard work, effort and innovation. The familiar cycle of land passing out of family hands in the third generation took place at Deltroit, as it had on so many other properties, despite Deltroit being one of the finest in the Riverina.

Once the deal with Kleberg was struck, the Corbett family at Billapalap became the only members of the Richardson clan still remaining on the original family landholdings in the area. Even so, they were not direct descendants of either William or John Richardson (joint owners of Billapalap) but of Thomas Richardson, the eldest brother. One of his daughters, Louisa, had married Edward Corbett, and the couple had purchased their block from Florence Fraser (Louisa's first cousin) when Billapalap was broken up in the 1930s. In short, the strategy begun by William Richardson of increasing borrowings to maintain the grazing enterprise had ultimately proved fatal to the retention of the business, notwithstanding the increase in land prices and some extremely good market conditions for both meat and wool. The capital increase, however, on the original investment would have been enormous and no doubt of some considerable comfort to Jack in this difficult transition.

Shorthorn grazing winter crop at Deltroit, 2009

CHAPTER 15

Contemporary Deltroit

$\mathcal{B}$ob Kleberg of King Ranch, the new owner of Deltroit, had coveted Jack Fraser's Shorthorn herd for many years. In his own words:

> [T]hat herd compared favourably with the best Shorthorn cattle I ever saw, England, Argentina, United States, anywhere! [...] I was busy looking all over Australia, trying to acquire the very best Shorthorn heifers and cows that could be purchased, for joining with Santa Gertrudis bulls. I really did want the Frazier [*sic*] Shorthorns! To get them, I bought the entire 6,000 acre Deltroit freehold and improvements, 450 purebred Shorthorn cows and about 10,000 sheep that were on the place.[1]

Key among the reasons for Kleberg's purchase of Deltroit were also the pasture renovations that Jack had carried out, his artful[2] conservation of the land and, last but not least, the beautiful lucerne flats along the Hillas Creek. The lucerne hay that could be cut twice a year at Deltroit was of particular interest to Kleberg since, parallel to his cattle breeding operations, he had a Quarter Horse stud that he was developing at Milton Park, the King Ranch Australian headquarters, situated in Bowral, just south-west of Sydney. It was here, on about 3000 acres of rolling countryside, that Kleberg bred superior Quarter Horses both for sale and for use on his larger Australian properties. After the purchase of Deltroit, some of the rich lucerne would be sent down to Milton Park[3] as feed for the horses and the Santa Gertrudis cattle that Kleberg was always improving.

Out of family hands

Precisely when and how Kleberg and Jack first came to meet is not known, but it was doubtless through their connections in the cattle industry. Through word of mouth, Kleberg would have become aware of Jack's reputation for always buying the best Shorthorn bulls at the Sydney Royal Show and for having the highest-quality commercial Shorthorn herd in the country. Moreover, breeders knew that Kleberg was on the lookout for top-quality Shorthorn, and both Kleberg and Jack were friends with the extremely charming and debonair Scottish Baron, Lord Lovat, himself a Shorthorn breeder. Indeed, Kleberg counted Lovat, who visited Australia regularly from his home at Beaufort Castle in Inverness, as among his closest friends,[4] and the introduction could easily have come through him.

Kleberg and Jack had a great deal in common and it is not hard to imagine the two men getting along famously. Both had inherited their properties, which had been established by their respective grandfathers. They understood not just the pressures of business, but also the responsibility that came with family inheritance. Neither was given to pretence, but were serious cattlemen striving for excellence in their livestock operations. Both men were fond of whiskey,[5] but neither man allowed alcohol to affect his performance. Instead, they both used it to retreat for a few hours at a time from the myriad of decisions affecting their properties or the welfare of their families. Kleberg, like Jack, had only one child — a daughter whom he treasured — and, by a bizarre coincidence, had also married a woman with the maiden name of Campbell! With so much in common, it was no wonder that Jack felt comfortable selling Deltroit to Kleberg, whom he no doubt trusted to perpetuate his life's work. Having done all he could to ensure a future for his cherished Shorthorns and his land, Jack moved with his wife, initially to Sydney and then to Queensland, where he lived until his death in 1977.

A new corporate era

By the time that he purchased Deltroit, Kleberg had established a considerable empire in Australia as well as in other parts of the world beyond Texas. In all cases of foreign investment, his strategy was to go into partnership with successful local businessmen and pastoralists and to use them to run his operations. Forming a partnership with three very able Australians — Sir Rupert Clarke, a pastoralist and investment banker; Peter Baillieu, a property manager and grandson of W. S. Robinson (at that time Australia's most successful entrepreneur and businessman); and Sam Hordern, a leading agriculturalist — Kleberg established a solid management team to look after his interests.

Aside from his first Australian venture, Risdon Station, bought in 1951, Kleberg had purchased three further commercial and fattening properties in eastern Queensland — Elgin Downs, New Twin Hills and Avon Downs — with an aggregate of 600,000 acres. The icing on the cake, however, was the purchase in 1959 of the iconic three-million-acre Brunette Downs in the Northern Territory, where Jack had been supplying young bulls for many years. By all accounts, the Shorthorn herd at Brunette Downs was very leggy and the Deltroit bulls were being used to improve the stock to a more beefy conformation.[6] Once purchased by King Ranch, Brunette Downs was restocked using Santa Gertrudis bulls over the Shorthorn females.[7] With these acquisitions, King Ranch demonstrated great faith in the future of the Australian beef industry, and it was into this extensive portfolio of six other Australian properties (including Milton Park) that Deltroit was absorbed in 1963. Together, these holdings became the largest overseas investments made by King Ranch and the laurel wreath that crowned Kleberg's latter years.[8]

Now part of a huge beef-producing operation that stretched from Australia to the United States and beyond, Deltroit entered a period of corporate ownership. The loyal overseer Billy Simpson, who had served the Fraser family for forty years, stayed on for about six months during a handover period to Brian Bennett, the first manager under King Ranch. Bennett maintains that while the Shorthorn herd were exceptional, Deltroit had become rundown in the last years of Jack's ownership. There was an

infestation of thistle in some of the paddocks, which needed clearing before being sown with phalaris, clover and rye grass to prevent this problem recurring. Large amounts of superphosphate were spread, as in Jack's day, in order to maximise the productivity of the pastures. The entire flock of sheep was sold, save for a few hundred wethers. These were fattened over twelve months and shorn in the Deltroit shearing shed, which was by now quite dilapidated, having seen hundreds of thousands of sheep pass through its stands.

Bennett was succeeded after two years by George Crouch, a well-known property manager in the Riverina who had carried out the original inspection of Deltroit with Kleberg before the purchase was finalised.[9] Subsequently, Crouch became the pastoral supervisor for King Ranch based at Milton Park, with overall responsibility for all their properties in Australia. Upon Crouch leaving Deltroit, Geoff Schmidt took over as manager between 1967 and 1971. Schmidt confirms that Kleberg's main interest in Deltroit was to upgrade his Santa Gertrudis cattle by using the outstanding Shorthorn females bred by Jack. In conjunction with a natural breeding program, some Deltroit cows were artificially inseminated with semen taken from Santa Gertrudis bulls based at Milton Park. Gradually, the Shorthorn numbers were increased from 450 to about 800 or 900 breeding cows, and the remaining sheep were sold. As anticipated by Kleberg, Deltroit proved to be an ideal base for the development of the Santa Gertrudis, which, for a time, became the top-ranking breed in Australia.

Apart from a dry period in 1968, the seasons were favourable in the initial years of King Ranch ownership and, instead of scarcity of feed being a problem, the main issue was that the pasture, especially the phalaris, could sometimes be too rich. This problem was overcome by feeding a magnesium supplement to the cattle in powder form sprinkled on lucerne hay. Although a fairly labour-intensive exercise, there was a team of four full-time men, including Schmidt, employed on Deltroit in this period. While there were some vehicles on the property, stock work was mostly done on horses supplied by Milton Park.

After Geoff Schmidt and his wife, Janet, left to manage Winderadeen, a property near Yass, Peter Stuart Fox was appointed manager. He and his wife, Patricia, lived in the Deltroit homestead as their predecessors had done. Although the structure of the house was still sound, it had already needed updating by the time the Frasers left. Only the bare minimum of work was carried out by King Ranch, and, although the managers and their families did all they could to care for it, the homestead lacked the proper maintenance that it really deserved.

Stuart Fox managed Deltroit from 1971 to 1978, during which time the cattle yards were upgraded and the program of pasture improvement continued, largely with the spreading of yet more superphosphate. The practice of growing and cutting lucerne on the creek flats for use at Deltroit and Milton Park was also carried on as before. To further enhance the Santa Gertrudis, four additional Shorthorn bloodlines from various places, including Eringoarrah at nearby Wantabadgery, were introduced at Deltroit. As an experiment, some Shorthorn cows were crossed with Brahman bulls and the female progeny was then covered by purebred Santa Gertrudis.

During this era, there were several dry years when cattle had to be sent north to one of the King Ranch properties as there was insufficient feed at Deltroit. Then, in 1974, there was a very wet winter and the whole Gundagai district was seriously flooded all the way to Mundarlo and Hillas Creek. Just east of the Deltroit homestead, a bridge that had been erected by King Ranch over the creek a few years earlier in order to join the two halves of the property was almost washed away. The bridge was subsequently moved about a kilometre further up the creek, where the banks were steeper and the crossing wider.

The end of Kleberg's reign

A couple of months after the flood, Kleberg died in Texas, having suffered a short illness. With the loss of such a highly driven and tenacious president and the competing claims of his extended family, some of the King Ranch properties were liquidated and their management structure dismantled. In particular, the Australian property holdings, though probably King Ranch's most promising assets,[10] were sold, Deltroit being among the first to go in 1978. The sale to livestock carrier Finemores and its partner, Mango Pastoral Company, a livestock trader in which Finemores also had a stake, was popularly regarded as a steal at $138 an acre.

The new owners sold the remaining cattle and used Deltroit largely for fattening sheep destined for both the domestic and overseas markets. At any one time, sheep numbers were as high as 26,000 on the property, but most were only there for a few weeks before being sold.[11] Nonetheless, Deltroit began to look rundown or 'flogged' with the grazing of such a large mob, especially as 1978 was another year of below-average rainfall. The former King Ranch manager, Stuart Fox, continued working at Deltroit for a few months and living in the homestead before he himself moved on, whereupon a new manager was installed in Isobel Fraser's former cottage.

Finemores and Mango Pastoral held Deltroit for only one year. In that short time, the general verdict in the district was that the property became overgrazed and that no attention was paid to the maintenance of pastures. In fact, the reverse is true; the new owners had begun an accepted program of pasture renovation that was cut short by the unexpected break-up of their partnership. When the two partners had bought Deltroit in 1978, the property had already been suffering for several years, both from lack of direction since Kleberg's death and a reduced budget imposed by his heirs. Finemores and Mango Pastoral implemented a widely recognised method of pasture improvement through 'chewing out' the paddocks, extensive spraying and the planting of 2100 acres of grain, mainly wheat but also some oats.[12]

When these measures were not immediately succeeded by the sowing of new pastures and the spreading of superphosphate, they left the impression that little or no care had been given to the health of the land, which looked to have been utterly spoiled. Moreover, it seems that in the intervening period before a new buyer was found, weeds of every kind took hold on the bare ground and the homestead stood empty and forlorn. William Richardson and his grandson Jack Fraser would doubtless have wept at the aspect of neglect that Deltroit wore in this period.

The Barr-Smiths

Fortunately, in early 1979, Deltroit fell into private hands again. Tom Barr-Smith, from a well-established rural family in Adelaide, purchased the property and it became a family home for himself, his wife Jenny, and their children. A manager, John Fuller, was appointed to resume the program of pasture maintenance and improvement after this had been interrupted by the change of owners. A Shorthorn herd was re-established using Bundaleer bloodlines from South Australia, and a flock of fine wool Merino sheep was introduced. The old woolshed, which was by now almost a wreck, burnt down and was replaced with a new, bonded structure.

Probably the Barr-Smiths' most lasting contribution to Deltroit was their imaginative renovation of the homestead and garden, both of which had been sadly neglected. Retaining all the marble fireplaces, the stained-glass windows, the elaborate cornicing and all but one of the pressed metal ceilings, they repaired and redecorated the whole of the inside of the homestead and built an extension at the north end, incorporating the former servants' quarters that became the kitchen and main entrance. A separate sitting room, which led into the new kitchen, was also built across the northern side of the house. Sadly, the memorable black- and white-tiled hallway with the name 'Deltroit' spelled across its width had to be taken up as, by that point, the tiles were broken and chipped.

In the garden, a huge amount of clearing was necessary. The Frasers' sunken garden had already disappeared, a casualty of the King Ranch era, and the tennis court was hidden among the undergrowth. The wisteria on its frame was still intact and retained but has since been taken down to encourage more light into the house. One of the most beautiful garden features for which the Barr-Smiths' were responsible is the large dam that they created in the horse paddock below the eastern side of the house, in front of the original entrance. Today, this is surrounded by poplar, willow and cana lilies, providing a sanctuary for a variety of birds and a nesting ground for the small snake-necked turtles found in the Hillas Creek.

Stockhorse beneath
ancient river red
gums by Hillas
Creek at Deltroit

Anthony Crichton-Brown

In 1990, the Barr-Smiths sold Deltroit to my husband, Anthony Crichton-Brown, an Australian businessman then living and working in London. Extremely driven and highly successful, Anthony was, at the age of forty-seven, Chief Executive of the Lumley Insurance Group, one of only three privately-owned insurance underwriting companies left in the world. He had worked for the Lumley Group since his early twenties, starting off as a clerk selling property and casualty insurance in Australia. Working his way to the top of the Lumley Group, Anthony gained a wide experience of business. He became not only very familiar with the management of risk, but also with the management of people. He does admit, however, that risk management in the insurance industry is 'a picnic' compared to that of the Australian agribusiness, where unpredictable weather patterns, markets, animal disease, fire and vermin, can nullify in a single event, all other projections.

Anthony's father, Sir Robert Crichton-Brown, was doubtless a role model for his son, who still refers to him affectionately as 'Boss'. A former Honorary Treasurer of the Australian Liberal Party, Sir Robert held, from the 1950s onwards, various important executive and non-executive positions in industry and commerce in Australia and the UK, including being Chairman of The Commercial Banking Company of Sydney,

Vice Chairman of National Australia Bank and Executive Chairman of Rothmans International. He had an entrepreneurial flair, having established a whaling operation at Moreton Island in Queensland just after the Second World War, before such things became outlawed. Unlike many fathers in his position, he was able to motivate Anthony to succeed on his own merits.

Aside from being a clever businessman, Anthony was and still is an action man, counting among his many passions flying fixed-wing aircraft, ocean racing and polo. Together with his father, Anthony was part of the winning crew in the Sydney to Hobart Ocean Yacht Race in 1970, an annual event in which Anthony competed on many occasions. He was also a member of the victorious Australian team that won the Admiral's Cup in the UK in 1967. An amateur polo player both in Australia, where he grew up, and later in the UK, he became Vice Chairman of Guards Polo Club in Windsor Great Park in 2000. Upon his retirement from this position in 2005, Anthony was described by Lord Patrick Beresford, in an article written for the club magazine, as being 'remembered for his impeccable manners, modesty, sportsmanship and affection for his ponies' and 'an inspiration to us all'.

Anthony
Crichton-Brown
at Deltroit, 2011

Prior to purchasing Deltroit, Anthony had little experience of farming, other than spending time as a boy, when home from boarding school at Tudor House and then Geelong Grammar, on the small family holding, Woodbury Farm, at Bowral near Sydney. Far from being a rural-based family, Anthony's parents used the farm as a weekend and occasional holiday retreat. In fact, Anthony's father was so concerned that his son might favour a life on the land over what he perceived to be a more lucrative and satisfactory one in the city that he sold Woodbury Farm in 1973. Thus encouraging his son to pursue a city career, Anthony was later able to bring to Deltroit a perspective gained from being in the 'cut and thrust' of the wider business community, not simply from being born into the rural scene.

A new challenge

Married firstly to Edwina Sparke-Davies, with whom he had three children, Samantha, Georgina and Matthew, Anthony and his family lived in Sydney before moving to the UK in 1987. Anthony purchased Deltroit three years later, but, being an absentee owner, he appointed a full-time manager, Jeff Chalmers from Wagga Wagga. Chalmers and his wife, Wendy, along with their three children, came to live in the old cottage that had been the home of Isobel Fraser. Over the next fifteen years, various overseers were also employed, each accommodated in the former Junction Hotel. There was also a series of young station hands and jackaroos, including Dave McMahon from the Adelong district who lived mainly in the jackaroos' quarters by the manager's cottage.

Anthony took on Deltroit with his usual energy and zeal, determined to create and maintain a property of the highest standards. He authorised Chalmers to implement an extensive program of improvements, both in terms of infrastructure and pasture renovation. New yards, laneways and fences were put in at considerable cost, and over 130,000 trees were planted, including a potentially valuable ironbark plantation. In addition, a new four-bedroom manager's residence was built in place of Isobel Fraser's former home. A local agronomist, Mark Lucas, was regularly consulted to advise on pasture improvement, which included the sowing of perennial pastures and lucerne as well as various winter crops. Additionally, he recommended up-to-date grazing techniques to protect the new pasture renovations. A livestock consultant, Ross Jelbart from Wagga Wagga, also regularly visited to discuss potential livestock sales and purchases and to keep an eye on livestock condition.

A breeding herd of high-quality Shorthorn was built up using bloodlines supplied chiefly by Gerald Spry, a well-known local stud breeder based in Mangoplah near Wagga Wagga. Spry had a reputation unrivalled in the district for the best Shorthorn genetics, which Anthony used to create a Shorthorn herd of about 500 breeding cows. In addition, a fat lamb and wool operation of about 3000 breeding ewes was introduced using fine wool Merino crossed with Dorset and Dohne rams. Every March, the sheep were shorn over a period of about ten days in the new Deltroit shearing shed put up by the Barr-Smiths. While all this was being achieved at considerable expense, Anthony and his family continued to live full-time in the UK, where he had become Chief Executive of Lumleys (later also becoming Chairman). With this big job, Anthony managed to visit Deltroit only a

Inspecting crops at Deltroit, December 2010. From left: Mark Lucas, Dave McMahon, Jack Byrnes.

couple of times a year for a few days at a time, in between Lumley Board meetings in Australia and New Zealand. Notwithstanding his absentee status, Anthony was always very closely involved with Deltroit's management and development.

All the time that he was in the insurance industry, Anthony hankered after a life in the great outdoors. His second daughter, Georgina, had returned to Australia, where in a quirk of fate she not only married Angus Campbell, the great nephew of Dor Fraser, but was also living on a property, Redmire, near the small New South Wales town of Taralga that 150 years before had been the childhood home of William Richardson's wife, Mary. Partly inspired by his daughter's experience and partly out of a heartfelt passion for the land that he owned on Hillas Creek, Anthony himself began to spend more time at Deltroit.

Anthony's thirty-year marriage to Edwina was dissolved early in the year 2000, whereupon he and I were married a short time later. Then, after almost six years of splitting our time between London and Deltroit, we came with our five-year-old daughter, Antonia, to live here permanently in April 2006. Once resident at Deltroit full-time, Anthony naturally wished to be

Deltroit team, March 2010. From left: Anthony Crichton-Brown, Brett Maher, Dave McMahon, Romain Devaud and Peter Webb.

more 'hands on' than his previous absentee status had permitted. He and Chalmers agreed to part company and Chalmers, who had worked hard and with great loyalty at Deltroit for seventeen years, left in July 2007, taking up another managerial position on a property not far from Gundagai. Anthony kept on the highly committed and responsible team then in place of station hand Dave McMahon, whom he promoted to overseer; Romain Devaud, a station hand from New Caledonia; and Brett Maher from the Adelong district, who had chief responsibility for the large homestead garden and its surrounds, but who spent increasing amounts of time on water supply and other maintenance issues on the property.

A drought beyond all others

Our time at Deltroit to date has been characterised by the worst drought in New South Wales since the Federation Drought of 1895 to 1903. Beginning around the middle of 2001 but not showing its teeth until late 2002, this extensive and gruelling period of well-below-average annual rainfall continued almost unabated until October 2010. Three times, the usually reliable Hillas Creek ran dry during the summer months, initially for six weeks in January 2008 and then for similar periods in 2009 and 2010. Large holes were dug in the sandy creek bed using the property's front-end loader in an attempt to find water for stock. An existing bore on the creek operated by a windmill, close to the cattle crossing and where the original Deltroit bridge had once been, also dried up, and it was necessary to drill three more bores in search of underground water on the south side of the property, among the hills. The large lake in front of the homestead all but disappeared, and the garden could not be watered while the creek was either very low or completely dry. Water in the homestead was brown and bitter from lying at the bottom of the tank, collecting dust and leaves. It was strictly rationed and we came very close to purchasing water for domestic use.

In the summer months during this period, it was once so fiercely hot that the top blew off the thermometer on the back verandah, where the temperature rose over 50 degrees Celsius in the western sun. Day in, day

Last remaining
sheep being
mustered along
Deltroit Road,
2008

out, the air was thick and heavy, with an eerie stillness that warned of danger. The possibility of fire was a constant worry, and working outside in what felt like a giant furnace was a debilitating and truly humbling experience. Occasionally, massive storm clouds would gather in the late afternoon sky that rumbled loudly with thunder and flashed menacingly with lightning, but all too often only a few millimetres of rain would fall, encouraging thousands of ants and tiny black flies to swarm in the sultry air. On the worst days in summer, hot winds from the north-west would blow unrelenting across the property, turning the outdoor furnace into a fan oven. Kicking up dust and pollen, stripping leaves from the trees hanging limp with thirst, and parching the dry, brittle landscape further, the winds were a frightening addition to the existing fire danger. Anyone who has lived in Australia through this kind of climatic phenomenon is unlikely to ever forget it.

The modern Deltroit woolshed and sheep yards, 2008

Anthony and I sometimes wondered what we had done, leaving not just the city, but also the temperate climate of England, behind us. Although the homestead was by then fully air-conditioned, having been modernised and renovated further in 2000 (enlisting the services of the outstanding builder from Wagga Wagga, Mick Baker), this was of little benefit when so much activity was necessarily outside. Moreover, just the sight from the windows of the brown, dusty paddocks littered with dead timber and stock lying exhausted in the stifling shade was enough to make anyone feel defeated by the heat. Even the large new swimming pool along the southern side of the homestead provided no relief in these conditions, being almost as warm as the outside air temperature. In those long, drought-afflicted summers, it seemed as if modern Deltroit had become as much a test of endurance for its occupants as it had ever been for the early settlers in the district, including William Richardson and his family.

Cattle crossing Hillas Creek during drought, 2008

Our lifestyle today

Antonia Crichton-Brown with her dog, Pirate

Once the weather cooled down, however, family life at Deltroit was pleasant, though isolated and sometimes monotonous compared to what we had been used to in London. Until very recently, we did not leave the property regularly for weekends in Sydney or Melbourne, as many people expected us to do. Aside from biannual visits to London, usually of about a month at a time, we stayed at Deltroit as much as possible to build a life there for ourselves and our daughter. We went horse-riding and mustering together, read history books aloud at the dinner table, played the piano and listened to the radio, challenged each other to games of tennis, cricket and billiards and, at the weekends, watched DVDs and TV costume dramas when there were no house guests to enliven the company. However, now that Antonia has gone away to school in Sydney, the pattern of our lives has begun to change.

Antonia commenced her schooling at a London preparatory school before making the transition firstly to St Patrick's, the private Catholic school in Gundagai, and then, after two years, to the state school, Gundagai Public. Since July 2011, she has been a pupil at Ascham in Sydney, where she is now a boarder. Prior to this latest move, Antonia became involved in many sporting activities in the district and rode every year in the annual agricultural shows at both Gundagai and Adelong. Such occasions continue to draw the community at Hillas Creek and the surrounding area together, but generally there are now fewer social activities in the locality for interaction with neighbours.

Not only have the lives of graziers become busier on the land, as properties can no longer sustain the size of workforce that they once did, but their 'off-farm' interests and social life are growing increasingly spread out now that Sydney and Melbourne are only four or five hours' drive away or a one-hour flight from Wagga Wagga. Nevertheless, there are still several notable occasions when the locals meet, including the Wagga Wagga

View over lake towards Deltroit homestead, 2011

Picnic Races, the annual Mundarlo Fire Brigade dinner, Easter Sunday and Christmas Eve at Mundarlo Church followed by refreshments at the Austins' Mundarlo homestead, New Year's Eve drinks by the river at Yabtree arranged by Fred and Noella Horsley, and occasional but legendary woolshed parties hosted by Ian and Fiona Horsley at Gundillawah.

Holistic management

Living 'above the shop', Anthony always spends a good proportion of his time working, rising early and retiring late, whether during the week or over the weekend. There is always stock or water to check, or research, planning and budgeting to do on the computer. The drought was a turning point for Anthony in the running of Deltroit, which had been managed by Chalmers using a grazing method known as 'set stocking'. Grazing methods are critical in the efficient management of both pastures and livestock, maximising the utilisation of grasses and animal performance as well as ensuring optimum plant regeneration. Under set stocking practices, animals are grazed in small mobs but left in one place for prolonged periods, allowing them to select certain plants over others. The stock is only moved on an ad hoc basis, and the paddocks, if they are large but not numerous, often receive little or no rest, which, in the case of perennial pastures especially, reduces their longevity and productivity as the density of vegetation declines.

At Deltroit, set stocking over the years had resulted in some excellent livestock performance, but had also denuded the perennial pastures of their most nutritious feed. Being in their paddocks indefinitely, the animals had sufficient time to graze selectively on the most palatable and high-quality plants. During the years of drought, when the area's average annual rainfall of 650 millimetres (26 inches) was not met, scarcity of feed was exacerbated by the set stocking method that had been employed. By early 2003, it became a common sight at Deltroit to see the cattle and sheep being fed hay and silage three times a week because there was not enough grass in the paddocks. This sorry state of affairs persisted until 2008, resulting in huge additional feed costs — much of which, in hindsight, could have been avoided by selling stock or sending them away on agistment. As is so often the case in the pastoral industry, we bet the wrong way on the weather breaking and it became too late to implement any other measures.

Instead, Anthony became interested in a relatively new approach to farming: holistic management, a method that was proving particularly successful in drier regions around the world. Increasingly aware that, at Deltroit, set stocking prevented pasture regeneration, Anthony sought advice from Bruce Ward, a former farmer turned environmental educationalist based in Sydney, who was building up an holistic management client base near Holbrook, 100 kilometres south towards Melbourne. There, Ward's ideas, many of which were originally developed by Zimbabwean biologist and farmer Allan Savory, had been put into practice with some spectacular results in terms of pasture regeneration, soil health and livestock performance.

Broadly, Ward advocated a planned grazing system in which stock are grazed in much larger mobs, usually for short periods in a number of paddocks. Animals are moved frequently onto fresh pasture in a clear grazing pattern that gives them less time to over-select. This helps prevent the destruction of the more nutritious plants, while also giving the pasture more time to regenerate than with a set stocking system. Additionally, the manure and trampling effect of so many animals in such an intensive environment encourages a faster, more vigorous re-growth of pasture that has only been lightly grazed, instead of decimated by too prolonged an exposure. With the promotion of greater ground cover, more sunlight is harvested by the plants through photosynthesis, more moisture is retained in the soil, and there is more biodiversity. The corollary of this is also that there is less soil erosion and salinity.

Inevitably, the sheep at Deltroit were the first casualty of this new approach. Since they are more liable than cattle to eat any remaining pasture closer to ground level, where feed is scarce, they therefore slow the recovery time of the plants. The entire flock of 2000 sheep was sold in 2008 and, until mid-2010, sheep were not to reappear at Deltroit and even then only in small numbers as agistment stock belonging to other graziers. In this way, sheep numbers could be more easily controlled than having a permanent mob on the property.

Large and regular stock movements have become a feature of life at Deltroit, cattle sometimes being moved several times a week in accordance with a graze plan. This takes into account an estimate of the grass available on entry, the daily consumption per animal, the desirable amount of grass to remain in the paddock on departure and the prevailing season. All these factors are relevant in maximising the chance of proper and speedy regrowth once the paddock is vacated. With a large number of paddocks, plenty of laneways all around the property and a well-established cattle crossing over the creek, Deltroit is well organised for these frequent stock movements.

Shorthorn and Angus cattle grazing perennial pasture at Deltroit, 2010

Expanding the enterprise

By the time that the new holistic management program was implemented, Deltroit had become part of a growing pastoral business known as Coolong Pastoral. Partly as a response to the drought and partly to achieve economies of scale, Anthony had purchased another property, Humula Station, 40 kilometres to the south of Deltroit, in December 2006. History was repeating itself in that the Richardsons had also been compelled to purchase Billapalap for the same reasons. Humula, however, was much smaller, being only 2500 acres of undulating pasture, but in a higher rainfall area than Deltroit and on a permanent waterway, the Umbango Creek. Here, Anthony established an Angus cattle-breeding operation of about 500 head, following the market trend towards this breed. In 2007, Anthony created an Angus herd of 500 breeders at Deltroit, in addition to the existing Shorthorn, and began an Angus–Shorthorn cross-breeding venture using stock from Humula. This resulted in a higher livestock performance than that achieved with purebred cattle due to the hybrid vigour of the combined breeds.

The grazing methods advocated by the holistic management system were also implemented at Humula. The station hand at Deltroit, Romain Devaud, was promoted to overseer at Humula, where he went to live full-time in a small cottage. Substantial improvements were carried out, including the erection of new cattle yards and the planting of more trees. The Humula homestead, which was an earlier but much more modest building than the one at Deltroit, had undergone a large number of alterations and was in good condition. By a coincidence that further illustrates the small, entrenched community in the area, Peter Webb, who was a great nephew of Cyril Crowe, the former overseer at Deltroit for two generations of Frasers, undertook to live in the Humula homestead as caretaker with his wife, Judy.

In March 2010, Anthony bought Toronga Station near Hay, comprising 85,000 acres of vast, open and almost treeless Riverina plains. Roughly 400 kilometres west of Deltroit, the land was so flat that it was possible to see the curvature of the earth on a clear day. Unlike most of Deltroit, the pasture was neither thick and varied nor spread like a carpet, but patchy and uneven, with saltbush and a short understorey of native grass predominating. However, the property had access to the Murrumbidgee River and some 8500 acres of prepared irrigation country, meaning that a variety of crops could be grown. In owning Deltroit, Humula and Toronga — each of which has a different rainfall and seasonal profile yet is located within reasonable proximity to the others — Anthony's strategy was to establish a more diversified agribusiness with scale economies derived from the combined utilisation of labour, machinery and pasture, together with the flexibility to 'finish' young stock on the eastern Riverina country that enjoyed a higher rainfall.

As Australia, along with the rest of the world, was mired in the global financial crisis and traditional safe havens for investors, including residential property and even bank deposits, became uncertain, Anthony saw investing in agricultural land as a sensible option, especially if it provided more scale and diversity within his existing business. Anthony kept on the full-time manager at Toronga, Jack Byrnes, and put him in charge of the overall Coolong Pastoral business. Toronga became a breeding station for the purebred Angus and crossbred cows as well as home to a flock of Dorper sheep, a high-fertility, easy-to-manage breed that is used for meat and thrives on the type of pasture predominating on the Hay plains. Additionally, Anthony maintained a rice-growing operation at Toronga utilising the water resources that he now had available.

A land of flooding rains

The year 2010, which saw the purchase of Toronga, began as unbearably hot and dry, identical to the previous nine years. In February, however, the weather changed suddenly, and at Deltroit alone there were 103 millimetres of rain — well above the monthly average of 40 millimetres. In a turnaround over the next seven months that none of the locals could really believe, rain fell steadily in the whole area, exceeding its average in every month except June. The 420 millimetres of rain that fell at Deltroit by October that year was still 164 millimetres short of the annual average. Nevertheless, the water table had risen to such an extent that when another 142 millimetres fell in just four days (14–17 October), the Hillas Creek rose more than six metres with alarming speed, bursting its banks and ripping through Deltroit as it gushed with mighty force into the Murrumbidgee River.

Submerging some of the creek flats in over a metre of water, the flood at Deltroit and along the Hillas Creek valley was probably the biggest since white settlement in that area and dramatically changed the predicament of the previous nine years. The Hillas Creek, which had suddenly become a swirling torrent of muddy water as treacherous as any stormy sea, washed away the Deltroit bridge and several metres of creek frontage. Fortunately, due to quick work by Anthony and his team, assisted by Ian Hardy, a friend from Holbrook, who happened to be driving by, there were no stock losses at Deltroit nor any damage to the house and garden. Nonetheless, ten

View over Deltroit and Hillas Creek, 2011

kilometres of fencing was either lost entirely or damaged, and timber was dumped by the floodwaters in odd and inconvenient places. For many weeks afterwards, Deltroit became a quagmire and it was difficult to drive a vehicle or even ride a horse over many of the paddocks.

Further downstream from Deltroit, the Hillas Creek roared through Yabtree and poured into the Murrumbidgee, which was now at bursting point, swelled by floodwaters from the huge catchment area around Gundagai. East of Deltroit, the township of Adelong was inundated by the swollen waters not of the Hillas but of the Adelong Creek. The main street became a river, the area was declared a natural disaster zone, and millions of dollars of damage to farms, businesses and homes was incurred.

Six weeks later, a second period of soaking rain, beginning on 2 December, caused massive flooding at Mundarlo, with the Murrumbidgee rising over ten metres and destroying a valuable crop of canola belonging to the Austin family. This time, however, although the Hillas Creek rose dangerously high, Deltroit was not inundated and no further damage was sustained. Notwithstanding these unexpected and unprecedented episodes in the district, the rainfall figures for the Hillas Creek area in the last twenty years clearly show a downward trajectory that is hard to ignore. Whatever is happening elsewhere, the climate at Hillas Creek would appear to be changing beyond the pattern of established variability.

A pastoral powerhouse

Today, by common consent, the pasture, shade timber and biodiversity at Deltroit are healthier than they have been for many decades, with prodigious ground cover in all paddocks due not only to the recent rains, but also perhaps, more importantly, to the holistic management program. By simultaneously addressing the health of the soil, the plants and the livestock, Anthony has achieved a level of sustainability and productivity at Deltroit that has probably never been present before in its colonial history. In some paddocks, where grasses have always skimmed the ankle, they now grow so tall that even the horses are wary of treading amongst them. Anthony is proud to say that he is 'a grass farmer', growing pasture to 'sell' to his own stock or those on agistment. It is this grass-growing activity that has become Anthony's main priority. With such an advance in the long-term wellbeing of the pastures, Deltroit has once again become a 'model' property, just as it was described by a contemporary observer one hundred years ago. In the words of leading agronomist Mark Lucas:

> I probably have not dealt with a more responsive property in terms of productivity improvement ... Deltroit ranks in the top end of livestock properties throughout New South Wales and Victoria.

Deltroit slopes in mid summer
showing new bore, 2009

Conclusion

*T*he evolution of Deltroit into one of the finest properties in the Riverina is not just important for its own sake. While the details contained in these pages are specific to Deltroit, the history of the property is nonetheless emblematic of what was happening during the same period on other landholdings, particularly in New South Wales. Similarly, the emergence of a settlement at Hillas Creek contemporaneous with the development of Deltroit itself has implications far beyond the immediate area. At both Deltroit and Hillas Creek, a microcosm of Australian social history took place and continues today, complete with all the colour and diversity that human frailty and a brittle environment impose.

Unless the details are recorded now, much information will be lost to future generations as local knowledge thins and photographs lose their meaning. Inevitably, Australia has grown away from its agricultural roots, and the stories of properties like Deltroit and small bush settlements such as Hillas Creek are disappearing amid this shift. It seems likely that, given the absence of any diaries and memoirs, both William and John Richardson, the first selectors at Deltroit, were themselves too busy making history in the vast and fertile expanse of the Murrumbidgee basin to record all that they did, knew and observed, leaving this task to their successors.

There are many elements in the history of Deltroit that accord with the stories of other properties, but one of the key similarities is that Deltroit was maintained in the same family for the traditional timeframe of three generations before being sold. The saying goes, 'The first generation build it, the second enjoy it and the third lose it', usually due to increasing debt necessitated by a combination of poor seasons and markets, as well as death duties (which have now been abolished). Few families have been able to overcome this well-established pattern in Australian pastoral history, and the Richardson and Fraser family was itself not immune.

By contrast, those families neighbouring Deltroit — the Horsleys and the Derricks — have all remained in the district into the fifth generation and continue to occupy the same landholdings, albeit reduced, as their forebears. Neither did any part of Billapalap last in Richardson and Fraser hands beyond three generations, with the exception of a block purchased in the 1930s by Thomas Richardson's descendants, the Corbett family, who still retain this land today. As in the case of Deltroit, the Pearces and the Crains, whose land bordered the once extensive boundaries of Billapalap, still occupy areas first grazed by family members five generations ago.

Where the history of Deltroit differs from so many other similar properties is in its inheritance by two female heirs, Florence and Isabel Richardson, and the subsequent management of the whole grazing enterprise by the eldest sister, Florence, until her death in 1936. Much of the story of Australian pastoralism is a male one, with few women being able to stand the isolation and the hardships involved. That said, by the time the Richardson girls inherited Deltroit, it was not only an established property with a luxurious homestead, but was already in a relatively well-populated district. Even so, the trend in those days was still for the wife to defer to her husband, yet this did not happen between Florence and her spouse, Charles Fraser. Oral testimony both from family descendants and former employees is very clear in highlighting that it was Florence who was in charge. These days, of course, there are many women running their own properties or herds, so what was unusual in the 1920s, when the Richardson girls inherited Deltroit, no longer applies today.

Another feature of Deltroit's history that was relatively new at the time concerns the sale of the property. When it passed out of Richardson and Fraser hands, it was sold to a huge international beef-producing company, King Ranch in Texas. Foreign investors such as this have become increasingly widespread in Australia, where there is currently no restriction on the purchase of agricultural land by foreign buyers from places such as China, the Middle East and the United States. In the present economic climate, where the traditional safe havens of urban property, the stock market and even cash deposits are increasingly volatile, shrewd investors are turning to agricultural land as the most stable investment. Moreover, countries like China have begun to recognise that their own rural industries are being encroached upon by the explosion of urbanisation and growth, and are now seeking more farmland overseas to meet the increasing food demands of their population. In contrast to the nineteenth century, the greatest migration to the Australian rural sector is no longer people, but capital.

This phenomenon of increasing foreign interest in Australian rural property is helping to make traditional family farming a thing of the past. Deltroit, like so many properties in Australia, was typical in being run for many years both within and across the generations of the same family. Originally, the two Richardson brothers, William and John, were in partnership together, and their nephews John, Al and Harry Larkin were all, at various times, part of the labour force. In those early days and up until quite recently, it was usual for a father, his brothers and their respective sons (if they had any) to all be involved in some way and to work alongside each other, providing companionship and support in their joint endeavour. Sometimes, even a grandparent was part of the workforce if he was fit enough. Such a setup is now becoming rare, especially as the younger generation are frequently opting for an urban lifestyle.

Rarer still is the number of families entering the farming sector for the first time with a view to working the land themselves. The necessary financial, physical and emotional commitment, when compared to the income returns, is seen as too great. On the other hand, if a property of several thousand or more acres is sold, nowadays it is increasingly unlikely to be bought by a family already based on the land, unless they have considerable capital reserves and a need to achieve economies of scale. Such a property is more likely to be purchased either by one of the growing number of foreign investors, usually a company, or by an individual from the city, looking either for a weekend retreat or a lifestyle change. Anthony and I are a prime example of these realities. Anthony came, mid-career, from a city-based business background and now both lives and works on the property full-time. Notwithstanding this, the ownership history of Deltroit is distinctly different from many other properties that began as a family enterprise. The fact that Deltroit returned to private hands after a long period of corporate ownership (by King Ranch and then Finemores) is an unusual cycle and there is no known precedent for it in the area.

Even though Deltroit is now back in a family structure, the style of managing the property and living there is entirely different from how it was in the past. Once Deltroit prospered, William Richardson and his heirs became removed from the daily toil associated with being a grazier and, at one point, employed a minimum of eight full-time workers on the property and another six in the homestead and garden. Today, despite its high productivity and sustainability, Deltroit is run with a comparatively slim workforce — namely, a manager based 400 kilometres away on the property at Hay and only two full-time men at Deltroit itself. Moreover, Anthony does much of the physical work, too, having become a key member of the team in a work environment where former class distinctions no longer matter. Similarly, in the homestead, one full-time housekeeper/cook is employed to maintain the house and look after its occupants, including family and guests. A young student from Charles Sturt University in Wagga Wagga comes twice weekly to help exercise the horses used for both mustering and general riding. Life at Deltroit has thus become a curious blend of gracious, almost baronial living, coupled with hard, physical work not just for the employees but also for the employers.

The lifestyle of physically working one's own property is now commonplace for most graziers throughout Australia and began again not long after the Second World War. By general consent, country Australia changed beyond all recognition from the 1950s onwards, due partly to the sharp rise in labour costs. Wages rose to such an extent that they fell out of step with the realities of farm income, which is often uncertain and sometimes negligible, especially in periods of prolonged drought. With labour costs so high, it was no longer viable for many graziers to employ managers, overseers or even station hands and jackaroos. In consequence, graziers became part of the labour force in much the same way as many of the original settlers were when they first depastured stock on Australian soil. Almost every property around Deltroit and along the Hillas Creek valley bears witness to this development, and the only exceptions are where the owner is too elderly to work or is an absentee landlord.

Being able to afford only a diminished labour force, graziers looked for ways to make their properties more efficient. Many landholdings were consolidated and mechanised, thereby reducing the need for men, but creating widespread unemployment on the land and loss of opportunities. Increasingly, people were forced to move away to the towns and cities, especially if they had a skill that they could utilise there. Frequently, only those with no other option stayed behind. People's spirits declined along with the job market, and the sense of pride that they used to exude in their work and in their appearance more or less disappeared. Once again, in many parts of Australia, the bush became a place of melancholy, monotony and often despair, an atmosphere that could be felt acutely around Deltroit and along the Hillas Creek valley during the recent ten-year drought. Only in exceptionally good seasons, after plenty of rain at the right time, does this air of despondency lift, bringing new hope into people's lives.

In addition to properties suffering through a reduced labour market, many becoming poorly maintained and neglected, country towns and smaller settlements have also either stagnated or crumbled. Adelong and Gundagai are good examples — the number of young families living there has reduced dramatically in the last thirty years, and the handful of shops and cafés have struggled to survive against the competition in the much bigger centre of Wagga Wagga. Adelong was recently given a reprieve by the establishment of a large paper mill at nearby Tumut, but Gundagai looks depressed, in spite of some new buildings and the steady traffic that passes through daily on the Hume Highway between Sydney and Melbourne. The main settlement of Hillas Creek itself, once an important local centre, disappeared long ago with the demise of the school, the pub and the post office. For the people at Deltroit and those in the surrounding district, there is no longer a place in the vicinity where they can go regularly to congregate, to wind down and to talk and, as in many other rural areas, the strong sense of community that prevailed for over a hundred years has more or less vanished.

Ironically, this general malaise in the bush, which affects landowners and workers alike, has not weakened the reluctance of those born on the land to leave their own holdings or the rural way of life. This powerful inclination to stay, whatever the economic realities, is as evident on properties neighbouring Deltroit and in the general vicinity as it is elsewhere in the country. These 'bushies', as they are affectionately known by city dwellers, have a deeply rooted attachment to the land that comes not just from being born in a particular place, but from working it themselves and watching the struggles of their parents doing the same. It gives them an affinity to nature and the vast open spaces akin to a spiritual or religious connection. Many are reluctant to experience life beyond their birthplace, even for a short time, and in this they have a very different mentality to that of the four Richardson brothers born into the farming community of Westmorland in the 1830s. They had a restless spirit, in spite of generations of Richardsons before them who had farmed in the Upper Eden Valley. Setting out as young men for the Victorian goldfields, they took part willingly in one of the greatest adventures life could offer them in that period of history.

The strong attachment to their land held by the residents of the Hillas Creek valley and their determination to stay where they are reinforces the already deep sense of continuity that prevails in the area, as in other country locations, in spite of modernisation and reduced job opportunities. Apart from almost two centuries of farm 'improvements', the silent, empty landscape, disturbed only occasionally by the raucous cry of flocks of cockatoos or the demonic laugh of a kookaburra, has experienced few changes since white settlement began. The descriptions by early surveyors of rounded hills and grassy slopes, of eucalyptus trees and granite rocks, of high ridges and a slanting creek meandering along the valley floor, remain as true today as they were then. Extended and uninterrupted views along the Hillas Creek valley stretch for miles, with only the movement of stock and wildlife and the occasional vehicle discernable in the landscape.

Moreover, just as with other pastoral communities around Australia, the rhythms of the farming calendar at Deltroit are the same as they have been for many generations — beginning with joining and progressing through pregnancy testing, calving, lambing, marking, drenching, weaning, shearing and fattening. In between these events, there might also be some ploughing, sowing and harvesting, depending on the season. The weather plays a significant role at Deltroit, as it does everywhere in Australia, both on the outcome of many of these activities and on the revenue stream of the property. However, the newly implemented holistic management program at Deltroit goes a long way towards mitigating the impact of the climate, especially the drier seasons.

To what extent the droughts will recur in future, only time will tell, but they have always been a periodic presence in the Hillas Creek valley as they are right across the continent. Deltroit is not alone in changing its grazing strategies to anticipate further years of dry and the widely predicted negative effects of global warming. Other properties in the area and further afield are finding ways to manage these issues and are moving away from strict set stocking patterns towards various rotational grazing methods. Science in many forms, including biology, agronomy, ecology, genetics and horticulture, is playing an ever-increasing role in maintaining the health of pastures and livestock as well as ensuring high productivity. Perhaps it will help to close the enormous gulf in understanding that currently exists between those who live on the land and those who work in the cities, as without these new measures the food source of every Australian is ultimately jeopardised.

In spite of the innumerable odds against success, Deltroit has not only endured, but, at the time of writing, is flourishing. Whereas many similar properties have been grazed out or subdivided, and their homesteads and outbuildings allowed to fall into ruin, Deltroit continues to set a high standard all round in modern pastoralism. Today, it can look forward to a new chapter in its illustrious history, since Anthony and I recently put our cherished home on the market. Family responsibilities in England, Antonia's education and a desire to travel are the reasons for this decision. Our greatest hope is that Deltroit will be sold to someone who appreciates its beauty and history as much as its exceptional productivity.

One hundred and fifty years is a long time in the life of any business, yet Deltroit continues to sustain its unrivalled reputation. Notwithstanding the initial isolation from a major centre; the primal force of the Australian sun; the recurring droughts, fires and floods; the problems of labour; the physical, backbreaking demands of working the land; and, last but not least, the constant but often subliminal fear known to all country people that disaster might be just around the corner, human purpose has prevailed at Deltroit over an environment that does its best to thwart it. The dream that William Richardson began and later realised, of a pastoral enterprise on a scale far beyond his boyhood imaginings, thrives today in a world of climate change, carbon taxes and uncertain markets. If William returned from the grave, there is no doubt he would be very proud.

Shorthorn moving along Deltroit laneway, 2008

Richardson Family Tree

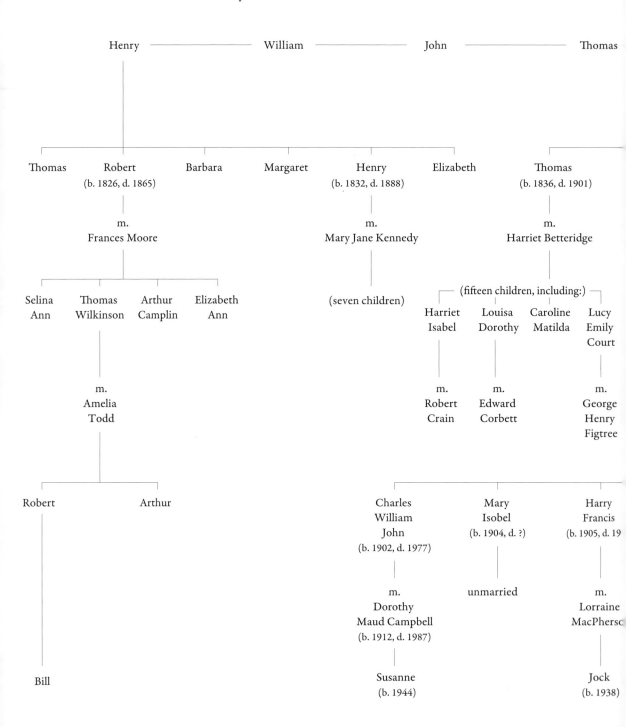

Note: Dates of birth and death have only been given for the more important characters appearing in the narrative.

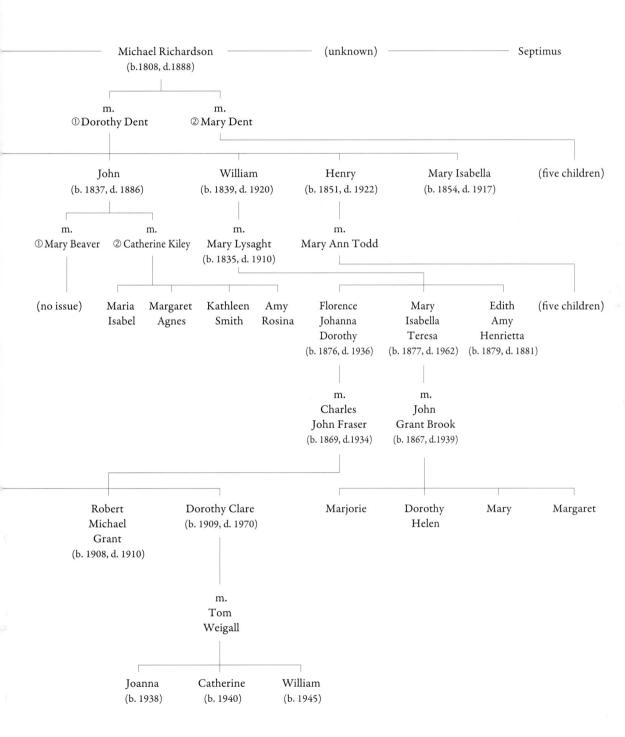

Michael Richardson ———— (unknown) ———— Septimus
(b.1808, d.1888)

m.   m.
① Dorothy Dent   ② Mary Dent

John   William   Henry   Mary Isabella   (five children)
(b. 1837, d. 1886)   (b. 1839, d. 1920)   (b. 1851, d. 1922)   (b. 1854, d. 1917)

m.   m.   m.   m.
① Mary Beaver   ② Catherine Kiley   Mary Lysaght   Mary Ann Todd
                          (b. 1835, d. 1910)

(no issue)   Maria   Margaret   Kathleen   Amy   Florence   Mary   Edith   (five children)
        Isabel   Agnes   Smith   Rosina   Johanna   Isabella   Amy
                                    Dorothy   Teresa   Henrietta
                                 (b. 1876, d. 1936)   (b. 1877, d. 1962)   (b. 1879, d. 1881)

                                   m.   m.
                                 Charles   John
                                 John Fraser   Grant Brook
                                 (b. 1869, d.1934)   (b. 1867, d.1939)

Robert   Dorothy Clare   Marjorie   Dorothy   Mary   Margaret
Michael   (b. 1909, d. 1970)   Helen
Grant
(b. 1908, d. 1910)

              m.
             Tom
           Weigall

      Joanna   Catherine   William
      (b. 1938)   (b. 1940)   (b. 1945)

Lysaght Family Tree

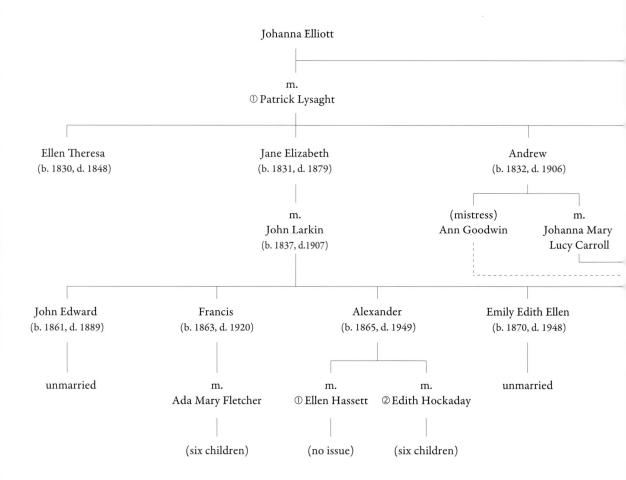

*Refer to Appendix A for the continuation of this branch.

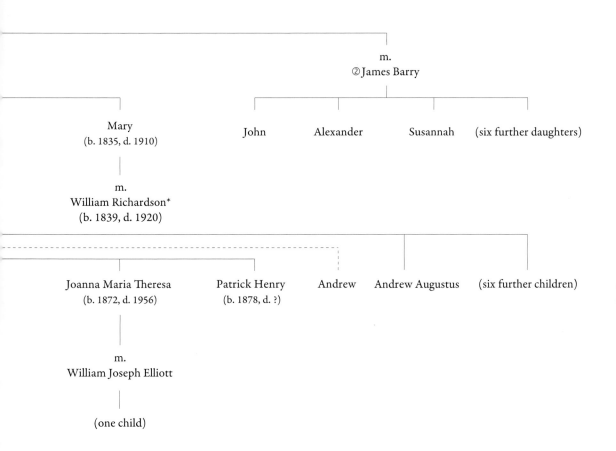

m.
②James Barry

Mary
(b. 1835, d. 1910)

John   Alexander   Susannah   (six further daughters)

m.
William Richardson*
(b. 1839, d. 1920)

Joanna Maria Theresa
(b. 1872, d. 1956)

Patrick Henry
(b. 1878, d. ?)

Andrew   Andrew Augustus   (six further children)

m.
William Joseph Elliott

(one child)

Appendix C

List of Licensees of the Junction Hotel [1]

John Griffiths (local selector)	November 1868 – August 1877
Amos Simpson (brother-in-law of John Griffiths)	August 1877 – January 1879
Ann Upton (sister-in-law of John Griffiths)	January 1879 – July 1880
William Beaver (local selector, John Richardson's brother-in-law and brother of Robert Beaver, licensee of the Mundarlo Inn)	July 1880 – June 1883
Edward Donnelly (married to Susannah Barry, Mary Lysaght's half-sister)	June 1883 – January 1885
Robert Williams	January 1885 – February 1895
Arthur James Cooper (local selector and formerly a publican at the Mundarlo Inn)	February 1895 – December 1903
Ambrose Edward Finney (formerly a publican in South Gundagai)	January 1904 – February 1905
Edward John O'Dwyer (from Mount Adrah)	February 1905 – July 1907
John Ross (brother-in-law of Edward O'Dwyer and a former miner)	July 1907 – August 1910
Michael Bernard Carmody (formerly a publican in Victoria)	August 1910 – January 1914
Margaret Carmody (widow of the above)	January 1914 – November 1916

List of Teachers at the Hillas Creek School [2]

Unnamed female	1876
Arthur McCorkill (resigned)	February 1877 – March 1878
Charlotte Hill (dismissed)	July 1878 – May 1879
Maud Crowe (transferred)	June 1879 – October 1880
Daniel Cox (deserted post and dismissed)	February 1881 – June 1881
William Adams (dismissed)	August 1882 – December 1884
Robert Cooper (transferred)	January 1885 – June 1885
George Hewitson (school closed)	July 1885 – November 1886

Endnotes

CHAPTER 1

1   *Tumut & Adelong Times*, 4 May 1900.

2   Michael Norton JP, 'A Rambling Review of the Past', *Gundagai Independent*, 1 December 1938.

3   Trevor Langford Smith, 'Murrumbidgee Land Settlement, 1817 to 1912', in G. H. Dury and M. I. Logan (eds.), *Studies in Australian Geography* (London: Heinemann Education Books, 1968), p. 99.

4   Letter from Henry Bingham dated 24 June 1841, reprinted in *The Australasian Chronicle*, 18 September 1841, p. 4.

5   Peter Rimas Kabaila, *Wiradjuri Places* (Jamison Centre, ACT: Black Mountain Projects, 1995–1998), p. 12.

6   Thomas Keneally, *Australians: Origins to Eureka* (Crows Nest, NSW: Allen & Unwin, 2009), p. 400.

7   'Report of the Select Committee on the Condition of Aborigines', *Morning Chronicle*, 17 December 1845.

8   Letter from Henry Bingham, dated 24 June 1841.

9   'Report of the Select Committee on the Condition of Aborigines'.

10   Letter from Henry Bingham, dated 4 November 1844, reprinted in *Sydney Morning Herald*, 23 November 1844.

11   Guy Fitzhardinge, 'Attitudes, Values and Behaviour: Pastoralists, Land Use and Landscape Art in Western New South Wales', PhD thesis, University of Western Sydney, 2008, available from *http://arrow.uws.edu.au:8080/vital/access/manager/Repository/uws:2378*.

12   W. K. Hancock, *Discovering Monaro: A Study of Man's Impact on His Environment* (Cambridge: Cambridge University Press, 1972), p. 65.

13   Dr John Rudder and Christopher Kirkbright.

14   NSW Electoral Roll 1903; *The Wagga Wagga Advertiser*, 9 November 1914; and *Wagga District News*, 11 November 1914.

15   *Tumut & Adelong Times*, 1 June 1900.

16   *The Wagga Wagga Advertiser*, 19 January 1907.

17   *NSW Government Gazette*, 29 September 1848.

18   Wallace Horsley, 'Yabtree 1829–1972', paper delivered to the Wagga Wagga & District Family History Society on 16 October 1972.

19   *Sydney Morning Herald*, 13 August 1835.

20   G. L. Buxton, *The Riverina 1861–1891: An Australian Regional Study* (Melbourne: Melbourne University Press, 1967), p. 18.

21   Emily Horsley, unpublished notes on the history of Yabtree.

22   Refer to the Map of the Pattern of Land Acquisition at Deltroit on page 52.

23   R. F. Horsley's diaries, entry dated 30 May 1876.

24   R. F. Horsley's diaries, entry dated 28 June 1882.

CHAPTER 2

1   Bleatarn Tithe Map and Apportionment of 29 January 1846, WDRC 8/77, Cumbria Archive Centre, Kendal.

2   *Post Office Directory of Westmorland and Cumberland* (London: Kelly & Co., 1858), courtesy of the Cumbria Archive Centre, Kendal.

3   Mark Blackett-Ord, 'Warcop's Strangest Portrait', *The Cumberland and Westmorland Herald*, 21 October 2006.

4   Margaret E. Shepherd, *From Hellgill to Bridge End: Aspects of Economic and Social Change in the Upper Eden Valley circa 1840–1895* (Hatfield, UK: University of Hertfordshire Press, 2004), p. 117.

5   ibid, p. 118.

6   *The Cumberland and Westmorland Herald*, 11 December 1880.

7   Will of Thomas Richardson, proved 10 January 1829.

8   Will of Michael Richardson (1808–1888); and information from Judy Jeffrey, great-granddaughter of Joseph Richardson.

9   Shepherd, *From Hellgill to Bridge End*, p. 130.

10   ibid, p. 121.

11   ibid, p. 130.

12   Census of England and Wales for the years 1861 and 1881.

13   *The Cumberland and Westmorland Herald*, 11 December 1880.

14   Shepherd, *From Hellgill to Bridge End*, p. 167.

15   Obituary of William Richardson, *Gundagai Times*, 11 March 1920.

16   Bleatarn Tithe Map and Apportionment, 29 January 1846.

17   Census of England and Wales for the year 1851.

18   *The Cumberland and Westmorland Herald*, 11 December 1880.

19   Shepherd, *From Hellgill to Bridge End*, pp. 229–230.

20   *Gundagai Independent*, 11 March 1920.

21 Shepherd, *From Hellgill to Bridge End*, p. 234.

22 Census of England and Wales for the year 1851.

23 P. H. Mannex, *Topography and Directory of Westmorland and Lonsdale North of the Sands in Lancashire* (London: Simpkin, Marshall & Co., 1849), courtesy of the Cumbria Record Office, Kendal.

24 Information from Judy Jeffrey.

CHAPTER 3

1 Shepherd, *From Hellgill to Bridge End*, p. 302.

2 ibid, p. 284.

3 *Westmorland Gazette and Kendal Advertiser*, 30 June 1855, and numerous subsequent issues.

4 *Westmorland Gazette and Kendal Advertiser*, 25 October 1851, p. 5.

5 ibid.

6 *Westmorland Gazette and Kendal Advertiser*, 22 November 1851, p. 2.

7 Letter from New Zealand to R. R. Bradley, dated 8 May 1854, reprinted in full in *Westmorland Gazette and Kendal Advertiser*, 4 November 1854.

8 Shepherd, *From Hellgill to Bridge End*, p. 334.

9 Information from Bill Richardson, great-grandson of Robert Richardson.

10 Obituary of Robert Richardson, *Tumut & Adelong Times*, 2 October 1865.

11 Information from Judy Jeffrey.

12 Portion 12 Parish of Mundarlo, CP66.243, available at the CSU Regional Archives; Wagga Wagga Lands Office; NRS18810, Conditional Purchase Registers, 1862–1938: SA29/123–127.

13 Census of England and Wales for the years 1861 and 1871.

14 Letter from James Cooper Stewart to his father in Scotland, dated 27 September 1857, MS12425 & 12507, BOX 3395/1(a-b), Manuscripts collection, State Library of Victoria.

15 *The Age*, 4 September 1857.

16 Information from Jock Fraser, great-grandson of William Richardson.

17 Information from Bill Richardson.

18 Obituary of Thomas Wilkinson Richardson , *The Border Mail*, 2 July 1929.

CHAPTER 4

1 Information from Jock Fraser.

2 *Gundagai Independent*, 11 March 1920; and *Tumut Advocate*, 16 March 1920.

3 *Tumut & Adelong Times*, 11 March 1920.

4 *Gundagai Independent*, 11 March 1920

5 Information from Jock Fraser.

6 Shepherd, *From Hellgill to Bridge End*, pp. 188–197.

7 Information from Jock and Sue Fraser, great-grandchildren of William Richardson.

8 Will of Michael Richardson (1808–1888).

9 *Gundagai Independent*, 11 March 1920; and *The Pastoral Review*, March 1920.

10 Portion 13, Parish of Mundarlo, CP67.2845, available at the CSU Regional Archives; Wagga Wagga Lands Office; NRS18810, Conditional Purchase Registers, 1862–1938: SA29/123–127.

11 Obituary of Thomas Richardson, *Adelong & Tumut Express*, 30 July 1901.

12 *Town & Country Journal*, 16 March 1872.

13 *Town & Country Journal*, 29 May 1880.

14 Jennifer Lambert Tracey, 'Gold on the Adelong!: An Historical Archeological Landscape Study of the Adelong Goldfield 1853–1916', in Ruth S. Kerr and Michael MacLellan Tracey (eds.), *Proceedings of the Australian Mining History Association 1996 Conference* (Canberra: Australian Mining History Association Inc, University of Western Australia & Home Planet Design and Publishing, 1997), pp. 64–67.

15 Information from Grant Figtree, great-grandson of Thomas Richardson.

16 Obituary of Thomas Richardson.

17 Portion 8, Parish of Euadera, CP62/50/SA209/50, available at the CSU Regional Archives; Wagga Wagga Lands Office; NRS18810, Conditional Purchase Registers, 1862–1938: SA209/50.

18 *Tumut & Adelong Times*, 1 March 1866.

19 Manning Clark, *A Short History of Australia*, (Camberwell, VIC: Penguin, 2006), pp. 100–101.

20 Buxton, *The Riverina 1861–1891*, p. 21.

21 Buxton, *The Riverina 1861–1891*, p. 54.

22 *Gundagai Independent*, 11 March 1920.

23 CP67.2845 and CP66.4197, available at the CSU Regional Archives, SA209/50.

24 *Tumut & Adelong Times*, 22 January 1866.

25 R. J. E. Gormley, Card Indexes on Wagga district, biography and history (MLMSS.672/8-9), accessed as the CSU Regional Archives.

26 CP66.4197 and CP67.2845, available at the CSU Regional Archives, SA209/50.

27 *NSW Government Gazette*, No. 83, 3 April 1868, pp. 998–999.

28 CP66.64, available at the CSU Regional Archives, SA209/15.

29 Amendment to *The Crown Lands Alienation Act 1875*, section 9.

30 CP66.4198, available at the CSU Regional Archives, SA209/50.

31 Langford-Smith, 'Murrumbidgee Land Settlement 1817 to 1912', p. 105.

32 Book 133, No 882, from the records at the Department of Lands NSW, Sydney.

33 Amendment to *The Crown Lands Alienation Act 1875*.

34 *Tumut & Adelong Times*, 22 January 1866.

35 Cliff Butcher, *Gundagai, A Track Winding Back* (Gundagai, NSW: A. C. Butcher, 2002), p. 58.

36 Various Crown Plans, but especially on Portion 20, Parish of Yaven.

Chapter 5

1 John Winston-Gregson, 'Colonial Archaeology in the Eastern Riverina', MA thesis, Menzies Library, Australian National University, 1982.

2 Letter from Thomas Scott Townsend to the Surveyor General, dated 18 September 1848, from the 'Surveyor General – Letters received 1822–55' file, Reel 3092, Item 2/1583B, State Records NSW.

3 CP66.382, available at the CSU Regional Archives; Wagga Wagga Lands Office; NRS18810, Conditional Purchase Registers, 1862–1938: SA/29/123–127.

4 *Government Gazette*, 31 December 1867.

5 Information from Bobbie Matheson, great-granddaughter of John Griffiths.

6 Richard Gormly, NSW Hotels, 1838-1900, ML reel CY 1528.

7 *Gundagai Times*, 21 April 1875.

8 *Gundagai Times*, 8 February 1868.

9 Family papers in the possession of Bobbie Matheson.

10 *Gundagai Times*, 27 May 1892.

11 Letter from Daniel Cox to District Inspector D. S. Hicks, dated 26 June 1881, Hillas Creek School file, Item 5/16270.1, State Records NSW.

12 Letter from Daniel Cox to District Inspector D. S. Hicks, dated 9 February 1881, Hillas Creek School file, Item 5/16270.1, State Records NSW.

13 Letter from District Inspector D. S. Hicks to the Chief Schools Inspector, dated 24 April 1881, Hillas Creek School file, Item 5/16270.1, State Records NSW.

14 *Gundagai Times*, 12 October 1888.

15 Portion 18, CP66.382, available at the CSU Regional Archives; Wagga Wagga Lands Office; NRS18810, Conditional Purchase Registers, 1862–1938: SA/29/123–127.

16 *Wagga Wagga Express*, 20 December 1879.

17 *Gundagai Times*, 3 April 1883.

18 *Wagga Wagga Express*, 30 September 1916.

19 Ross Petty and David Denholm, 'The Great Southern Road', paper delivered to the Wagga Wagga & District Family History Society.

Chapter 6

1 Petition to the Postmaster-General of New South Wales, dated 24 June 1873, in the Hillas Creek Post Office file, Part 1, Series SP32/1, Box 321, National Archives of Australia.

2 Letter from J. Griffiths to T. Channon, dated 29 July 1873, in the Hillas Creek Post Office file, Part 1, Series SP32/1, Box 321, National Archives of Australia.

3 Letter from J. Hoskins to the Postmaster-General of New South Wales, dated 23 June 1873, in the Hillas Creek Post Office file, Part 1, Series SP32/1, Box 321, National Archives of Australia.

4 *Gundagai Times*, 12 July 1879.

5 Winston-Gregson, 'Colonial Archeology in the Eastern Riverina'.

6 Letter from W. Bootes to the Secretary, Postmaster-General's Office of New South Wales, dated 6 January 1873, in the Hillas Creek Post Office file, Part 1, Series SP32/1, Box 321, National Archives of Australia.

7 Hillas Creek Post Office file, Part 1, Series SP32/1, Box 321, National Archives of Australia.

8 Robert Lee, 'Linking a Nation: Australia's Transport and Communications 1788–1970', *Australian Heritage Council* (University of Western Sydney, 2003), available at *http://www.environment.gov.au/heritage/ahc/publications/commission/books/linking-a-nation/index.html*.

9 William Lees, *Coaching in Australia: A History of the Coaching Firm of Cobb & Co., with a Guide to the Present Coaching Routes in Brisbane* (Brisbane: Carter-Watson, 1917).

10 *Wagga Wagga Express*, 15 November 1858.

11 *Wagga Wagga Express*, 4 June 1859.

12 Letter from Thomas Scott Townsend to the Surveyor General, dated 18 September 1848.

13 *Gundagai Times*, 9 November 1869.

14 Report by Postal Inspector Moyse, dated 7 June 1880, in the Hillas Creek Post Office file, Part 1, Series SP32/1, Box 321, National Archives of Australia.

15 Report by Postal Inspector Moyse, dated 7 August 1880, in the Hillas Creek Post Office file, Part 1, Series SP32/1, Box 321, National Archives of Australia.

16 See, for example, letter from J. H. Miller to Postmaster General, dated 7 April 1905, in the Hillas Creek Post Office file, Part 1, Series SP32/1, Box 321, National Archives of Australia.

17 Letter from Robert Williams to the Secretary, Postmaster General's Office of New South Wales, dated 17 December 1890, in the Hillas Creek Post Office file, Part 1, Series SP32/1, Box 321, National Archives of Australia.

18 Letter from Postal Inspector Francis to Postmaster General of New South Wales, dated 13 September 1912, in the Hillas Creek Post Office file, Part 1, Series SP32/1, Box 321, National Archives of Australia.

Chapter 7

1 Fitzhardinge, 'Attitudes, Values and Behaviour'.

2 John Pickard, 'The Transition from Shepherding to Fencing in Colonial Australia', *Rural History* (Vol. 18, No. 2, 2007), p. 143.

3 Pickard, 'The Transition from Shepherding to Fencing in Colonial Australia', p. 147.

4 *Tumut Advocate*, 16 March 1920; and *Gundagai Independent*, 11 March 1920.

5 Early Parish Maps for Cunningdroo and Gumly Gumly; and CP67/57, 68/66/68/67 available at the CSU Regional Archives; Wagga Wagga Lands Office; NRS18810, Conditional Purchase Registers, 1862–1938: SA29/123–127.

6 George Seymour, 'My Early Days', reprinted in the *Gundagai Independent*, November 1925.

7 Information from Ken Galvin, station hand at Deltroit (1945–1957).

8 Hancock, *Discovering Monaro*, p. 63.

9 Fitzhardinge, 'Attitudes, Values and Behaviour'.

10 Hancock, *Discovering Monaro*, p. 109.

11 ibid, p. 110.

12 Clark, *A Short History of Australia*, p. 195.

13 Hancock, *Discovering Monaro*, p. 109.

14 *Gundagai Times*, 12 February 1924.

15 *NSW Government Gazette*, No. 111, 20 September 1848.

16 *The Hobart Courier*, 23 June 1857.

17 *NSW Government Gazette*, No. 111, 20 September 1848.

18 Mortgage between Thomas Usher Elliott and John and William Richardson, dated 7 March 1873, Old System Vendors Register, Indexes 11858–11899, Book 135-73.

19 Probate file of John Richardson.

20 *Sydney Morning Herald*, 9 June 1887.

21 *Tumut & Adelong Times*, 4 May 1900.

22 Book 179, No. 525, from the records at the Department of Lands NSW, Sydney.

23 Mortgage between Thomas Usher Elliott and John and William Richardson.

24 Stock Brands Directory of NSW, 31 December 1951, available at the Wagga Wagga Lands Office.

25 Information from Ken Galvin.

26 *Tumut & Adelong Times*, 4 May 1900.

27 Information from Jock Fraser.

28 Diaries of R. F. Horsley, 28 February 1876.

29 Book 383, No 293, from the records at the Department of Lands NSW, Sydney.

30 Dairies of R. F. Horsley, various entries between 1876 and 1889.

31 *Town & Country Journal*, 2 January 1886.

32 Diaries of R. F. Horsley, 18 April 1888.

33 Emily Horsley, unpublished notes on the history of Yabtree.

34 *Gundagai Times*, 25 May 1888.

35 *Tumut & Adelong Times*, 4 May 1900.

36 Buxton, *The Riverina 1861–1891*, p. 247.

37 *Tumut & Adelong Times*, 4 May 1900.

38 *Gundagai Times*, 18 March 1924.

Chapter 8

1 R. J. E. Gormly, Card Indexes on Wagga district, biography and history (MLMSS.672/8-9), accessed at the CSU Regional Archives.

2 Seymour, 'My Early Days'.

3 Diaries of R. F. Horsley, 28 February 1876

4 *Gundagai Times*, 30 April 1897.

5 Entries dated 26 February 1900 and 19–29 January 1903.

6 *The Windmill Journal* (published by the Morawa District Historical Society), Vol. 2, No. 3, p. 11.

7 Emily Horsley, unpublished notes on the history of Yabtree; and Map of the Parish of Yaven, Edition 1, 1883.

8 *Gundagai Times*, 2 January 1875.

9 Emily Horsley, unpublished notes on the history of Yabtree.

10 *Tumut & Adelong Times*, 11 November 1904.

11 *Gundagai Times*, 6 January 1905.

12 *Gundagai Independent*, 7 January 1905.

13 *Gundagai Times*, 30 April 1870.

14 *Gundagai Times*, 25 June 1870.

15 Butcher, *Gundagai*, p. 91.

16 *Gundagai Times*, 3 July 1891.

17 Seymour, 'My Early Days'.

18 *Gundagai Times*, 12 July 1892.

19 *Gundagai Times*, 19 July 1900.

20 Seymour, 'My Early Days'.

21 Information from Ken Galvin.

Chapter 9

1   *Gundagai Times*, 5 July 1910; *Gundagai Independent*, 6 July 1910; and *Tumut & Adelong Times*, 8 July 1910.

2   Information from Joanne Flack, descendant of Edward Elliott, uncle of Mary Richardson (née Lysaght).

3   ibid.

4   Assisted Immigrants Index 1839–1896, State Records NSW.

5   *Gundagai Times*, 5 July 1910.

6   Pat Williamson, *Around Wowagin* (Goulburn, NSW: Taralga Historical Society, 2004).

7   Information from Joanne Flack.

8   Assisted Immigrants Index 1839–1896, State Records NSW.

9   *Wagga District News*, 11 November 1914.

10 *Sydney Morning Herald*, 20 December 1878.

11 Emily Horsley, unpublished notes on the history of Yabtree.

12 *Yass Courier*, 17 May 1865.

13 ibid.

14 *Sydney Morning Herald*, 20 December 1878.

15 Gaol register number 8522/79, Berrima Gaol Photographic Description Book, NRS 2021, State Records NSW.

16 Information from Susan James, great-granddaughter of Susannah Barry.

17 *Gundagai Times*, 14 May 1882; see also, Danny Webster, *Police of Adelong & Distict, 1788 to 1901* (Adelong, NSW: D P. & Y. E. Webster, c. 1992).

18 *Gundagai Times*, 6 June 1874.

19 Police register of police appointments (1861–1892), NRS 10943, State Records NSW.

20 *Town and Country Journal*, 24 January 1880; and Allan M. Nixon, *Stand and Deliver!: 100 Australian Bushrangers 1789–1901* (Melbourne: Lothian, 1991).

21 Information from Patricia Horsley and Fred Horsley, great-grandchildren of R. F. Horsley.

22 Information from Joanne Flack.

23 *NSW Government Gazette*, 1837, p. 234.

24 Frank Osborne, *Osbornes in Early Illawarra* (Illawarra Historical Society, Inc., 2000).

25 *Illawarra Mercury*, 7 September 1906.

26 Information from Jock Fraser.

27 Information from Bill Richardson.

28 *The Border Mail*, 2 July 1929.

29 Information from Bill Richardson.

30 Information from Jock Fraser.

31 Obituary of Joseph Lambert, *Tumut & Adelong Times*, 16 January 1903.

32 Information from Jock Fraser; and Lyle Allen, late resident of the Adelong district.

33 In the possession of Joanne Flack.

34 *Wagga Daily Advertiser*, 9 November 1914.

35 Diaries of R. F. Horsley, entries dated 29 July 1878 and 2 September 1879.

36 Emily Horsley, unpublished notes on the history of Yabtree.

37 Diaries of R. F. Horsley, entry dated 3 March 1888.

38 ibid, entry dated 19 May 1888.

39 ibid, entry dated 15 December 1888.

40 Information from Patricia Horsley and Barbara Bohm, granddaughter of Frank Larkin Horsley.

41 *NSW Government Gazette*, 11 June 1881.

42 The Grand Lodge, Sydney.

43 Information from Grant Figtree.

44 Information from Gary Waters, great-grandson of Thomas Richardson.

45 Information from Grant Figtree.

46 Probate file of John Richardson.

47 *Town and Country Journal*, 27 March 1886.

48 *Sydney Morning Herald*, 9 June 1887; see also *Gundagai Times*, 7 June 1887.

49 Book 374, No. 465, from the records at the Department of Lands NSW, Sydney.

50 *Gundagai Times*, 19 March 1886.

51 NSW Electoral Roll for the year 1915.

Chapter 10

1   Memorandum of District Inspector Flannery, dated 11 December 1874, Hillas Creek School file, Item 5/16270.1, State Records NSW.

2   *Sydney Morning Herald*, 14 March 1921.

3   Inspection Report by District Inspector Hoskins, dated 7 February 1877, Hillas Creek School file, Item 5/16270.1, State Records NSW.

4   Letter from District Inspector Hicks to Chief Inspector, dated 24 April 1881, Hillas Creek School file, Item 5/16270.1, State Records NSW.

5   Letter from District Inspector Cox to District Inspector Hicks, dated 26 June 1881, Hillas Creek School file, Item 5/16270.1, State Records NSW.

6   Memorandum of District Inspector Hicks to Chief Inspector, dated 6 March 1882 and subsequent notations, Hillas Creek School file, Item 5/16270.1, State Records NSW.

7   Memorandum of District Inspector Hicks to Chief Inspector, dated 8 October 1881, Hillas Creek School file, Item 5/16270.1, State Records NSW.

8   Application for aid to a Provisional School, dated 29 December 1879, Item 5/18263.3, Yaven Yaven School file, State Records NSW.

9   ibid.

10   *Albury Banner*, 21 December 1883.

11   ibid.

12   *Geelong Advertiser*, 1 April 1857.

13   Brian Maher, *Planting the Celtic Cross: Foundations of the Catholic Archdiocese of Canberra and Goulburn* (Canberra: B. Maher, 1997).

14   Emily Horsley, unpublished notes on the history of Yabtree.

15   Isaac Hebb, *The History of Colac and District* (Melbourne: Hawthorn Press, 1970), p. 32.

16   Dawn Peel, *Year of Hope: 1857 in the Colac District* (Colac: D. Peel, 2006), p. 95.

17   ibid, p. 112.

18   Hebb, *The History of Colac and District*, pp. 123–124.

19   Peel, *Year of Hope*, pp. 84–85.

20   *Victorian Government Gazette*, 15 October 1858.

21   Peel, *Year of Hope*, p. 113.

22   Maher, *Planting the Celtic Cross*, p. 254.

23   Letter from John McCaig to Edward Doyle, dated 26 April 1860, Geelong record series, Higgins Collection at Geelong Heritage Centre.

24   Letter from John McCaig to Edward Doyle, dated 7 July 1860, Geelong record series, Higgins Collection at Geelong Heritage Centre.

25   Pay sheets, May–June 1858, Geelong record series, Higgins Collection at Geelong Heritage Centre.

26   Letters from John McCaig to Edward Doyle, dated 29 December 1859 and 1 January 1860, MS 11642, Manuscripts collection, State Library of Victoria; also letters dated 26 April 1860 and 28 October 1861, Geelong record series, Higgins Collection at Geelong Heritage Centre.

27   Terms and Conditions of Sale, 12 March 1861, Geelong Historical Records Centre.

28   *Geelong Advertiser*, 24 October 1862; and *Victoria Police Gazette*, 30 October 1862.

29   John McCaig, letter to the editor, *Queensland Daily Guardian*, 30 October 1865.

30   Anne McLay, *James Quinn: First Catholic Bishop of Brisbane* (Toowoomba: Church Archivists' Society, 1989).

31   *Queensland Daily Guardian*, 22 February 1866.

32   Information from Patricia Horsley and descendants of John McCaig in Fiji.

33   McCaig, letter to the editor, *Queensland Daily Guardian*, 30 October 1865.

34   *Fiji Times*, 6 July 1892.

35   Obituaries of Catherine McCaig, *Grenfell Record*, 18 November 1929; and Dennis McCaig, *Gundagai Independent*, 4 August 1927.

36   Information from Patricia Horsley.

37   *Gundagai Times*, 29 December 1876.

38   *Gundagai Times*, 27 December 1878.

39   *Gundagai Times*, 29 Decemeber 1876.

40   *Gundagai Times*, 20 April 1880.

41   *Gundagai Times*, 28 June 1880.

42   Emily Horsley, unpublished notes on the history of Yabtree.

43   ibid.

44   ibid.

45   Information from the various grandchildren of Florence and Isabel Richardson.

46   Information from Philip Bowring, grandson of Isabel Richardson.

Chapter 11

1   *Freeman's Journal*, 2 June 1900.

2   *The Catholic Press*, 9 June 1900.

3   *Tumut & Adelong Times*, 29 May 1934.

4   *Tumut & Adelong Times*, 30 August 1917.

5   *Adelong Argus*, 17 March 1903.

6   ibid.

7   Information from Betty Malloy, granddaughter of William Paine.

8   *Gundagai Times*, 3 and 14 February 1905.

9   Gundagai photograph collection (1887–1927) by Dr C. L. Gabriel, National Library of Australia.

10   *Tumut & Adelong Times*, 23 May 1902.

11   ibid.

12   Tribute to C. J. Fraser, *Tumut & Adelong Times*, 29 May 1934.

13   Obituary of C. J. Fraser, *Gundagai Independent*, 7 May 1934.

14   *Adelong Argus*, 10 March 1903.

15   Obituary of C. J. Fraser, *Gundagai Independent*, 7 May 1934.

16   ibid.

17   Information from Archives Office, Kincoppal-Rose Bay School.

18   *The Catholic Press*, 15 March 1902.

19   *The Catholic Press*, 4 June 1903.

20   Information from the grandchildren of Isabel Richardson, especially Ben Blackden, Philip Bowring, Anthony Bowring, Stephen Wright, Philippa Berry and Jane Kemmis-Betty.

21   Information from Joanne Flack.

22   *Adelong Argus*, 17 March 1903.

23   In the possession of Joanne Flack.

24   *Tumut & Adelong Times*, 1905.

25   Census of England and Wales for the year 1871.

26   Alan Brooke, 'The Brooks of Larchfield Mill', a privately commissioned study by the grandchildren of Isabel Richardson, March 2009; and the Obituary of George Brook, *Huddersfield Examiner*, 28 January 1888.

27   Brooke, 'The Brooks of Larchfield Mill'.

28   ibid.

29   Information from Ben Blackden and Philip Bowring.

30   Information from Philip Bowring.

31   Brooke, 'The Brooks of Larchfield Mill'.

32   Obituary of George Brook, *Huddersfield Examiner*, 19 August 1893.

33   Information from Anthony Bowring.

Chapter 12

1   Old Systems Vendor Register, Book 700, Deed No. 352, from the records at the Department of Lands NSW, Sydney.

2   Information from Helen Dickinson, NSW Land Research Specialist, based on the title documents from the records at the Department of Lands NSW, Sydney.

3   *Adelong Argus*, 17 February 1903.

4   ibid.

5   ibid.

6   *Gundagai Independent*, 9 May 1903, 25 May 1904 and 6 July 1904.

7   *Adelong Argus*, 17 February 1903.

8   Monks Hardy Exhibition held at the Wagga Wagga Council Chambers, 2009.

9   *Adelong Argus*, 17 February 1903.

10   ibid.

11   *Adelong Argus*, 17 March 1903.

12   ibid.

13   ibid.

14   *Gundagai Independent*, 6 July 1904.

15   Information from Jock Fraser.

16   Information from Joanne Flack.

17   UK outbound passenger lists (1890–1960), State Library of New South Wales.

18   ibid.

19   Obituaries of Mary Richardson, *Gundagai Times*, 5 July 1910, and *Tumut & Adelong Times*, 8 July 1910.

20   *Tumut & Adelong Times*, 1 May 1904.

21   *Gundagai Independent*, 11 March 1920.

22   *Gundagai Independent*, 15 October 1917.

23   Information from Jock Fraser.

24   *Tumut & Adelong Times*, 11 March 1920; and *Gundagai Independent*, 11 March 1920.

25   *Tumut Advocate*, 16 March 1920.

26   *Tumut & Adelong Times*, 11 March 1920.

27   Letters from Emily Larkin to Registrar of Probates, dated 13 December 1934 and 3 January 1935, Probate file of William Richardson, State Records NSW.

Chapter 13

1   Information from Jock Fraser.

2   *Gundagai Independent*, 7 May 1934.

3   Information from Ken Galvin, former Deltroit station hand.

4   Information from Patricia Horsley.

5   Information from Jock Fraser and Ken Galvin.

6   *Gundagai Independent*, 6 July 1936.

7   Information from Ken Galvin.

8   Information from Helen Russell, daughter of Cyril Crowe.

9   *Tumut & Adelong Times*, 16 February 1971.

10   Information from Helen Russell.

11   Information from Ken Galvin.

12   Information from Sue Fraser, granddaughter of Florence Fraser.

13   Information from Helen Russell and Ken Galvin.

14   Information from Ken Galvin.

15   Information from Sue Fraser and Patricia Horsley.

16   Information from Patricia Horsley.

17   Information from Ken Galvin.

18   Information from Gail Arnold, granddaughter of Al Larkin.

19   Pearce diaries, entry dated 21 February 1903.

20   ibid, entry dated 13 September 1905.

21   ibid, entries dated 2 April 1903 and 31 July 1905.

22   ibid, entry dated 16 June 1901.

23   ibid, entries dated 18 May and 22 June 1903.

24   Information from Neville Lucas, grandson of Al Larkin.

25   Information from Lyle Allen and Ken Galvin.

26   Information from Toby Corbett, great-grandson of Thomas Richardson.

27   Information from Lyle Allen and Ken Galvin.

28   *Adelong Argus*, 24 June 1902.

29   Information from Gail Arnold.

30   Information from Ken Galvin.

31   Information from Jock Fraser.

32   ibid.

33   ibid.

34   Information from Lyle Allen.

35   Information from Patricia Horsley.

36   Information from Fred Horsley.

37   Emily Horsley, unpublished notes on the history of Yabtree.

38   Information from Fred Horsley.

39   Information from Patricia Horsley, Fred Horsley and Sue Fraser.

40   Information from Patricia Horsley.

41   *Gundagai Independent*, 22 November 1923, 18 Feb 1924; *Canberra Times*, 12 June 1931; and *Sydney Morning Herald*, 1 September 1932.

42   *The Advertiser*, 14 December 1926.

43   Information from Gundagai Shire Council.

44   *The Pastoral Review*, May and June 1934.

45   Information from Jock Fraser.

46   Information from Lyle Allen.

47   Information from Ken Galvin.

48   Information from Lyle Allen.

Chapter 14

1   *Gundagai Independent*, 7 May 1934; *Tumut & Adelong Times*, 8 May 1934.

2   Information from the late Diana Eckersley, youngest sister of Dor Fraser (née Campbell).

3   *Tumut & Adelong Times*, 4 June 1935.

4   *Sydney Morning Herald*, 1 March 1912.

5   *Sydney Morning Herald*, 18 March 1936.

6   Information from Sue Fraser.

7   *Sydney Morning Herald*, 18 March 1936.

8   Information from Jane Kemmis-Betty, granddaughter of Isabel Brook.

9   Information from Goudhurst Local History Society.

10   Information from Anthony Bowring.

11   Information from Philip Bowring and Philippa Berry, grandchildren of Isabel Brook.

12   Information from Philippa Berry.

13   *Gundagai Independent*, 6 July 1936.

14   Information from Sue Fraser.

15   Information from Sue Fraser.

16   Information from Lyle Allen.

17   Information from the late Cyril Webb, nephew of Cyril Crowe.

18   Information from Lyle Allen.

19   Information from Fred Horsley.

20   *Tumut & Adelong Times*, 27 February 1940.

21   Information from Cyril Webb and Ken Galvin.

22   Information from Sue Fraser.

23   Information from Sue Fraser.

24   Information from Fred Horsley.

25   Information from Bill Derrick, resident of the Mundarlo district.

26   Information from Sue Fraser and Ken Galvin.

27   Information from Sue Fraser.

28   *The Pastoral Review*, May 1951.

29   Information from Ken Galvin.

30   Information from Sue Fraser.

31   Information from Ken Galvin.

32   Information from Sue Fraser and Ken Galvin.

33   Information from Sue Fraser.

34 *Gundagai Independent*, 15 October 1917; and information from Ken Galvin.

35 Information from Ken Galvin.

36 Information from Sue Fraser.

37 Information from Ken Galvin.

38 Information from Helen Russell.

39 Information from Yvonne Peel, daughter of Reg Whiting.

40 Information from Patricia Horsley.

41 Information from Ken Galvin.

42 *The Young Witness*, 15 July 1949; *Tumut & Adelong Times*, 19 July 1949.

43 Information from Sue Fraser.

44 Information from Ken Galvin.

45 Information from Simon Eckersley, nephew of Dor Fraser.

46 Information from Sue Fraser.

47 Information from Ken Galvin.

48 Information from Patricia Horsley.

49 Information from Fred Horsley.

50 Information from Yvonne Peel.

51 Information from Patricia Horsley.

52 *The Pastoral Review*, August 1953.

53 *The Pastoral Review*, July 1953.

54 *The Pastoral Review*, January 1959.

Chapter 15

1 Thomas Lea, 'In the Crucible of the Sun', privately published in 1974 in the USA for King Ranch, p. 60; available at the Library of Congress, Catalogue Card Number 74-76840.

2 Information from Sue Fraser.

3 Information from Geoff Schmidt and Peter Stuart Fox, former managers at Deltroit.

4 John Cypher, *Bob Kleberg and the King Ranch: A Worldwide Sea of Grass* (Austin: University of Texas Press, 1996), p. 71.

5 ibid, p. 45.

6 Information from Geoff Schmidt.

7 *The Pastoral Review*, January 1959.

8 Cypher, *Bob Kleberg and the King Ranch*, p 184.

9 Information from Geoff Schmidt and Peter Stuart Fox.

10 Cypher, *Bob Kleberg and the King Ranch*, p. 184.

11 Information from Kevin McMahon of Mango Pastoral Company.

12 Information from Kevin McMahon.

Appendices

1 Compiled from Hillas Creek Post Office file, Part 1, Series SP32/1, Box 321, National Archives of Australia; and R.J. Gormly, Notes on NSW Hotels, 1838-1900 (MLMSS 672/1).

2 Compiled from the Hillas Creek School file, Item 5/16270.1, State Records NSW.

Select Bibliography

Books and articles

Butcher, Cliff. *Gundagai, A Track Winding Back*. Gundagai, NSW: A. C. Butcher, 2002.

Buxton, G. L. *The Riverina 1861–1891: An Australian Regional Study*. Melbourne: Melbourne University Press, 1967.

Campbell, David. *Evening under Lamplight: Selected Stories*. St Lucia: University of Queensland Press, 1987.

Clark, Manning. *A Short History of Australia*. Camberwell, Vic.: Penguin, 2006.

Cypher, John. *Bob Kleberg and the King Ranch: A Worldwide Sea of Grass*. Austin: University of Texas Press, 1995.

Denholm, Zita. *T.Y.S.O.N.: The Life and Times of James Tyson, Pastoral Pioneer, 1819–1898*. Wagga Wagga: Triple D Books, 2002.

Gormly, J. *Exploration and Settlement in Australia*. Sydney: D. S. Ford, 1921.

Hancock, W. K. *Discovering Monaro: A Study of Man's Impact on His Environment*. Cambridge: Cambridge University Press, 1972.

Hebb, Isaac. *The History of Colac and District*. Melbourne: Hawthorn Press, 1970.

Kabaila, Peter Rimas. *Wiradjuri Places*. Jamison Centre, ACT: Black Mountain Projects, 1995–1998.

Keneally, Thomas. *Australians: Origins to Eureka*. Crows Nest, NSW: Allen & Unwin, 2009.

Lambert Tracey, Jennifer. 'Gold on the Adelong!: An Historical Archeological Landscape Study of the Adelong Goldfield 1853–1916', in Ruth S. Kerr and Michael MacLellan Tracey (eds.), *Proceedings of the Australian Mining History Association 1996 Conference*. Canberra: Australian Mining History Association Inc., University of Western Australia & Home Planet Design and Publishing, 1997.

Langford-Smith, Trevor. 'Murrumbidgee Land Settlement, 1817 to 1912', in G. H. Dury and M. I. Logan (eds.), *Studies in Australian Geography*. London: Heinemann Education Books, 1968.

Lea, Tom. *In the Crucible of the Sun*. Kingsville, TX: King Ranch, 1974.

Lee, Robert. *Linking a Nation: Australia's Transport and Communications 1788–1970* (online book), Canberra: Australian Heritage Council, 2003, available at *http://www.environment.gov.au/heritage/ahc/publications/commission/books/linking-a-nation/index.html*.

Lees, William. *Coaching in Australia: A History of the Coaching Firm of Cobb & Co., with a Guide to the Present Coaching Routes in Brisbane*. Brisbane: Carter-Watson, 1917.

Lindley, David. *Early Gundagai: Thomas Lindley (1807–1862), emancipist in Southern New South Wales* (2nd revised edn). Yass, NSW: T. Greensmith & Co., 2005.

Luders, Peter E. *Gundagai and the Lands of the Two Rivers: A Story of Region and Colony, State and Nation*. Sunnybank Hills, Qld.: BookPal, 2010.

Maher, Brian. *Planting the Celtic Cross: Foundations of the Catholic Archdiocese of Canberra and Goulburn*. Canberra: B. Maher, 1997.

Mannex, P. H. *History, Topography and Directory of Westmorland and Lonsdale North of the Sands in Lancashire*. London: Simpkin, Marshall & Co., 1849 (courtesy of the Cumbria Record Office, Kendal).

McLay, Anne. *James Quinn: First Catholic Bishop of Brisbane*. Toowoomba: Church Archivists' Society, 1989.

Morris, Sherry. *Wagga Wagga: A History*. Wagga Wagga: Council of the City of Wagga Wagga, 1999.

Morrison, Alec. *When Wool was King: The Inside Story of Australia's Wool Industry*. Sydney: R. M. Williams Publishing, 2009.

Nixon, Allan M. *Stand and Deliver!: 100 Australian Bushrangers 1789–1901*. Melbourne: Lothian, 1991.

Osborne, Frank. *Osbornes in Early Illawarra*. Illawarra Historical Society, Inc., 2000.

Peel, Dawn. *Year of Hope: 1857 in the Colac District*. Colac: D. Peel, 2006.

Pickard, John. 'The Transition from Shepherding to Fencing in Colonial Australia', *Rural History*, Vol. 18, No. 2, 2007.

Post Office Directory of Westmorland and Cumberland. London: Kelly & Co., 1858 (courtesy of the Cumbria Archive Centre, Kendal).

Shepherd, Margaret E. *From Hellgill to Bridge End: Aspects of Economic and Social Change in the Upper Eden Valley circa 1840–1895*. Hatfield, UK: University of Hertfordshire Press, 2004.

Webster, Danny. *Police of Adelong & District, 1788 to 1901*. Adelong, NSW: D P. & Y. E. Webster, c. 1992.

Williamson, Pat. *Around Wowagin*. Goulburn, NSW: Taralga Historical Society, 2004.

Newspapers and Periodicals

Adelong & Tumut Express

Adelong Argus

The Advertiser

The Age

Albury Banner

The Australasian Chronicle

The Border Mail

Canberra Times

The Catholic Press

The Courier (Hobart)

The Cumberland and Westmorland Herald

Freeman's Journal

Geelong Advertiser

Grenfell Record

Gundagai Independent

Gundagai Times

Illawarra Mercury

Morning Chronicle

NSW Government Gazette

The Pastoral Review (later *The Australian Pastoralists' Review*)

Queensland Daily Guardian

Sydney Morning Herald

Town & Country Journal

Tumut Advocate

Tumut & Adelong Times

Victorian Government Gazette

Wagga District News

The Wagga Wagga Advertiser (later *The Daily Advertiser*)

Wagga Wagga Express

Westmorland Gazette and Kendal Advertiser

Yass Courier

The Young Witness

CIVIL AND ARCHIVAL RECORDS

Assisted Immigrants Index 1839–1896, State Records NSW.

Bleatarn Tithe Map and Apportionment of 29 January 1846, WDRC 8/77, Cumbria Archive Centre, Kendal.

Census of England and Wales for the years 1851, 1861, 1871 and 1881.

Conditional Purchase Registers, 1862–1938: SA29/123–127; Wagga Wagga Lands Office, NRS18810, CSU Regional Archives.

Early Parish Maps for Yabtree, Mundarlo, Tarcutta, Dutzon, Cunningdroo and Gumly Gumly.

Gaol register number 8522/79, Berrima Gaol Photographic Description Book, NRS 2021, State Records NSW.

Gormly, R. J. E. Card Indexes on Wagga district, biography and history (MLMSS.672/8-9), CSU Regional Archives.

———. NSW Hotels, 1838-1900, ML reel CY 1528.

Higgins, W. and W., Solicitors, Papers, Geelong Heritage Centre.

Hillas Creek Post Office file, Part 1, Series SP32/1, Box 321, National Archives of Australia.

Hillas Creek School file, Item 5/16270.1, State Records NSW.

Letter from James Cooper Stewart to his father in Scotland, dated 27 September 1857, MS12425 & 12507, BOX 3395/1(a-b), Manuscripts collection, State Library of Victoria.

Letters of Edward Doyle, MS 11642, Manuscripts collection, State Library of Victoria.

NSW Electoral Rolls for the years 1903, 1908 and 1915.

Police register of police appointments (1861–1892), NRS 10943, State Records NSW.

Records at the Department of Lands NSW, Sydney.

Stock Brands Directory of NSW (delete date), available at the Wagga Wagga Lands Office.

Surveyor General – Letters received 1822–55, Reel 3092, Item 2/1583B, State Records NSW.

UK outbound passenger lists (1890–1960), State Library of New South Wales.

Various certificates of birth, death and marriage in New South Wales, Victoria and the United Kingdom.

Various probate files, State Records NSW.

Various probate files, UK Register of Probates.

Yaven Yaven School file, Item 5/18263.3, State Records NSW.

UNPUBLISHED SOURCES AND FAMILY HISTORIES

Brooke, Alan. 'The Brooks of Larchfield Mill', privately commissioned study by the grandchildren of Isabel Richardson, March 2009.

Fitzhardinge, Guy. 'Attitudes, Values and Behaviour: Pastoralists, Land Use and Landscape Art in Western New South Wales', PhD thesis, University of Western Sydney, 2008, available from http://arrow.uws.edu.au:8080/vital/access/manager/Repository/uws:2378.

Horsley, Emily. Notes on the history of Yabtree.

Horsley, R. F. Diaries, 1826–1891.

Horsley, Wallace. 'Yabtree 1829–1972', paper delivered to the Wagga Wagga & District Family History Society on 16 October 1972.

Matheson, Bobbie. Family papers in the possession of.

Pearce, John Joseph. Diaries, 1899–1912 and 1914–1916.

Petty, Ross and Denholm, David. 'The Great Southern Road', paper delivered to the Wagga Wagga & District Family History Society.

Winston-Gregson, John. 'Colonial Archaeology in the Eastern Riverina', MA thesis, Australian National University, 1982.

Pictorial Credits

Sincere thanks to the following individuals, families, organisations and archives that have kindly granted permission for their photographs or images to be reproduced in this book:

Gail Arnold: pages 105, 109 (top), 219

Peggy Bell: page 74

Grandchildren of Isabel Brook: pages 60, 183, 188, 189, 190, 191, 192, 193, 195, 209, 220, 238

Toby Corbett: page 46

Val Corbett: pages 31, 33 (bottom), 35, 36

Crowe family: pages 216 (left and right), 250

CSU Regional Archives, Wagga Wagga: page 101

Cumbrian Archive Centre: pages 30, 38

Cutler family: page 80

Simon Eckersley: pages 203, 204 (top and bottom), 206 (top), 236

Figtree family: page 52

Joanne Flack: pages 184–185

Jock Fraser: pages 213, 223 (bottom), 229, 248 (right top and bottom)

Sue Fraser: pages 132, 169, 172, 175, 200, 201, 214, 215, 216 (middle), 217, 223 (top), 225, 226, 232, 234, 235, 240, 241, 244, 245, 246, 247, 248 (left), 249, 251, 252, 255, 256

Ken Galvin: pages 222, 253

Historic Environment Records, West Yorkshire: page 187

Horsley family: front cover, pages 70–71, 119, 145, 147, 148, 154, 158, 160, 161, 166, 170, 194 (top and bottom), 198 (top), 224 (top and bottom), 231

Bundle Horsley: pages 198 (bottom), 212

Sue James: page 141

Justice and Police Museum Collection: page 139

Bobbie Matheson: pages 73, 78

National Archives of Australia: pages 88, 94

National Library of Australia: pages 178, 179, 180

Sedbergh School Archives: pages 39, 40, 41

Tony Sheffield: inside front cover, pages 18–19, 68, 85, 196, 280, 286

Stuart Smith: page 228

State Library of Victoria: page 50, 63, 163

State Records NSW: page 137

Garry Waters: pages 44, 48

The Weekly Times (Newspix / News Ltd): page 271

Loris White: page 96

Wollongong City Library and Illawarra Historical Society: page 142

All other images not otherwise attributed are in the personal possession of the author.

Acknowledgments

I am indebted to many people far and wide without whose support this book could not have been written. They include the following: Antonio Albert, the late Lyle Allen, Gail Arnold, Frank and Diana Austin, Tom and Jenny Barr-Smith, Peggy Bell, Brian Bennett, Philippa Berry, Ben Blackden, Celia Blackden, Roger Boissier, Anthony Bowring, Philip Bowring, Debbie Burgess, Mary Burns, Toby Corbett, Bryan Corrigan, Mary Crowe, Leo and Marie Cutler, Zita Denholm, Helen Dickinson, Judy Echin, the late Diana Eckersley, Simon Eckersley, Lleanne Epp, Grant and Rose Figtree, Joanne Flack, Jock Fraser, Sue Fraser, Ken Galvin, Vivienne Gate, Patricia Guina, Brigid Hains, Carol Herben, Bruce Horsley, Fred and Noella Horsley, Ian and Fiona Horsley, Patricia Horsley, Sue James, Judy Jeffrey, Jane Kemmis-Betty, Jillian Kolhagen, Jenny Krohn, Bobbie Matheson, Ruth McEwen, Sherry Morris, Michelle Nichols, Kerry Pearce, Dawn Peel, Bill Richardson, Helen Russell, Geoff Schmidt, Cathy Smart, Peter Smith, Stuart Smith, Richard and Janetta Streeter, Peter Stuart Fox, Garry Waters, Judy and Peter Webb, the late Ken Webb, Loris White, Col Wilkinson, John Winterbottom, the late Miles Wright, and Stephen Wright.

Above all, my thanks go to Val Wilkinson from Tumut, whose assistance and encouragement in researching this book have been invaluable; and to David Tenenbaum, Adolfo Aranjuez and Ning Xue of Melbourne Books.